Mundane Reason

Mundane reason

*Reality in everyday and
sociological discourse*

Melvin Pollner

*University of California,
Los Angeles*

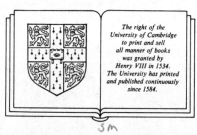

The right of the
University of Cambridge
to print and sell
all manner of books
was granted by
Henry VIII in 1534.
The University has printed
and published continuously
since 1584.

Cambridge University Press

Cambridge
New York   New Rochelle   Melbourne   Sydney

Published by the Press Syndicate of the University of Cambridge
The Pitt Building, Trumpington Street, Cambridge, CB2 1RP
32 East 57th Street, New York, NY 10022, USA
10 Stamford Road, Oakleigh, Melbourne 3166, Australia

First published 1987

Printed in Great Britain at the University Press, Cambridge

British Library cataloguing in publication data

Pollner, Melvin
Mundane reason: reality in everyday and sociological discourse.
1. Ethnomethodology. 2. Reality.
I. Title.
121'.3   HM24

Library of Congress cataloguing in publication data

Pollner, Melvin.
Mundane reason.
Bibliography.
1. Sociology – Methodology. 2. Ethnomethodology.
3. Traffic courts – Social aspects – Case studies.
I. Title.
HM24.P62 1987   301'.01'8   87-30946

ISBN 0 521 32184 0

9-26-90

CE

This book is dedicated to
the memory of my parents,
Isidore and Pauline Pollner

Contents

Preface

> The aspects of things that are most important for us are hidden because of their simplicity and familiarity. (One is unable to notice something – because it is always before one's eyes.) The real foundations of his enquiry do not strike a man at all. Unless *that* fact has at some time struck him. – And this means: we fail to be struck by what, once seen, is most striking and most powerful.
>
> (Wittgenstein 1951: 50)

One of ethnomethodology's contributions to the understanding of social life is its capacity to produce a deep wonder about what is often regarded as obvious, given or natural. Whether it be the interpretation of documents, the utterance of 'uh-huh' or the flow of everyday interaction, ethnomethodology has provided a way of questioning which begins to reveal the richly layered skills, assumptions and practices through which the most commonplace (and not so commonplace) activities and experiences are constructed.

Ethnomethodology's second contribution is an extension of the attitude of wonder to the discourse and practice of the human sciences (and, more recently, the natural sciences as well). It has striven, with various degrees of success, to make problematic the ways in which disciplines concerned with human behaviour conceptualize, research, and account for human behavior. The resultant inquiries have suggested that the production of 'objective' or scientific accounts of human behavior are themselves permeated by rich, subtle practices and assumptions which are typically ignored or unrecognized – just as they are in everyday life.[1]

The following research partakes of both dimensions of ethnomethodological wonder. It asserts, argues and at times shows that aspects of both everyday and sociological discourse, practice and inquiry are dependent upon assumptions about the nature of 'objective reality', to wit that there is an objective determinate order independent of the acts of observation or description through which it is known. The assumption of an 'out there', 'public' or 'objective' world is a central feature of a network of beliefs about reality, self and others which comprise what I shall call *mundane reason*. For most contemporary Western adults, the assumption of an objective reality is virtually self-evident (and thus truly mundane). Yet a tradition of philosophical skepticism, Eastern epistemology, phenomenological investigations, certain forms of 'pathological' experience and what some purport to be the cutting edge of physics (O'Flaherty 1984) suggest that the epistemology and ontology implicit in everyday and scientific discourse is historical, contingent – and even wrong. These whisperings from other traditions and disciplines are not amplified by me into a voice encouraging a new or 'correct' ontology. Rather, I use them in varying degrees of explicitness as ways of moving 'outside' of mundane discourse so as to grasp it as a folk idiom. The thrust and spirit of part of my analysis is not how limited mundane reasoners are for failing to see the threats and alternatives to mundane discourse, but how ingenious they are in sustaining it.

The analysis, however, is not entirely an appreciation of the genius of mundane reason and mundane reasoners. The claim that the objective determinate order is but an 'assumption' which founds both everyday and social scientific discourse has critical implications for the latter. Specifically, it implies that the human sciences may be naively founded on a problematic supposition and thus may comprise a *folk discipline*, that is, a form of inquiry which is not so much 'about' members' assumptions as it is ensnared by and an expression of those assumptions. The modification of the sociological imagination necessary to disentangle sociology from mundane reason is an extraordinary complex undertaking. As is perhaps already obvious, the assumption of an objective world, what Husserl (1962) characterized as the 'natural attitude', is the basis of a discourse which includes some of the most cherished conceptual possibilities of Western culture. The very distinction between 'truth' and 'error', for example, presupposes an objective reality with regard to which 'descriptions' or 'experience' (themselves terms I shall later submit are derivations from within mundane reason) may be compared. Thus, suspension of the assumption of objective reality may reverberate to some of the primordial terms and possibilities of sociological analysis. Does, for example, suspension of the assumption entail abandoning a concern with 'truth' or 'error'? Does it imply that sociological discourse cannot be 'about' anything? And what of this very discourse through which the structures, antinomies and paradoxes of mundane reason are presented. What is its status in relation to what it purports to talk about?

These are the kinds of questions which I did not intend to ask at the outset of my inquiry but which thrust themselves in my path as I explored mundane reason and considered its implications for sociology.

This investigation of mundane reason is both substantive and methodological. Substantively, the study addresses the nature and practice of mundane reason, especially as expressed in the courtroom, a setting of interest because of the extensiveness of mundane reasoning, and in selected forms of sociological analysis. Mundane reason is viewed as an idiom or 'language game' (Wittgenstein 1953) constituted through deep assumptions regarding persons and reality. In a fashion akin to an anthropologist, we examine how members of the 'tribe' of mundane reasoners use their beliefs about reality to make inferences, raise and resolve puzzles and exercise tact and ingenuity. Methodologically, the study explores the implications of mundane reason for the social sciences and sociology especially. Insofar as mundane reason comprises an activity of the 'tribe', to what extent does mundane reason infiltrate the discourse of those who would be students of tribal life? What consequences for sociology flow from naive participation in the mundane idiom? To what extent, if any, can sociology transcend mundaneity?

There is an unusual warp and woof to the following chapters and a word on how the loom was constructed will help to discern the pattern I tried to weave. This study began as an ethnomethodological investigation of traffic court transactions. The traffic court was chosen because of the opportunity it afforded to explore central ethnomethodological concepts and concerns (Garfinkel 1967): accounts and accountability, legal and everyday rationality, practical management of activity, the interpretation of indexical expressions and so forth. Moreover, at the time, I had begun to appreciate the ways in which 'truth', the proffering of some determinate version of 'what really happened', was not the province of the scientist but a construction produced in and through practical activity: traffic court was interestingly thick with just such activity. Thus, the initial vision for my research was of a blend of substantive ethnographic description and more formal ethnomethodological analysis of 'practices' for producing the sensible, orderly, intelligible features of traffic court transactions, especially versions of 'what really happened'. At the same time I was intensely aware of one of the few ethnomethodological methodological admonitions: beware of confounding the topics of one's studies with the resources for studying them (Cicourel 1964; Garfinkel 1967). In subtle ways, the warning goes, sociologists have naively employed and taken for granted the self-same

skills, practices and suppositions as members of the society. The confounding has the consequence, as I indicated earlier, of rendering
sociology a folk discipline: sociology becomes naively ensnared in the
very practices it ought to be describing. The methodological warning
turns into a substantive recommendation: the ethnomethodologist is to
search out these hidden resources and describe the ways in which they
are used by members in the construction of 'rational', intelligible or
'accountable' action and discourse.

Over the course of observation of several traffic courts, the methodological aspect of my study gained ascendance. I became intrigued with the
way in which I was trying to produce a determinate version of how the
judge was trying to produce a determinate version of 'what really
happened'. To be sure, the substance of judges' and my concerns was
different, as were our practices and the circumstances within which we
deployed them: the judge, for example, made decisions in real time with
on-lookers immediately present while I made mine in academic time at
my carrel with only imagined on-lookers (though real ones would
eventuate). Yet we participated in an abstract conceptual 'space' which
seemed similar. We were both addressed to entities and events which
were presumably possessed of their own determinate structure or
orderliness. Could this dichotomy through which we cast ourselves as
inquirers over and against 'real' structures be one of the taken for granted
resources I had been warned about? The assumption of an objective
world seemed so difficult to grasp as an 'assumption' and so deeply
entwined in any form of inquiry or, indeed, social activity that I decided it
was either a truly foolish or a truly profound topic. The taken for granted
character of the assumption, the obviousness (i.e. how could it be
otherwise?) of the reasoning which it founded and mundane reason's
pervasive presence in the society suggested the possibility of uncovering
a major and consequential construction. Thus I elected to shift my focus
from the traffic court *per se* to the traffic court as the site of mundane
reason. And mundane reason became the primary focus.

The shift in levels entailed a transformation of the underlying organization of the study. Initially, I envisioned a study which would illustrate,
apply and deepen ethnomethodological concepts and reveal the taken
for granted aspects of the 'accomplishment' of traffic court. While the
path of such an investigation was hardly clear, the grass had been pressed
by those who went before and there were some guideposts. Mundane
reason by contrast is virgin terrain with even fewer guides and guideposts.[2] Accordingly, the study was transformed from an expedition

within more or less established conceptual boundaries to a reconnoi-
tering of a new territory. The following chapters, then, probe and
delineate what mundane reason might be and experiment with ways and
concepts for conceiving and describing its construction and use.[3]

Because mundane reason is intricated in the discourse through which
conventional naturalistic-positivistic inquiry, lay or professional, casts or
understands itself, the terms and concepts of positivistic inquiry are
unsuited for penetrating mundane reasoning: in important ways these
terms and concepts *are* mundane reasoning. Thus, one must struggle to
secure a vocabulary and an attitude for moving beyond the positivist
discourse. At times this has meant reliance on certain anthropological
contrasts and *gedanken* experiments. At other points the pursuit of the
basic assumptions pertaining to the subject-object duality backs one into
philosophy, most especially the work of those whom Rorty (1979) calls
the 'edifying' philosophers such as Wittgenstein and Heidegger. Indeed,
as one moves to the limits of mundane discourse, one's entire attitude
and analysis may assume a distinctly philosophical even metaphysical
tenor. This I suspect is unavoidable if only because analysis of the
structures which provide for empirical description will perforce require
one to step out of the mundane frame and into 'philosophy' (cf. McHugh
et al. 1974). There are powerful ideas and insights to be had on the
margins of sociology and philosophy. I have occasionally used some of
these 'marginal' ideas as wedges to crack through mundane reason or
'ladders' (Wittgenstein 1961) to try to climb beyond it.

The increased generality and abstraction of concern placed a great
empirical burden on the materials gathered from observation of traffic
court transactions. Initially, traffic court transactions were of interest in
their own right: the new focus, however, transformed them into
instances of mundane reasoning. Aside from what I might claim to know
about mundane reason as a commonsense reasoner and sociological
practitioner, the courts were the only sites of mundane reason for which I
had extensive and detailed materials. Thus, there is a tension between
the generality of my claims about mundane inquiry and reason on the
one hand and the empirical materials through which my claims are
illustrated let alone substantiated on the other. Although my empirical
cup may be less than full, I take comfort from the fact that it is not bone
dry – especially given that it is served in a context which has been casual
in regard to concrete, actual, ongoing activity. The efforts of Wittgenstein, Heidegger and others to explore the contingent or accomplished
character of everyday ontology and epistemology have typically relied

upon the stock in trade of philosophical analyses – the remembered or imagined example (Heritage 1984). Insofar as empirical attentiveness among philosophical inquirers is used as a standard, the empirical materials here are distinctive rather than deficient.

Chapter 1 argues that conventional sociological inquiry has unwittingly committed itself to certain assumptions about the nature of social reality. Sociological inquiry takes for granted a subject or observer confronting an objective and determinate order shared or sharable with other observers. This network of mundane assumptions is the source of sociological goals (to know the world, i.e. the social order, accurately and comprehensively); methodological concerns (objectivity); and fundamental autobiographical conceptions of self (inquirers inquiring into the world). The mundane assumptions are similar to those made and used by everyday actors as they carry out their own practical investigations. Persons in everyday life also suppose a real and intersubjective domain. The conflation of lay and social scientific epistemology may belie a failure of the sociological imagination. I argue it does! Instead of naively appropriating and operating within everyday assumptions, these assumptions and their use ought to comprise a central topic of sociological investigation.

Chapter 2 begins the exploration of mundane assumptions about the nature of reality. In traffic court, as in other sites of mundane inquiry, intelligible or 'accountable' (Garfinkel 1967) inference and interpretation of reality rests upon assumptions about the objective, determinate and coherent nature of concrete events and objects. These assumptions are not explicitly articulated but their force is evident in the ways in which judges, defendants, and others make or refute claims about 'what really happened' or assert that claims are impossible or implausible.

Chapter 3 explores the ways in which mundane reason's suppositions about reality though unfounded and vulnerable when viewed from the 'outside' are preserved through mundane reasoners' unwitting ingenuity.[4] Mundane reason provides a range of solutions or explanations to puzzles which might be otherwise seen as crises regarding the assumption of a shared objective world. In traffic court, for example, conflicting accounts of what is assumed to be a real and intersubjectively available order of events is not treated as evidence that reality is radically 'subjective'. Rather, parties to the disjuncture search out and propose the ways in which the world was observed or described was faulted or problematic. Through the artful formulation of these solutions mundane reasoners reproduce the 'self-evident' character of mundane assumptions about reality.

The great variety of candidate solutions generated by mundane reason to account for disjunctive claims about or experiences of reality means that there is considerable latitude in the resolution of any concrete disjuncture. In Chapter 4 I develop an analytic characterization of the process of resolution through which some claims/experiences are 'authorized' and others discredited as representations of reality. The resolution of disjunctures involves a 'politics of experience' (Laing 1967) through which one experience is empowered as definitive of the real and others are deemed erroneous or subjective. I use this framework to examine the ways in which sociological analysts are often involved in a politics of experience with those they study or theorize about. Sociological concepts ranging from 'false consciousness' to 'interpretation' to 'subjectivity' itself are the product of a politics in which the analyst has authorized his or her own version of reality by reference to which lay members are found to be deficient witnesses of 'what's really happening'. These concepts suggest how deeply mundane reason permeates sociological analysis.

Chapters 2, 3 and 4 are concerned in the main with assumptions about the nature of 'hard' or 'material' events such as cars, stoplights and roads. Mundane reasoners, however, may also treat 'abstract', 'symbolic' or 'constructed' orders as objective, that is, as existing independently of reaction, observation or perception. Though from a point outside the system in question mundane reasoners may demonstrably be shown to be constructing a world, they nevertheless experience and describe themselves as 'reacting to' or 'reflecting' an essentially objective domain or world. In Chapter 5 the outside ontology of the 'construction' of deviance (as provided by societal reaction theory) is juxtaposed with the inside ontology of 'reflection' (as expressed in the formulations of judges). The juxtaposition affords insight into how mundane reasoners are able to disattend the constructive or creative aspect of their activity so as to encounter a domain or world which seems to be 'always already there'. An aspect of mundane reasoners' accomplishment is their remarkable and endless capacity to formulate a 'mundane auto-biography' and represent themselves as standing over and against an objective field of events and relations.

Not only do mundane reasoners have distinctive ways of formulating their relation to reality, they have distinctive ways of reflecting upon that relation. Mundane reflection, however, is deeply tied to mundane assumptions and practices and thus is incapable of grasping the processes through which mundane worlds are constituted. Chapter 6 considers the ways in which mundane reflection is shaped by mundane reason and thus precluded from radical self examination. Mundane reason's incapacity for radical reflection, it is suggested, is not a deficiency or fault but an aspect of the very processes through which mundane worlds are constituted.

Ethnomethodology's precocious claim to stand apart from sociology stemmed from its attempts to move 'outside' of conventional sociological discourse and praxis. To free oneself of deep conventions and convictions requires distance or marginality. The impulse to move to the edge and beyond of sociological discourse, however, dominated the earlier programmatic statements in the form of declarations of difference and disjuncture (e.g. Zimmerman and Pollner 1970). These declarations were not wrong but they were incomplete. The discovery of practice is not the end of investigation but the beginning of a dialogue with and within sociology. Thus, what should also have been said is that ultimately ethnomethodology must bring its insights back to sociology, either to ask substantively how a particular discourse and practice arise or to pursue, at the methodological level, the implications of these practices for the self-understanding of sociology. By virtue of its concern with taken for granted practice, ethnomethodological inquiry must strive to transcend the constitutive and constraining character of the dominant form of life and the practice, language and experience which it cultivates in order to 'see' them at all. But it also must – if it is to contribute to an understanding of social life – return to sociology to understand those practices in their larger social context and to consider their significance for a form of social life concerned with forms of social life. Chapter 7, the concluding chapter, 'returns' to consider mundane reason in terms of structural and historical processes. Mundane reason, it is suggested is not simply the product of the local work of mundane reasoners, for it is also shaped by longer term and larger scale dynamics. I also return to consider several vexatious issues in the study of mundane reason, such as the extent to which sociology can move beyond mundane reason.

Acknowledgements

The influence of Aaron V. Cicourel and Harold Garfinkel is so pervasive in the following pages that I cannot easily state the nature or extent of my indebtedness. Cicourel has been my mentor, colleague and friend for many years. He has sustained me, challenged me and taught me, all in the right proportion and at the right time. Garfinkel, through his writings and seminars, introduced me to the extraordinary organization of the ordinary and to the conception of radical inquiry which is at the heart of my study.

An author could not ask for two better colleagues and friends than Renee Anspach and Robert M. Emerson. At various junctures when I felt spent, their encouragement and counsel were deeply appreciated sources of strength. I have had the benefit of thoughtful commentary on one or another aspect of the manuscript or the ideas contained in it from Donald Cressy, Kathy Ferguson, David Goode, Michael Lynch, Michael Phillipson, Mark Peyrot, George Psathas, Emanual Schegloff, Howard Schwartz, D. Lawrence Wieder and Don H. Zimmerman. None of my friends and colleagues has read the final version and some have not seen any version. Thus, they can hardly be responsible for whatever failings or errors the final version may contain. They should be credited, however, for contributing to whatever merit the work may have, for it surely would have been less without their response.

I am indebted to the judges who gave of their time and knowledge to assist me in gathering materials. Judge Joseph Lodge was especially helpful

As Alfred Schutz noted, the thinker departs from and returns to the world of everyday life. My wife Judy and children Leslie and Adrian made my return the sweetest part of my voyages and lovingly prepared me for the next sojourn. I am thankful for the warmth and concern of my father-in-law and mother-in-law, Isadore and Sylvia Abramson.

A version of Chapter 3 was published as 'Mundane Reasoning' in *Philosophy of the Social Sciences* (1974) 4:35–54; a version of Chapter 4 was published as 'The very coinage of your brain: the anatomy of reality disjunctures' also in *Philosophy of the Social Sciences* (1975) 5:411–30; portions of Chapter 5 were published as 'Sociological and common sense models of the labelling process' in Roy Turner (editor) *Ethnomethodology* Harmondsworth: Penguin (1974) 27–40.

1

The problem of mundaneity

Sociology has not of late dreamt Comte's dream. Few persons entertain the thought, particularly in the embarrassing presence of linguistics and, until recently, economics, that sociology is or could become the Queen of the Social Sciences. Indeed, for some, sociology's claim to presence in the court, let alone any sort of title, often seems precarious. The complexity of social affairs, the infiltration of values, and the impoverished character of the methods of theoretical analysis are but a few of the reasons advanced to dampen sociology's pretensions. Nevertheless, from both the point of view of practitioners within the discipline and critics without, sociology's aspiration to the throne, while possibly amusing, is understandable. That is to say, what is of issue generally is the extent to which sociology has or can realize itself as a rigorous science. Whether or not sociology ought to envision itself as responsible to the idea of science is essentially undisputed.

Yet, that ambition, which has marked sociology since its inception, is not beyond question. Specifically, it is possible to render problematic not merely the adequacy of sociology *qua* science but the primordial matter as to whether or not it is a science which sociology ought to be. Instead of asking to what extent does sociology approximate the conventional model of a science, we may ask whether it is science which sociology ought to approximate. Such a question, however, retains the integrity of the basic phenomenon to which sociology addresses itself: it merely renders the method of address problematic. It is possible to go one step further. Not only may we question the utility or desirability of sociology's methodology, we may inquire into the very nature of sociology's phenomenon as well. Specifically, sociology may be examined for the extent to which its subject matter is properly conceived.

As is obvious, perhaps, such questions are possessed of peculiar properties. They are 'radical' questions in that they cannot be resolved by an appeal to the normal operating procedure of the discipline to which they are put. Whether or not sociology's phenomenon ought to be A or B and whether or not its foundational methodology ought to be X or Y is not amenable to answer or solution in the same way that questions formulated within the confines of sociology's 'normal paradigm' are resolved (Kuhn 1970). They cannot be answered within the normal paradigm because it is precisely the normal paradigm which is under consideration.[1] 'Radical questions' are radical in that they question the taken for granted foundations of the discipline from within which they are asked. The primordial questions of 'What is the phenomenon?' and 'How is it to be approached?' are asked on a bridge unsecured at either end: a bridge, moreover, which traverses an abyss whose walls are sheer paradox. An example of the perplexities that can be encountered by 'radical' questioning is furnished by considering the peculiar consequences of a global polemic against sociology's phenomenon, and the method through which it is investigated. In one sense there is an 'argument' or critique; and yet in another there is none. The conventional sense of a critique dissipates when an entire discipline is comprehensively challenged – from its conception of its subject matter to the conception of its method – because then one is not so much offering a challenge as formulating an alternative discipline (Scheffler 1967: 82; Shapere 1964: 391).[2] If there is disagreement with respect to both method and phenomenon, and if the disagreement is on a global level as opposed to the particular, then the structural conditions which provide for the possibility of 'rational' debate and communication are nullified.[3] Unlike disputes which may occur 'within' a particular discipline and which call for particular remedy or reform, a radical critique of the sort we have described demands an alteration of a discipline's foundation in such a fashion that the discipline is no longer recognizable to itself. To ask of sociology that it alter its phenomenon and fundamental methodology is to ask sociology to cease to be what it now takes itself to be.

These paradoxes and perplexities are but a taste of things to come. Our investigations depart from a perspective which is, for the most part, profoundly and necessarily alien to the current presuppositions and practices of sociology. Our investigations are alien to the practices and presuppositions of sociology – or at least strive to be alien – because it is these very foundational presuppositions and practices which comprise our inquiry's central concern. We seek to move outside the space (Spencer 1982) of conventional sociological discourse in order to focus upon and learn how sociological inquiry or any mode of inquiry is constituted through the use of primordial suppositions and sustained

through practices of reasoning which treat those suppositions as incorrigible (Gasking 1965) givens.

Foundational suppositions and practices are ordinarily not the focus of
sociological or everyday inquiry because they are constitutive of the very
possibility of inquiry. From 'within' inquiry, the assumptions are often so
deeply taken-for-granted and the practices applied so subtly that
inquirers regard them as given, unalterable and self-evident. Sociology's
ambition to be a science is but an expression of its deep, one might say
naive, commitment to a network of suppositions and practices, which, I
propose, ought first and foremost comprise a topic of study. But to
embark on such a study requires first that we gain distance from, and, in
this sense, become alien to, sociology's aspiration to be a science.

The strangeness of sociology as a science

In order to provide a sense of the strangeness of sociology as science, it is
necessary to try to transcend the limitations of conventional Western
thought which accords to the sciences a peculiar sort of primacy or
privileged status. Toward this end, I want to present a conversation
between two strangers to the world. Let us call them transcendental
strangers or, perhaps, 'transcendental anthropologists'. One stranger,
the 'Student', has been assigned the task of doing an anthropological
analysis of the world. The other stranger, the 'Mentor', is a thesis
supervisor or something of the sort. They speak on the occasion of the
Student's return.[4]

Student: Mentor, as you know, my task was to do an anthropology of man.
When I reached the world, I was not sure how to begin. My methods were
unformulated; my phenomenon unclear. After a period of drift and turmoil, I
stumbled upon practitioners of 'science'. They were many in number and
diversely situated over the earth. For hundreds and hundreds of years, they as a
body had been engaged in acquiring knowledge of the world. They had an
immense accumulation of factual material organized under the auspices of
theoretical frameworks and an immense variety of technical practices for securing
factual materials. (Imagine an inventory of all the conventional virtues attributed
to the sciences.) Indeed, they even had what they called 'social sciences', whose
specific concern was an elucidation of the 'social world', and they had accumulated a vast literature reporting the results of their endeavors. I found that my
task had been done in principle. Therefore, I have duplicated the literature, and I
propose that our concerns are being cared for. Here, then, is the *American
Sociological Review*, *American Journal of Sociology*, *Public Opinion Quarterly* . . . *Rules
of Sociological Method*, Weber's . . .
Mentor:[5] Incredible! You have committed the most peculiar of errors. If I

understand you correctly, you have taken a procedure indigenous to the world and used it as a means of producing descriptions of the world. If that is what you have done, then you have misconceived your task. Do you not see that the procedures you refer to as the 'social sciences' are integral features of the world you set out to examine? Have you not used as a resource what well might have been the phenomenon? These journals that you present, aren't they the stories that story-tellers tell?

Student: But it wasn't just any story they were telling. You must recognize, Mentor, that the scientists had developed special ways of analyzing the world so as to produce 'stories', as you call them, which were superior to any which had hitherto been produced. The stories, unlike those of the 'layman', were compilated in accord with the most rigorous of criteria – criteria which assured that were others to examine the world, they, too, would tell the same story. They were concerned with the degree of correspondence between their stories and the referent of the stories; and they took great caution in the preparation of the stories so as to assure correspondence or, at least, to assure that there would be public ways of ascertaining whether the stories were correct. (Imagine an extended inventory of all of the ideals of scientific inquiry.) True, the stories were stories; but they were, as the scientists said, 'objective' and unequalled in their accuracy.

Mentor: I am not doubting what you say. But when I hear you recount what you were told, I hear only a description of how scientists talk so as to lay claim to having produced definitive stories of the world. That is, I hear what you say as a description of activities which go on in the world under the name of science. You, too, should have heard the claims in that way. That way of talking, that way of reasoning, was not to be taken over by you as your own way of talking, your own way of reasoning. That was the phenomenon. The activities in which the scientists engaged, the claims that they made, the ideals under whose auspices they claimed to have operated – all these are in-the-world, and thus at least part of what you should have attended to in your investigations.

Student: You mean, Mentor, I failed in my task because I trusted the sciences when I should have been far more critical. I should have determined, for example, whether indeed the sciences actually satisfied the criteria they posed for themselves and if, in fact, their descriptions were, as they say, empirically verifiable? Is that what you mean when you say I should have attended to the sciences as a phenomenon?

Mentor: No, I mean nothing of the sort. Your task was not to 'debunk' the world, not to reveal its faults, and not to see if the sciences were, in fact, what they made themselves out to be. It was not your task to find out whether the sciences and their accumulated products were 'right' or 'wrong', 'true' or 'false', 'correct' or 'incorrect'. Your task did not call for an evaluative concern because such evaluative concerns are themselves features of the sciences in particular and the world in general. Such evaluations are of interest only in the ways in which they are carried out by members in-the-world. Similarly, the notion of truth, the system of logic, the fact-finding and theorizing practices of the sciences are of no interest in ways other than as phenomena. And if such practices are claimed to be superior to those employed by what you have called 'laymen', then those claims are of equal interest as a phenomenon – and only as a phenomenon – for they, too, are in-the-world.

Student: I think I now see your point, Mentor. I should not be seduced by worldly practices and worldly reason for they are in the world. Worldly reason and worldly practices are what I have come to study and they therefore cannot provide me with answers. But given what you have said, is it not the case that even if I turn to study worldly practice and reason that I nevertheless fall prey to yet deeper and more subtle worldly practices? If I study worldly practice in all its forms, do I not become like worldly members in that I suppose a structure, an orderliness or even a disorderliness or structure in the first place, and that I seek in some fashion to explain, describe or 'know' that order? Members of the world often cast themselves in that relation to what they regard as 'nature' or 'social facts' or 'reality'. Thus even in deciding to study worldly practice and reason in the most comprehensive sense possible I seem to participate in a worldly structure nevertheless. And Mentor, if I somehow abandon or transcend this last structure through which I cast myself over and against 'the structure of worldly practice and reason', if I abandon all worldly practice, reason and structure so as to treat them as in-the-world, am I not left without a place to stand, so to speak? In depriving myself of this last resource, do I not thereby deprive myself not only of a topic, but the possibility of any topic? And if I . . .

Mentor: I see you have understood me well. Let us postpone the answers – if there are answers – for another time.

The Student represents the conventional social sciences: his initial naivete is the naivete of the social sciences. As the Mentor points out, the study of worldly activities and the use of science can in some sense be seen to be at odds with one another simply because science is a worldly activity. From the near-radical[6] perspective of the Mentor, the use of science by a transcendental anthropologist is akin to a conventional anthropologist's use of, say, the descriptions of activities proferred by tribal elders or produced by oracular methods as a means of providing a description of the people under consideration. Presumably, for the conventional anthropologist the descriptions offered by the tribal elders are part and parcel of the tribal life which the anthropologist wishes to describe.[7] They have no particular primacy over any other aspect of the order of activities they describe. Analogously, from the standpoint of a transcendental anthropological concern with socially organized activities, the theoretical and technical practices which comprise 'science' would not be resources, they would be instances of worldly practice and reason.

As a consequence of this re-orientation, empirical analysis, theoretical explication and even logic itself are rendered problematic, but without a concern for a corrective. Indeed, even the remedial self-concern which is characteristic of the sciences is rendered a feature of doing science. That is, the sciences' reflexive concern with themselves, explication of their foundational assumptions, examination of the relation between 'actual' practice and ideals and so on, are accorded the status of phenomena. Furthermore, given the Mentor's perspective, even the 'reflexive' sciences such as the social psychology of psychology, the sociology of sociology, of knowledge and of science are rendered integral features of science with no particular primacy or privileged ontological status *vis-à-vis* the order of affairs which they explicate.

As the Student's concluding questions and the Mentor's reluctance to answer them indicates, the development of the perspective of a transcendental or radical anthropology generates a number of extraordinary problems. For example, a radical disengagement from worldly reason and worldly practice is *not* assured by taking a 'step back'.[8] To be sure, the recommendation to conceive of science as worldly practice and worldly reason turns the sciences into 'topics' and expands the domain of worldly practice. The addition of yet another topic, as distinctive and reflexive as it may be, however, is an implicit acceptance, reiteration and reaffirmation of a network of formal relations and suppositions in which a 'subject', 'knower' or 'inquirer', is once again constructed and juxtaposed to what is variously known as the 'object', 'out there', 'reality' or 'social facts'.[9] Insofar as the schema of formal relations and the discursive space which it creates is reproduced, the transcendance intimated by the Mentor is not so much an escape from the house of commonsense as it is a change of floors, for the formal structures which provide for the possibility of a topic, remain unexamined and, indeed, unnoticed.

Sociology becomes mundane

Thus far, we have attempted to provide a sense of how sociology's patterning of itself in the image of the sciences is strange. We have proposed that instead of embracing science – and thereby being co-opted by worldly reason and practice – sociology might well have approached worldly reason and practice with a naivete which would have made what is now a resource of sociology into a topic (Garfinkel 1967; Zimmerman and Pollner 1970). But the program which relinquishes the 'privileged' status conventionally accorded to the sciences demands a radical transformation of the entire sense of the phenomenon. It is not merely a matter of adding yet another substantive concern to the list of topics already surveyed by the social sciences. Indeed, there already are sociologies of sociology, of science and of knowledge. In proposing that the sciences and worldly reason be rendered topics in their own right, the radical perspective has a vision of a phenomenon which transcends that which ever could be considered by the sciences even if the sciences do, in fact, exhibit a reflective concern with themselves. The phenomenon includes the very work whereby reflective and analytic concern; theorizing and analysis; observation and inquiry; the pursuit of truth and objectivity and the recognition of error and subjectivity; and a concern with and conjectures about the nature of reality in everyday and scientific contexts are constituted as intelligible possibilities. This work is not accessible within the space (Spencer 1982) of conventional inquiry for the work constitutes the space of conventional inquiry.

Sociology, like the rest of the sciences, and, for that matter, like all modes of inquiry, is directed to the explication and analysis of a world whose 'thereness' is essentially non-problematic. It is precisely in and through inquiry's preoccupation with a world already there that the network of assumptions and practices through which the thereness of the world is created is disattended. Inquiry gains a world but loses the work of worlding. For radical inquiry, by contrast, the phenomenon *par excellence* is not the world *per se* but worlding, the work whereby a world *per se* and the attendant concerns which derive from a world *per se* – truth and error, to mention two – are constructed and sustained.

Almost at its inception, sociology accepts and enters into a network of assumptions and concepts – an ontological space – which severely circumscribes what it might entertain as a phenomenon. Specifically, in entering the space in which a 'knower', 'inquirer', or 'subject' (in corporate or individual form) is conceptualized as striving to 'know', 'understand', or 'observe' what is variously designated as 'social facts', 'nature', or 'reality', the construction of that very ontological space is lost as a phenomenon. These conceptual distinctions, the assumptions from which they derive and the reasoning which they cultivate are precluded as topics for they comprise the space within which sociology will naively dwell. We may gain a deeper sense of how sociology comes to forfeit these assumptions as phenomena if we consider the moments at which sociology decides to employ these assumptions as resources.

In their rudimentary stages the social sciences often know themselves as a distinctive mode of inquiry by reference to practical inquiry, that is to say, the investigations carried out by the 'man in the street'. In turn, practical inquiry's recognition of itself as practical depends on the availability of contrasting alternatives, one of which is scientific inquiry. The two modes of inquiry are in this way dialectically dependent upon one another for the reflexive sense of themselves.[10] The presumed superiority of scientific inquiry requires reference to a perfectly matched inferiority of practical inquiry. When, for example, 'underlaborer'[11] philosophers of science, such as Earnest Nagel (1961), explicate the superiority of science, they do so by reference to the relatively impoverished character of practical investigations.[12] Thus, for instance, when the virtuosity of science's systematical nature is displayed, it is displayed in contrast to the more or less chaotic character of commonsense knowledge. The strengths of science are established by contrast to the weakness of alternative modes of inquiry. Because of the dialectic which obtains among modes of inquiry in order for them to be recognizable as distinctive and differentially valued modes, scientific and practical inquiry are cast into essentially competitive roles (Zimmerman and Pollner, 1970). The emergence of science casts its now-to-be-seen alternatives into the role of would-be aspirants in the race toward definitive knowledge of the particular domain to which the science is addressed.

We can get a sense of the essentially competitive relation between sociology and commonsense investigation from Durkheim's (1951) consideration of the potential uses of officially imputed causes of suicide (cf. Atkinson 1978). 'It seems natural to profit by this already accomplished work,' Durkheim speculates, for the official compilations, 'apparently show us the immediate antecedents of different suicides' (p. 148). But Durkheim's optimistic conjectures are short lived:

what are called statistics of the motives of suicides are actually statistics of the opinions concerning such motives of officials, often of lower officials, in charge of this information service. Unfortunately, official establishments of fact are known to be often defective even when applied to obvious material facts comprehensible to any conscientious observer and leaving no room for evaluation. How suspect must they be considered when applied not simply to recording an accomplished fact but to its interpretation and explanation! To determine the cause of a phenomenon is always a difficult problem. The scholar requires all sorts of observations and experiments to solve even one question. Now, human volition is the most complex of all phenomena. The value of improvised judgments, attempting to assign a definite origin for each special case from a few hastily collected bits of information is, therefore, obviously slight. As soon as some of the facts commonly supposed to lead to despair are thought to have been discovered in the victim's past, further search is considered useless, and his drunkenness or domestic unhappiness or business troubles are blamed, depending on whether he is supposed recently to have lost money, had home troubles or indulged a taste for liquor. Such uncertain data cannot be considered a basis for explanation for suicide.

Moreover, even if more credible, such data could not be very useful, for the motives thus attributed to the suicides, whether rightly or wrongly, are not their true causes (pp. 148–9).

According to Durkheim, the lay member is incompetent to determine the motivation of any particular suicide. Further, the motives, whether correctly assessed or not, are not the true causes of suicide. The lay member of the society is an incompetent investigator of specious circumstances. The lay member is naive with respect to the procedural aspects of investigation as well as to what it is that ought properly be investigated in the first place.

The naivete attributed to the lay member is not an incidental feature of the social sciences. The distinctiveness of the sciences requires reference to that which the sciences are not. The contrast is absolutely vital to the sense and possibility of a social science. Why, after all, should not ordinary talk about the social structures be adequate accounts of those structures? The answers to these questions and the idea of science itself turn upon the sciences' capacity to reveal modes of practical inquiry as essentially unable to arrive at 'universally valid truths' or at the structure of 'nature as it truly and objectively is'. Indeed, the notion of 'nature as it really is in and of itself', that goal toward which the sciences presumably converge, is itself invidiously juxtaposed to the now-to-be-seen vulgarity of the practical man's regard for nature. The idea of a social *science*, in short, is essentially dialectic. Its formulation as a *modus operandi* in the world is established by reference to what it is not and, because part of what it is not are the practices of the practical man, the idea of science is imbued with irony. The sciences, in the way in which they are what they are, make reference to the inadequacy of alternative modes of addressing the world.

In precisely what respect are the practices of the practical man portrayed as inferior to those of the sciences? The fact that they are both modes of inquiry should alert us to the major dimensions of the invidious contrast. Specifically, commonsense and scientific inquiry are cast in competitive relations with respect to their ability to discern and describe 'real', 'factual', or 'objective' structures of a particular domain. The nature of the competition is clearly articulated in Durkheim's (1938) *The Rules of Sociological Method*. As will be recalled, sociology is given the vision of its possibility by declaration of a factual order which is social and hence not within the province of psychology or biology, and a social order which is factual and hence demanding of methods of inquiry able to retrieve and make observable 'real' (as opposed to specious or imagined) structures. The lay member's grasp and observation of these social facts is hopelessly infused by *a priori* concepts, argues Durkheim.

At the moment when a new order of phenomena becomes the subject matter of a science, these phenomena are already represented in the mind not only by rather definite perceptions but also by some kind of crudely formed concepts. Before the first rudiments of physics and chemistry appeared, men already had some notions concerning physicochemical phenomena which transcended mere perception, such as are found, for example, mingled in all religions. The reason for this is that thought and reflection are prior to science, which merely uses them more methodically. Man cannot live in an environment without forming some ideas about it according to which he regulates his behavior. But, because these ideas are nearer to us and more within our mental reach than the realities to which they correspond, we tend naturally to substitute them for the latter and to make them the very subject of our speculations. Instead of observing, describing, and comparing things, we are content to focus our consciousness upon, to analyze, and to combine our ideas. Instead of a science concerned with realities, we produce no more than an ideological analysis. To be sure, this analysis does not necessarily exclude all observation. One may appeal to the facts in order to confirm one's hypotheses or the final conclusions to which they lead. But in this case, facts intervene only secondarily as examples or confirmatory proofs; they are not the central subject of science. Such a science therefore proceeds from ideas to things, not from things to ideas (Durkheim 1938: 14).

As realities *sui generis*, the social structures are demanding of a methodology which will mirror their features. The objectivity of the world *qua* objectivity requires objective procedure. It is at this point that practical investigations are found wanting – precisely because of their dialectically discovered practicality. That is, they are wanting because while they are concerned with the world – they do, for example, concern themselves with the causes of suicide as evidenced by the availability of the statistics whose utility Durkheim dismisses – they are infiltrated with prejudices and practicality. Practical inquiry fails because of an imperfect methodology; that imperfection being constitutively revealed when lay inquiry is considered under the auspices of the idea and ideals of science. Sociology as a science was to remedy these faults so as to be able to objectively explicate the order of affairs, 'social facts', which were only erroneously or subjectively analyzed and known by lay members.

The grounds and the terms of the implicit competition between the sciences and practical inquiry is furnished by the notion of the 'world'.[13] The sciences, like the modes of inquiry to which they are juxtaposed, are conceived as mutually oriented to an essentially objective nature. The substantive content of the world varies from discipline to discipline, of course, but in each instance the world is conceived to have an existence independent of the theoretical and technical practices in and through which it is explicated. And it is this existential thesis which constitutes the grounds within which the sciences proclaim their superiority over the specious or otherwise faulted character of practical inquiry. It is by reference to the essential facticity of the world that the sciences demonstrate the inappropriateness of the flawed methods of practical inquiry and the virtues of their own.

It is at precisely this point – the point where the sciences apparently triumph – that they can be seen to have both forfeited and presupposed what Merleau-Ponty (1962: 63) calls the 'phenomenon of the phenomenon'. It is here that the sciences succumb to a naivete regarding their own theoretical and technical activities and those of practical inquiry as well. It is here that the problematic character of the very availability of nature or world as an explicable (or for that matter inexplicable) objectivity disappears. If we may summarily refer to the structures which provide for the world's appearance as an independent object as the 'mundaneity' of the world, then it is precisely at the point when the sciences turn to the world that the 'mundaneity' of the world is lost as a phenomenon.

To be sure, the world is a phenomenon to both scientific and practical inquiry and the attitudes under whose auspices they are carried out. How does the world work? What will it do? What has it done?[14] But when considered under the auspices of such questions – no matter the ideals which govern the extent to which answers are to be pursued – the world is retained as an objective field. The wonder manifest in such questions is a wonder with the world as an already pre-constituted facticity. The wonder or perplexity is with the world as a being whose 'insidious presence' (Merleau-Ponty 1962: 41) as an object is simply taken-for-granted. What is specifically excluded from scientific and practical inquiry's puzzlement with the world is the ways in which inquiry manages to furnish itself with a world which can be the object of its concern.

In entering mundane space and competing with everyday mundane practitioners, sociology incurs a two-fold loss. It naively accepts and thus is oblivious to the mundaneity of its own inquiry. It does not consider the very assumptions and practices which makes possible its concerns with objectivity, truth, and description. It loses sight as well of the mundaneity of everyday life. Everyday practitioners in various ways presuppose and inquire into an objective order of social and physical fact. Once sociology accepts the mundane assumptions, it turns to everyday inquiry *not* as a phenomenon in its own right but as an inadequate means of theorizing about and inquiring into reality as it 'really' is. Thus, sociology feels enhanced by having produced deeper, more systematic, more comprehensive and more objective accounts and analyses of social reality. At the very moment of its elation, such as it is, however, there is reason for despair: it is at precisely that moment that mundaneity – the practices whereby the space of a knower, subject or agent standing over and against an objective world is created and sustained – becomes invisible and sociology becomes mundane.

Scientific and practical investigations as mundane inquiry

Scientific and practical investigations are cast in competition and thereby permit one another to manifest themselves as specific and distinctive modes of explicating the world. Each mode of inquiry, in the very way that it is inquiry, is concerned with explicating and analyzing a world whose facticity is 'obvious'. When considered with respect to their concern with a pre-given world, the sciences and their dialectically juxtaposed practical or everyday counterparts are instances of what we shall henceforth call *mundane inquiry*. Mundane inquiry is inquiry into a world (a domain, a field, a region), which is presumed to be independent of the mode and manner in which it is explicated.[15]

The presumption of mundane inquiry travels under a variety of titles. Husserl (1962: 91–100) calls it the 'thesis of the natural standpoint'. The natural thesis is a presupposition which in a typically implicit and inarticulate form pervades all concern for the world. It pervades all concern with the world, for it is the generally unquestioned 'belief' in the objective existence of the world.[16] It is the assumption of the world's independence from the concern under whose auspices it is considered. Husserl describes the belief this way:

I find continually present and standing over against me the one spatio-temporal fact-world to which I myself belong, as do all other men found in it and related in the same way to it. This 'fact-world,' as the world already tells us, I find to be out there, and also take it just as it gives itself to me as something that exists out there. All doubting and rejecting of the data of the natural world leaves standing the general thesis of the natural standpoint. 'The' world is as fact-world always there: at the most it is at odd points 'other' than I supposed, this or that under such names as 'illusion,' 'hallucination,' and the like, must be struck out of it, so to speak; but the 'it' remains ever, in the sense of the general thesis, a world that has its being out there. To know it more comprehensively, more trustworthily, more perfectly than the naive lore of experience is able to do, and to solve all the problems of scientific knowledge which offer themselves upon its ground, that is the goal of the sciences of the natural standpoint (ibid.: 96; italics deleted).[17]

Merleau-Ponty (1964a) writes of the *préjugé du monde* made by perception. The prejudice is not a substantive preconception of the world,[18] that is, a preconception which infiltrates perception so as to yield distorted or ideological representations of the world. Rather, the prejudice of the world, insofar as it characterizes mundane inquiry, is the pre-judgment of the world as a determinate and independent object. It is the pre-judgment which permits of the sense and possibility of a world in the first place, of a world which may be *subsequently* considered for the extent to which it is adequately apprehended and by virtue of which considerations of 'objectivity' and 'truth' may arise. This foundational thesis or prejudice draws together under the common heading of mundane inquiry not only the natural and social sciences, but varieties of practical inquiry as well. Mundane inquiry, in the very ways that it is recognizable to itself as inquiry, presupposes the essential objectivity of the world. Mundane inquiry, insofar as it remains a recognizable rational enterprise, examines a world whose facticity is essentially non-problematic.

The discussion of naivete, prejudices and assumptions may be disconcerting, particularly in light of the self-proclaimed ideals and actual practices of the sciences. After all, is not the superiority of the sciences founded upon their judicious self-scrutiny: a self-scrutiny instituted to eliminate or, at least, systematically articulate precisely such matters? Did not Durkheim (1938: 14–34) himself emphatically urge sociologists to 'Consider social facts as things' and, correlatively, that 'All preconceptions must be eradicated'? Do not these maxims, insofar as they are rigorously adhered to, promote the progressive purification of procedure and the asymptotic approximation of 'nature as it really is in itself'?

From 'within' mundane inquiry, these exhortations are not cause for embarrassment. On the contrary, it is compliance with dictates such as these which, from the point of view of the sciences, raise the sciences beyond the naivete characteristic of practical inquiry.[19] From 'without', however, the rigorous adherence to the Durkheimian maxims is the embodiment of Merleau-Ponty's *préjugé du monde*. It is precisely in turning to the world as 'thing' and in attempting to remove the 'idols' peculiar to the practical attitude that the sciences succumb to and manifest a naivete of the profoundest depth. In turning to the world and in being 'objective', the very mundaneity of the world is necessarily condemned to oblivion. It is necessarily lost as a possible thematic because the mundaneity of the world is not and cannot be 'merely another' feature of the world which can be uncovered and explicated by analysis. It cannot be explicated by analysis because mundaneity permeates and stands behind every act of inquiry. Its insidious ambience precludes its being noticed, described or manipulated for it is the mundaneity of the world which stands as the grounds for any and all such activities. Indeed, it is not so much that mundaneity is excluded as a topic, rather, insofar as the world, any world, is taken up in inquiry, mundaneity disappears as a possible topic. Mundaneity never provides the opportunity for inquiry to turn to it or not to turn to it, for mundaneity, presupposed as it is in all 'turning to', is really not an 'it'. It is not an object, for it is the work which provides for the possibility of objects in the first place.[20]

Mundaneity is essentially occult. Mundaneity cannot be seen because it is the ambient condition and grounds of all inquiry.[21] Further, the hiddenness of mundaneity is reiterated for any and all worlds. Thus, mundaneity is not rendered manifest by 'perceiving the perceiving', 'observing the observing', or any such reflective, second order or 'one step back' examination of attending to the world.[22] For even in reflexive self-consideration, inquiry is once again confronted by an objective domain in which the mundane work involved in its organization is nowhere to be found as a particular. Because reflective inquiry has its world or domain, e.g. the 'observing', the 'perceiving', etc., it reiteratively exhibits all of the formal properties of that which it considers. The naivete of mundane inquiry – that is, its necessary obliviousness to mundaneity – reasserts itself as soon as mundane inquiry turns its attention to *anything*, even if that 'thing' is 'mundane inquiry' or, for that matter, 'mundaneity' itself.[23]

Because mundaneity hides at any level of inquiry, 'transcendental anthropology' is at best a 'near-radical' discipline. Even after having relegated the sciences to the field of data, it turns to the field as an already constituted world which is now to be explored and explicated. The primordial foundations of the sense and possibility of 'inquiry' and 'world' remain unexplicated. In this way, transcendental anthropology is as naive as the Durkheimian program. As is perhaps obvious, the naivete of Durkheimian sociology is neither remedied nor radicalized by an appeal to a Weberian or 'subjectivist' (as opposed to Durkheim's 'objectivist') position. Weber's (1936) position and *Verstehen* sociology in general is sometimes regarded as antithetical to Durkheim's maxim, 'Treat social facts as things', and in many ways it is. For Weber, the social structures originated in, were sustained by, and constituted of meaningful courses of activity. Sociology's programmatic phenomenon, according to Weber, was not social facts *simpliciter*, but social-facts-as-interpreted-and-thereby-produced (Weber 1964: 101–4). Though the Weberian program entails a return to subjectivity, it is nevertheless as mundane and thus as naive, in our technical sense of the term, as Durkheim's.[24] Although Weber returns to the subjectivity of the actor, he returns to it as a mundane object, i.e. as a fact among facts. As the concern of *Verstehen* sociology, and in the very ways in which it is the concern, subjectivity is objectivated as a domain. That is to say, it is brought under the auspices of the natural thesis. Weber's methodology, insofar as he is explicit about it, is geared to retrieve the meanings which actors 'attach' to their activity (Weber 1964: 88). Those meanings – in the very ways in which they are available as examinable entities – are presumed prior to and independent of the method and manner in which they are addressed and made observable. The subjectivity of the actor, in short, is itself an objective field. The furniture of the world to which Weber turns is, indeed, different from Durkheim's, but it is furniture of the world nevertheless.[25]

A preliminary specification of mundaneity as a phenomenon

Mundane inquiry presupposes the world as a determinate definite object. In a sense, mundane inquiry regards the world as if it, mundane inquiry, had nothing to do with the world's presence. From the point of view of mundane inquiry, the world is an *a priori* facticity. Durkheim did not fabricate the social structures; he discovered them. Newton did not invent the universe; he described its functioning. Heisenberg's (1966) uncertainty principle does not obtain because Heisenberg said that it does; Heisenberg said that it does because it presumably obtains.[26] In each instance, mundane inquiry finds itself addressing a world which is presumptively independent of the theoretical and technical activities in which the world is taken up. Insofar as mundane inquiry finds itself explicating a world, it finds itself analyzing structures whose existence have nothing to do with the fact that they are being explicated. From the point of view of mundane inquiry the operations of which mundane inquiry is comprised are merely instrumentalities for explicating or making observable objective structures. Hence, the concern with the purification of procedure, elimination of biases, and the concern with whatever would distort or deflect the capacity to reflect and represent the real world (McHugh *et al.* 1974). In being directed to the explication of the world, mundane inquiry does not want to produce artifactual findings – findings which are more reflections of the particular method employed to retrieve real structures than they are representations of the structures themselves. Mundane inquiry always represents itself as oriented to reality.

Yet mundane inquiry is never able to provide an ultimate justification for its assumption of an objective world. Because it has access to its world only through particular perceptions, reasonings and operations, mundane inquiry is unable to determine the ontological status of its world – for such determination would involve yet other perceptions, reasonings or operations. Thus while mundane inquiry is directed to a real world, an order of events and relations which is independent of the operations through which it is observed, measured or explicated, the ultimate objective 'thereness' of mundane inquiry's world can never be fully demonstrated. In this sense mundane inquiry is founded on an assumption or belief which is indemonstrable from within mundane inquiry. Yet the belief in the world is presupposed by virtually any form of praxis:

At every moment of conscious life, we find ourselves within the perceptual world, amidst things and objects of the greatest diversity: natural objects as well as objects of value or cultural objects, inanimate things as well as animals. Within this world, there live with us our fellow-men to whom we are standing in relationships of the most various kinds. All those objects and things, living beings, fellow-men, etc., appear and are taken as real existents. They pertain to the real world which encompasses all existents including ourselves.

Living in the *'natural attitude'* (*natürliche Einstellung*), which is the attitude not only of everyday experience but also of any activity whatever (with the sole exception of radical philosophical reflection as carried out in specific phenomeno-logical considerations), we simply accept the existential character with which the perceptual world and whatever it contains present themselves. In all dealings with real mundane existents, in all perceiving, reasoning, exploring, planning, acting, etc., there is implied or involved the existential belief, i.e. belief in the existence of what concerns us. To be sure, the existential belief is not permanent-ly stated and formulated; the existential character of the things and beings encountered is not on every occasion disengaged, rendered explicit, and posited. Such rendering explicit and formulation through a judgment about existence is, of course, always possible. As a rule, however, the existential belief involved in all our activities assumes a rather implicit and inarticulate form. This belief is not so much a premise entailing consequences but rather a general thesis which, unformulated and unthematized, underlies and supports all mental activities and upon which we proceed in all our dealing with mundane existents (Gurwitsch 1966: 91–2).

A fruitful initial approach to mundaneity is to treat the assumptive nature of the real world (and related theses regarding its coherence and accessibility to others) literally. Thus one would approach mundane reasoning as one might approach the belief system of a culturally esoteric tribe. Mundane beliefs could be conceived of as a cultural system which patterns the actions and utterances of members and is drawn upon by them as a way of ordering their projects and circumstances. Conceived of as a cultural belief system, the analytic task would be to describe the nature of mundane beliefs or prejudices, the ways in which they constitute and constrain action and inference, the ways in which such beliefs are transmitted and acquired, and the institutional, historical and interactional processes contributing to their maintenance and reproduction.

The assumption of an objective reality does not stand as an isolated belief. It is embedded in a network of distinctions and beliefs by which it is implied and which in turn imply it. Although it is difficult to extract or define any element as more significant than another because of their mutually implicatory character, it is useful to begin by noting that mundane reason distinguishes the 'objective' from the 'subjective' realm. The ways in which the distinction is substantively articulated varies from context to context. At the most abstract level the distinction is referred to as the 'subject-object' or 'knower-known' duality. In more colloquial and concrete terms, the mundane division is appreciated and expressed as the distinction between the inner, subjective, personal or psychological domain on the one hand and outer, objective or public domains on the other. The essential feature, however, is that mundane reason distinguishes a subjective domain of some sort from an objective domain, which can be made the focus of inquiry and concern.

Mundane reason prefigures or stipulates the structure of objects in the outer or public domain. For mundane reason objects, events and processes in the outer world and the world as a general context are determinate, coherent and non-contradictory. These specifications comprise, as it were, mundane reason's ontology of objects. Mundane reason's ontology of objects in turn implicates mundane reason's anticipation of the nature of individual and collective experience. Specifically, mundane reasoners expect that accounts and experiences, individually and collectively, will reflect the (assumed) structure of reality. Thus, they anticipate that accounts of the real world will be determinate, coherent and compatible. The tacit assumption of mundane reason, to borrow from Merleau-Ponty (1962: 54), is:

that every instant experience can be coordinated with that of the previous instant and that of the following, and my perspective with that of other consciousnesses – that all contradictions can be removed, that monadic and inter-subjective experience is one unbroken text – that what is now indeterminate for me could become determinate for a more complete knowledge, which is as it were realized in advance in the thing, or rather which is the thing itself.

Mundane reason has several properties which it is useful to highlight in order to appreciate its distinctive texture and power. It is important to recognize, for example, that mundane beliefs are not empirical descriptions of how mundane reasoners actually experience or describe themselves or their relation to reality. Rather, they are stipulations which mundane reason holds to be incorrigibly (Gasking 1965) so about ego, others and reality. To be a mundane reasoner is to be accountable to the mundane stipulations. There are innumerable instances, for example, where individuals' accounts and experiences conflict or contradict one another. Such episodes, however, are not the occasion for dismissing mundane reason but rather the beginning of a search for how such a discrepancy could have occurred *given* the coherency and determinateness of the public domain. Thus, mundane reason is not an empirical version of reality but an *a priori* specification of its features in terms of which empirical claims are reviewed for their adequacy.

Mundane reason provides the resources for generating or constructing innumerable conceptual and discursive possibilities. At the most general or abstract level, the concept of truth, most especially the concept of truth as correspondence between a 'perception' or 'description' on the one hand and the 'real' on the other, obviously requires the distinction between 'knower' and an 'objective' or 'real' domain to which perceptions might (or might not) correspond. Indeed, the very notions of 'perception' or 'description' are intelligible possibilities only by virtue of the assumption of an enduring or invariant objective domain which is intended (not 'created') by perception. Relatedly, a wide range of subjective modalities are endowed with their specific sense by reference to mundane reason's canonical specification of a real world: 'dreams' and 'imagination', for example, are constructed in part by contrast to that which is not real or objective, as in 'It was *just* a dream'.

Mundane reason also provides the resources for formulating a range of philosophical conundrums, paradoxes and puzzles. By playfully permuting elements of the mundane idiom, for example, all manner of vexed questions may be posed: Is there really a reality? Does it exist when I am not conscious of it? How can I tell if I am dreaming or wide-awake? These puzzles, I underscore, are raised from within and by virtue of mundane reason. As a way of highlighting the generative potential of the mundane idiom, the ways it provides resources for innumerable concepts, puzzles and solutions, I use the terms (as I already have) 'mundane discourse' and 'mundane space'.

Mundane reason is also a resource in that it stands as a background scheme of interpretation which provides the intelligible or accountable character of mundane inference and interpretation. As a shared idiom or language game, mundane reason provides members with resources for the formulation and grasp of a range of claims, comments and concerns without their having to be articulated in so many words. For example, by virtue of mundane reason's supposition of one real world, contradictory experiences or reports are fraught with implications for assessments of the quality of the observations or the character of the observers, e.g. someone is lying. Mundane reasoners 'hear' those implications and may even anticipate and attempt to preclude them. The ways in which the mundane idiom comprises a background schema which enables such inferences and strategies I refer to as mundane hermeneutics.

Mundane reason may be operative within consciousness and inter-action at an extremely primordial level. The inability to compose, experi-ence or account for oneself in mundane terms may be very bewildering to oneself and to others. Because mundane distinctions include the very differentiation of inner and outer, the inability to re-present experience in these terms may induce great anxiety: individuals may fear they are losing their 'minds' or 'worlds'. Relatedly, individuals may orient to mundane reason so deeply that they are prepared to honor the ideali-zations at great cost to themselves. Sacks (1972c) indicates the level of sacrifice which persons are apparently prepared to make in order to be (ac)counted as good mundane reasoners:

it does seem to be the case, perhaps curiously so, that even when persons are under interrogation for possibly serious offenses, ones for which their lives may be at stake, confessions can be garnered by saying to them that what they have said at some point is inconsistent with what they have said at another point. One might imagine them to say 'How can it be inconsistent; I said both those things,' or et cetera. A preliminary investigation of the method of interrogation suggests that while exploration of what goes on in such situations is of great interest, it is by no means to be supposed that persons take lightly the reasonableness,

consistency, clarity, and so on, of their answers, and may well be more concerned with preserving their claim to consistency than their claim to innocence
(p. 444).

While conceptualizing mundaneity as a network of beliefs, or prejudices, provides a concrete point of departure, it is important to keep in
mind the limitations of the analogy (to say nothing of the more severe
problems of describing that which provides for the possibility of 'description'). The prejudices comprising mundaneity, for example, are very
different from beliefs about the substance of reality such as the belief that
God does (or does not) exist or even that a particular object does or does
not exist. Mundane prejudices are not about the substantive or particular
nature of reality but about formal properties such as the existence,
coherence and subjective accessibility of reality *per se*. In this sense
mundane beliefs comprise a folk ontology. It should also be clear that
what we refer to as the beliefs, assumptions or prejudices of mundane
inquiry are not distorting or obfuscating features of mundane inquiry.
Nor are we arguing for a purified form of mundane inquiry purged of its
prejudices which would thereby enable it to discern and describe the
world more perfectly. The prejudices are not ordinary prejudices (or to
put the matter somewhat differently they are extraordinarily ordinary)
for it is through them that mundane inquiry in a bootstrap-like fashion
permits itself to be. Purging these primordial prejudices would not
enhance or improve mundane inquiry, it would dissolve and destroy
mundane inquiry.

The consequentiality and profundity of these beliefs foreshadows
several methodological problems. In approaching the beliefs of a culturally strange society an observer benefits from the perspective of the
outsider and is able to see the contingent or problematic character of what
insiders may regard as natural, given or inevitable. In the case of
mundane reason, however, we are the insiders. Thus, we may expect
that the constructed and precarious character of mundane beliefs and the
practices through which they are sustained will not be as readily
transparent as the precariousness of the beliefs of a strange society or
esoteric group. Accordingly, we will have to furnish what Garfinkel
(1967: citing Spiegelberg) referred to as 'aids to a sluggish imagination'
through which we can loosen the claim which mundane beliefs make on
our experience. Husserl (1962) referred to the network of mundane
assumptions as the 'natural thesis' and by that characterization captured
the way in which it provided for our sense of a 'nature' independent of
ourselves *and* the 'obvious' and hence seemingly 'natural' character of

that attitude. Our investigation of mundaneity requires that as analysts we recognize that the natural attitude has a compelling force for those within its sphere, while at the same time we develop resources to highlight the ways in which its ostensible 'naturalness' is an historical (Carr 1974; Bernstein 1978) and interactional accomplishment.[27]

A deeper problem is foreshadowed in the recognition that the very conception of 'belief' is itself an expression or construction from within the mundane idiom. The assumption of an objective world, a determinate order 'out there', dialectically implicates a network of other mundane distinctions. The 'objective out there', for example, implies a 'subjective in-here'. It implies as well certain modalities through which individuals may experience reality such as 'perception' or 'observation' and modalities in which individuals turn from the real to the subjective as in 'imagination', 'hallucination' or 'dreams'. The assumption of an objective world implies and is implied by a network of other terms which provide for the intelligibility of 'objective world' just as 'objective world' contributes to the sense of other idiomatic derivatives. Thus, to teach a child how to represent his or her experience as 'dreams' requires reference to the 'real': representation of ones experience as 'perception of the real' in turn requires reference to some experience of the non- (or 'subjectively') real such as dreams. Thus, 'subjectivity' and 'objectivity' are twin-born, each pole dialectically elaborating and requiring the other.

The concept of 'belief' and 'assumption' forms part of this dialectically elaborated grammar. We learn to use 'belief' in conditions when the 'objective facts' are unknown or problematic and we want to indicate the tenuous character of our claim (cf. Coulter 1979; Needham 1981). As such, however, 'belief' arises in an idiom in which an objective domain (outside the discursive or perceptual activity) is presupposed with regard to which descriptions or claims may stand in greater or lesser degrees of correspondence. The notion of 'real world' or 'objective reality' is embedded in an extensive, pervasive language game which includes as an intelligible move or possibility the use of the very concept of 'belief' itself (Wittgenstein 1969). Thus, as attractive as the conception of mundaneity as a belief system may be as an initial point of departure, we shall ultimately have to develop a yet deeper conception of the ways of mundaneity. The conceptualization of mundaneity as assumptions or beliefs is not so much to describe mundaneity as it is to move within the idiomatic space of mundaneity itself.

A related issue involves the extent to which inquiry into mundaneity can be truly radical. Mundane inquiry, insofar as it is a distinctive and discriminable mode of concern with the world, presumably stands in contrast to other varieties of inquiry. If the definitive feature of mundane inquiries is their concern with an objective world, a world *per se*, then presumably modes of inquiry which do not concern themselves with a world *per se* comprise alternatives. From time to time we have alluded to the 'radical' perspective, and it is this perspective which furnishes the alternative. Radical inquiry does not concern itself with a world *per se*, but rather with the facticity of a factual world, the objectivity of an objective world, and so on. Whereas mundane disciplines address a world *per se* – a presumptively preconstituted order of natural or mundane existents and the relations which obtain among them – radical disciplines address mundaneity, that is, the practices through which a world *per se* is constituted and made available as an analyzable domain in the first place. Yet no sooner is the distinction between mundane and radical inquiry formulated than certain antinomies are awakened and come to the fore.

All inquiry has a domain which is presumptively independent of its being taken up in analysis. Indeed, without the presumption of an essentially objective world, inquiry loses its sense as inquiry. In speaking 'of' or 'about' the structure of mundane inquiry, in articulating the theses, practices and structures which comprise mundaneity, radical inquiry finds its object, so to speak, in attending to 'the attending to the world *per se*'. Radical disciplines, therefore, address a second-order world *per se*, but it is a world *per se*. Though substantively unique, the order of affairs addressed in radical inquiry exhibits the formal properties exhibited by the domain of mundane disciplines, e.g. the properties of mundane reason are presumed to be independent of the procedures through which they are made observable. In short, while the notion of radical inquiry is a convenient expository device, inquiry into mundaneity, by simple virtue of the fact that it is inquiry, is rendered mundane.

The organization of the investigations

Sociology, we have suggested, is deeply immersed in a network of assumptions regarding the nature of reality, knowledge and experience. They suffuse sociological discourse about reality and contribute to the conceptual space within which sociology defines itself, its projects and its issues. These assumptions are similar to those which inform the discourse and inquiries of persons in everyday life. Thus, sociology treats as a non-problematic resource what members of society treat as a non-problematic resource – the assumptions and practices which produce, preserve and comprise mundane reason. These assumptions and practices, we proposed, are deeply entrenched in social life. As such they are not the resources of sociological investigations, but their topic.

The most primordial assumptions are those pertaining to the existence of objective structures, their coherence and their accessibility to others – in effect, assumptions which comprise a folk ontology and a folk epistemology. The penalty for naively participating in these folk ontologies and epistemologies is that sociology becomes infiltrated and infused by historically delivered and reproduced structures to whose operation it is oblivious because those structures seem natural, given, or inevitable. We have indicated, however, that there may be limits to the extent to which our inquiry, ethnomethodology or sociology generally, can divorce themselves from or transcend mundane resources.

In the following we seek to explore what we have proposed is all too often taken for granted as a resource by the social sciences and neglected as a phenomenon – mundaneity. At least initially, this entails examining the ways in which the work of mundane reflections upon, descriptions of, and investigations into a real world, advance, use, and sustain certain 'beliefs' or 'prejudices' regarding the nature of reality and its accessibility to observation and description. We shall explore mundaneity through examination of and reflection upon materials collected from a setting marked by a recurrent if not abiding concern with the 'real world' – municipal traffic court.

The materials considered in the study were gathered over the course of observation of six municipal courts located in four different municipalities. The courts varied considerably in size, character, and tempo. Big City Court, for example, was reputed to be the largest court in the United States devoted exclusively to arraignments for traffic violations. The court might arraign as many as two hundred and fifty defendants in both a morning and afternoon session, five days a week. Collegeville Court, in contrast, was a service provided by a much smaller municipality for the area immediately adjacent to a university campus. It was in session one afternoon a week during which forty or so individuals, the majority of whom were students, might be arraigned. In many of the courts I was allowed to tape record arraignments or given access to tapes made by the courts themselves. I took field notes regarding whatever seemed to be interesting or notable about the interaction between judge and defendant. I was especially interested in judges' decision work and made an effort to talk to them about their work in general and in regard to particular cases or issues which had occurred in preceding sessions. These materials are of interest in a number of ways: their salience for the analysis of mundane reason is that the judge, defendant, police officers and other involved parties are often intensely and consequentially involved in describing, theorizing about and determining the 'real'.[28] Though hardly exhaustive or representative of all settings in which mundane reason is involved, the centrality of mundane reasoning in traffic court transactions makes the court an attractive setting in which to begin.

In both trials and arraignments, judge and defendant are oriented to determinations of 'what *really* happened on the highway'.[29] That is, they are concerned with a world which is presumptively independent of what anyone happens to think, say or judge it to be. In a trial for a traffic offense, for example, the judge is concerned with finding the 'facts' and these are, of course not equatable with persons' 'descriptions' of the facts. Indeed, the facts are facts precisely because they are impervious to the ways in which they are made observable. The recognized possibility of errors, distortions, and falsehoods, and, for that matter, the recognized possibility of veridical perceptions and truthful accounts, is tacit testimony to an orientation to a real and objective order of existence.

The judge is also oriented to the determination of the guilt or innocence of the defendant. The guilt or innocence is presupposed as a 'real' property of the defendant, that is, as possessed of a being independent of the judgmental acts in which it is determined. The judge, for example, recognizes that his assessment of the defendant's guilt may be 'correct' or 'incorrect'. In the use of such a distinction, we find ourselves again in the presence of an idiom – a mundane idiom – which presupposes the essential objectivity of the domain about which determinations are being made.

Whether it be the concrete occurrences on the highway or their status as legal events, they are addressed, spoken about and judged as possessed of a determinate and real structure, that is, a structure which exists independently of the fact that it is addressed, spoken about, and judged. It is precisely through this concern with a real world that the court satisfies the definitive criterion and, for that matter, the only criterion of mundane inquiry. Our concern, I should underscore, is not with the court as such. The court is of interest only as a particular instance of mundane inquiry and site of mundane reason. The focus of these investigations are the assumptions and practices which provide for what mundane reasoners recognize as intelligible, warranted or 'accountable' inference and discourse about reality. Though the materials employed in the study derive from a specific setting these investigations are not ethnographic.[30] The traffic court and traffic court transactions are not attended to as matters of interest in their own right, but as occasions for inquiring into, reflecting upon and illustrating the suppositions which infuse and make possible intelligible discourse about the real. Moreover, though we utilize transcriptions of transactions we do not consider them in terms of the sequential structure of conversation *per se*, but as expressions and examples of a discourse through which members may make inferences, pose problems and proffer solutions regarding the 'real world'.

These materials and the reflections they provoke regarding lay inquiry, however, are but one tier of concern. Not only shall we describe the nature of mundane reasoning as it occurs within a single everyday setting, we shall explore the various ways in which mundane reason informs and infuses sociological inquiry as well. Thus, the observations about mundaneity of traffic court transactions comprise a springboard for observations regarding the mundaneity of sociology.

2

Mundane idealizations

When mundane inquiry reaches out for the 'real', it is confronted by a paradox: the real is precisely that which is independent of its 'grasp', and yet it is available only through some sort of grasping. The 'facts of the case' for a judge, for example, are features of the world and are thus independent of the manner in which they are made observable. Yet, the facts are only available through a situated course of talking, pointing, representing, perceiving or thinking. Mundane inquiry, in its concern with the real, attempts to transcend the particularity and situatedness of its concern, and yet it finds that it is always situated, always particular.[1]

Mundane inquiry, in its concern with factual structures, is addressed to that which is independent of anyone's saying and doing. Yet mundane inquiry is a course of saying and doing. The 'saying and doing' sets for itself the seemingly paradoxical task of presenting that which, precisely insofar as the saying and doing is 'successful', will make itself available as having had nothing to do with the saying and doing. The concern with the 'in-itself', 'reality' and 'truth' is an essentially transcendental and paradoxical pursuit of mundane inquiry. From the point of view of mundane inquiry, a problem *par excellence* is how to objectively determine the real, the objective, the in-itself – *given* that the in-itself is available only insofar as it is for-us. The problem for mundane inquiry, in other words, is how to gain access to a world which transcends the situated explicative work through which it is made observable – *given* that mundane inquiry is irremediably situated.

Mundane inquiry's pursuit of the real is embedded in a network of assumptions regarding the nature of objects and events in the real world. Among these assumptions are expectations regarding the coherency, determinateness and non-contradictory character of the real. Because these assumptions are advanced or invoked prior to any actual determination, observation or description of reality, we refer to these assumptions as *idealizations* (Bachelard 1968; Husserl 1970) of reality. The idealizations serve as 'guides' in mundane inquiry's efforts to transcend itself and determine the real. More specifically, they function as constraints which the corpus of mundane determinations – reports, claims and experiences – of reality must satisfy insofar as it is to be counted as intelligible and rational. Thus, for example, in hearing a defendant's claim that he made both a left and a right turn simultaneously, we 'know' that both claims cannot be literally correct. The rapidity with which a judge and we ourselves arrive at such conclusions and the confidence with which we assert them reflect our immersion in and use of the mundane idealizations.

In this chapter, we first specify more precisely the nature of the mundane idealizations which as we indicated stipulate the determinate and coherent character of real world events and objects. We then proceed to examine the ways in which they are used in court to interpret accounts and to credit some claims and discredit others as possibly correct versions of 'what really happened'.

Mundane idealizations of reality

In his exploration of 'phenomenological ontology', William Earle (1968) offers a characterization of our *a priori* understanding or 'intuition' of the real. Although I shall not address his larger philosophical concerns, Earle's characterization of the nature of the understanding of the real furnishes an especially cogent rendering of mundane reason's idealizations of the object. Whereas Earle regards the 'intuition of the real' as invariant, universal and cognitive, I prefer to think of the 'intuition' as part of the language game which mundane reasoners and mundane inquirers use as the background for doing intelligible inference and interpretation of the real. It is helpful to begin by considering Earle's formulation of the problematic which is resolved through our intuition of the real.

Earle (1968) proposes that objects are either 'clear' or 'unclear'. The clarity of the object depends on the correspondence between the 'idea' (e.g. representation, conception, perception) we have of it or the way it appears on the one hand and what it is on the other. However, Earle argues, 'we have nothing but objects as they appear', that is, objects are always mediated through perception, reflection and accounts.

How then, can we ever know that some objects *are* more or other than what they *appear* to be? . . . Obviously we could not regard any idea as an unclear idea unless we knew what it was to be real. If we had no idea of what reality must be in its most formal sense, we could never know whether in any given case we had a true or adequate or clear idea of some reality or not. In fact, the very notions of truth, falsity, clarity, unclarity, etc., would lose all meaning (p. 74).

Translated into terms resonant with our current concerns, Earle is raising the issue of how we come to hear accounts or claims about reality as inadequate or faulted. How is it that we come to hear, for example, contradictory accounts as problematic, as jointly betokening a situation which cannot exist in the real world and as suggestive that at least one account is an inadequate rendering of reality? Earle proposes that our appreciation of the problematic character of representations, perceptions, or reflections is produced through an *a priori* understanding of the real. According to Earle, our intuition is a formal specification of what an object must be insofar, and in the way, that it is real.

The idea of reality is nothing but the formal idea of Being, which is explicated by the laws of thought. It is the idea therefore by Being, which is discursively rendered as self-identical, non-contradictory, and absolutely determinate. Such an idea has, in one sense, no finite content. It doesn't say what is self-identical, non-contradictory, and absolutely determinate. It presents simply the form of anything that makes any pretense to reality. If anything claims to be real it must obey these 'conditions', or it is ruled out *a priori* (p. 75: italics deleted).

The intuition of the real, then, specifies that regardless of substance, a real thing is determinate and non-contradictory. As a consequence of this intuition, Earle continues, we impose constraints on reasoning and discourse.

The violation of these laws results ontologically in non-being, judgmentally in the false and absurd, and propositionally in the non-significative. It is therefore no accident or happy stipulation that sentences within any assertive language are forbidden to contradict themselves. It is, of course, a stipulation; but it is more than a stipulation: it is the sole assurance that the language can be meaningful, i.e. an assertive language at all. Nor is it any happy coincidence that thought aims to move in accordance with the 'laws of thought'; it must on pain of not being the thought of anything real, i.e., not being cognitive thought. The formulation of the laws can be either ontological, logical, or linguistic; but these formulations are not equipollent. The character of reality is the ground which establishes the rules thought and language must obey if either thought or language is to be truly related to the real rather than to nothing; and thought or language which has no object or meaning is not thought or language at all, but has collapsed into a non-cognitive, mental or non-symbolizing physical event (pp. 80–1).[2]

For Earle, our intuition of the real is an ontologically correct insight into the nature of the real. I do not wish to engage Earle on this issue but simply to propose that from a sociological point of view Earle's account is a useful rendering of the version of objects to which mundane reasoners hold one another accountable in their reports about reality. Mundane reasoners suppose real objects to be a determinate, non-contradictory and coherent ensemble of aspects and (like Earle) mundane reasoners treat those suppositions as ontologically correct. These idealizations serve as a pre-delineation of the relations which must obtain among mundane inquiry's determinations of the world, because for mundane inquiry the idealizations are descriptive of the world's structure *qua* real object. Thus, mundane inquiry can anticipate the relations which obtain among observers' reports insofar as they report upon the self-same object.[3] Specifically, given the idealizations of the object, diverse explications of that object can be expected to display a unity and reciprocity irrespective of the material character of the object. Insofar as both defendant and officer explicate the same highway scene, for example, in the very way that they are describing the 'same scene', mundane reason has already prefigured the relations which must obtain among the accounts, insofar as they are to be counted as possibly correct. They must be non-contradictory. Unless one were versed in the mundane idealizations of the object, there would be no particularly compelling or intrinsic reason for puzzlement over contradictory reports on the self-same object. A stranger to mundane reason, for example, might not even *hear* the contradiction. Without idealization of the object, conflicting reports might be heard as the explication of an object which happened to include, say, the fact that it was moving at a speed of sixty *and* seventy-five miles an hour.[4]

The presupposition of a determinate, non-contradictory, self-identical and coherent world are beyond invalidation, for they legislate in advance what mundane inquiry can find in the first place. For example, given that a defendant and an officer conflict as to the direction of an automobile, the principle of non-contradiction might be regarded as 'invalid'. That is, were the *préjugé du monde* and its derivative idealizations suspended, then the occasion of a conflict might be the occasion not for deciding which of the two persons was in error (as it is in a system of mundane reason) and which was telling the 'truth', but an occasion for considering if, perhaps, the idealizations of the object were invalid and a car could have been travelling north and south simultaneously. But mundane reason is not a 'neutral' system: it is not prepared to suspend its foundational prejudices. Thus, as we shall see, on the occasion of contradictory observations of reality, it is not the mundane idealizations which are brought into question but the nature of the observations or the adequacy of the observers.[5]

We turn now to consider the ways in which the mundane prejudice and its derivative idealizations inform the practices of mundane inquiry at least insofar as these practices are manifest in the traffic court. For the traffic court judge, the reports of the defendant and of the officer stand in some unknown relation to the 'real' or 'actual' state of affairs. Insofar as the judge is interested in determining what 'really' happened, he is confronted with a vicious circle. The 'real' scene is precisely that which is independent of the manner in which it is made observable, i.e. reports. Yet the scene in question is available only through situated reports: the relation of these reports to the scene they describe is indeterminate. As we shall see, determinations of 'what really happened' or 'the truth' are founded on an anticipation of the formal structure of 'real things'.

Mundane reasoning and the wisdom of Solomon

An interesting and useful prelude to our examination of the use of mundane idealizations in contemporary traffic court, is furnished by a description of mundane inquiry in a much older court; the Old Testament account of King Solomon's decision regarding two women, each of whom claimed to have given birth to the same child. The account is written about and written for mundane reasoners. The use of mundane reason is evident in both the specifics of the text and, more interestingly, in what is left unsaid or omitted because of its presumed obviousness.

Then came there two women that were harlots, unto the king, and placed themselves before him.
And the one woman said, Pardon, my lord, I and this woman dwell in one house; and I was delivered of a child with her in the house.
And it came to pass on the third day after I was delivered, that also this woman was delivered: and we were together, there was no stranger with me in the house, only we two were in the house.
And this woman's son died in the night; because she had overlaid him.
And she arose in the midst of the night, and took my son from beside me, while the hand-maid slept, and laid him in her bosom, and her dead son she laid in my bosom.
And when I rose in the morning to give my son suck, behold, he was dead; but when I looked at him carefully in the morning, behold, it was not my son, whom I had borne.
And the other woman said, It is not so; my son is the living one, and thy son is the dead; and this one said, It is not so; thy son is the dead; and the other saith, It is not so; thy son is the dead, and my son is the living; thus they spoke before the king.

Then said the king. This one saith, This is my son that liveth and thy son is dead: and the other saith, It is not so: thy son is the dead and my son is the living.
And the king said, Fetch me a sword; and they brought the sword before the king.
And the king said, Hew the living child in two, and give the one half to one, and the other half to the other.
Then spoke the woman whose son was the living unto the king, for her love had become enkindled for her son, and she said, O pardon, my lord, give her the living child, and only do not slay it; but the other said, Neither mine nor thine shall it be, hew it asunder.
The king then answered and said, Give her the living child, and so not slay it; she is its mother.
And when all Israel heard of the judgment which the king had given, they feared the king; for they saw that the wisdom of God was in him, to exercise justice (Leesser 1913: 1 Kings III).

Solomon need not be told as we, the readers, need not be told that there is a problem. The disputed sequence of events has a determinate structure and thus both women's accounts cannot be correct. In turn, it is the knowledge that there is some determinate sequence which allows us to interpret the womens' utterances as 'accounts' or 'claims' whose correspondence to 'what really happened' is problematic. As mundane reasoners we hear the contradiction of claims and even, perhaps, project possible explanations of the contradiction. The contradiction is not grasped as heralding some new ontological possibility that reality is constituted through perception and thus there are as many realities as there are perceivers. Rather, we as readers may conjecture, one or another of the women is 'lying' or 'deluded'.

Solomon's plight is especially well developed from a mundane reasoner's point of view. While the disputed scene has an objective and publicly accessible structure, Solomon was not present at the actual scene and cannot render a direct judgment. Moreover, both women are categorized as harlots and hence the claims of one cannot be given privilege over the other on the basis of moral reputation. Finally, there was no 'stranger' in the house, hence no one who can give an impartial or objective account. In this fashion, Solomon's plight is classically mundane: he is denied direct access to a real and determinate but disparately characterized objective sequence, yet he has to make a specific decision about 'what really happened'. The artfully narrated hopelessness of the situation from a mundane point of view is precisely what allows Solomon to display that 'the wisdom of God was in him'. Solomon himself underscores the ostensible impossibility of the situation: 'This one saith . . . and the other saith, It is not so . . .'

Solomon's solution is predicated upon substantive commonsense assumptions about 'mothers' and knowledge of the formal properties of the real. Solomon reckons that real scenes have a determinate and coherent structure, that is, an aspect of a real world scene implicates other aspects with which it is compatible. If Solomon can locate such an aspect, moreover one which might reveal itself in the immediate situation, then he would be able to ascertain the real mother. For Solomon, 'real mothers' place the well-being of their own child above any other consideration. Solomon's proposal to hew the child in two is an occasion in which the implicitly postulated disposition of a real mother to save her child at any cost is allowed to express itself. The omniscient narrator assures us that Solomon's implicit reasoning regarding real mothers is valid, for we are told, 'then spoke the women whose son was the living'.

The appreciation of the point or upshot of the tale requires work on the part of the reader (as well as the women and Solomon). The intelligibility of their speech acts, the nature of the problem, the genius of the solution are constituted through a framework of assumptions about persons and the substantive and formal nature of 'reality'. Insofar as one does not or cannot bring the mundane idiom to bear, then the tale threatens to fragment into a mere description without a 'point'. The deployment of mundane reason as a background schema through which acts of inference and interpretation are provided with their intelligible or pointed character comprises what might be termed the hermeneutics (Palmer 1969) of mundane reason. In what follows we shall explore mundane hermeneutics especially in regard to mundane reason's idealizations of objective reality. Moreover, we explore the idealizations in a modern incarnation of Solomon's court (at least with regard to the occurrence of contradictory claims about reality) – traffic court.

The idealizations of mundane reason and the interpretation of accounts

In court, 'what really happened' is typically made available through verbal accounts. Obviously, to describe what really happened requires more than simply stating 'This is what really happened'. It is necessary to provide the details, the properties, the features of 'what really happened' in order to realize or make observable the state of affairs, which is the intended object of analysis. For example, 'what really happened' may be realized by reference to a specification of the vehicles, their speed, inferred intentions of the driver and a virtual infinitude of other possible details. The descriptions may be extended indefinitely by a progressive explication of its details and/or by explication of the encompassing context in which it takes places. The event proper may be elaborated by reference to the make of the car, the number of scratches upon it, their size and so on, as well as by an elaboration of the prevailing world situation. Because the scene is available for infinite explication, the specifically noted aspects do not exhaust or fully comprehend the scene of which they are details.

The specifically noted aspects realize the scene in an *adumbrated fashion*. They present the scene as that-about-which-more-could-be-said, about-which-further-inferences-could-be-made, and so forth.[6] In examining the officer's comments on a traffic citation, for example, a reader could anticipate other notable details, some of which are directly (i.e. logically) implied by the aspects noted on the ticket, and others which, while not directly implied, are possible in the sense they would not contradict the specific comments. Indeed, if one chose to expand the scope of the event proper, then ultimately the world and the universe itself – the totality of all states of affairs – are aspects which, however remotely and indefinitely, are implicated in the description of a particular situated event, such as an improper left turn.

An example of the way in which an account points beyond its explicit particulars to further possible aspects was provided when I asked a judge to review a citation. The judge went to the clerk's counter and selected, in what seemed to be an arbitrary fashion, a citation which had been discarded by a defendant who had already paid his fine. It contained the following information:

> *Day*: May 28   *Time*: 5:00 p.m.   *Day of week*: Tuesday
> *Sex*: Male   *Height*: 5' 2"
> *Hair*: Brown   *Weight*: 120
> *Eyes*: Blue   *Birthdate*: 12-7-11
>
> Violations(s): 21651 V.C. Divided highway driving to left of divided section; Driving W/B on wrong side of Shoreline Dr. against E/B traffic Approximate speed: 20 mph

The judge noted the following:

See, here it says nineteen-eleven (1911) – he's an oldster. Now the fact that it says which traffic he was driving against and the time when he did it tells me its murderous – its thick traffic. No business address so the guy is probably retired. So he wasn't doing it as if he were taking a chance. He just didn't know. He wasn't doing it intentionally. He was driving right into the sun. He probably didn't see or something. Now if it was an eighteen year old kid it's something else. There you have to search for what he was up to. The ticket tells you what he's like, what's he driving; does he work, anything about his occupation, where does he live, how old is he, can he pay, is he rich or poor. What was he driving? A fast car?

As evidenced by the judge's imputations, the ticket is only a partial explication of the totality of possibly notable particulars. From the point of view of the judge, the specifically noted aspects point to both an inner and outer horizon (Gurwitsch 1964: 237) of further possible determinations. For example, the scene proper is internally elaborated by reference to the type of traffic prevailing as indicated by the time of the offense; this, in turn, furnishes the grounds for the inference as to the type of intention required for one to go against such 'thick' and 'murderous' traffic. It is as if the specifically noted aspects leave 'gaps' or 'lacunae', which may be inferentially extrapolated. When considered under the auspices of the idealizations, the citation particulars present themselves as partial explication of their object; an explication which at once promises and is informed by a horizon of further determinations which, if known, would render the intended object complete.

The noted aspects, for the judge, are details of an essentially determinate scene. The aspects are not treated as a mere congery (Sorokin 1964: 12–16) of particulars, but rather as a unified ensemble which refer to and realize a scene-in-the-world. As such, the 'gaps' are regarded as being capable of determination subject to the constraints imposed by the already specified particulars. Because it is the noted particulars which furnish the gaps in the first place, in the sense that they are the initial specification of the object, the solution to the gaps is already anticipated and implied by the explicit aspects of the scene (Gurwitsch 1965). To be sure, the extent to which further determinations are constrained, pre-structured or implied by the explicit aspects is variable. There is a latitude in the degree of certainty with which undisclosed aspects of the object may be anticipated. The 'oldster' in the citation may have known precisely what he was doing: he may have been 'young at heart' or, perhaps he was suicidal. Nevertheless, the scene, in the way that it is realized as a scene-in-the-world, presents itself, for the judge and for mundane reason in general, as one whose further determination is, to a varying extent, but always to some extent foreshadowed by this initial description (Gurwitsch 1965: 21).[7]

The process of interpretation through which the judge organizes the disparate pieces of information into a possible version of a scene in the world is guided by mundane suppositions regarding the coherency and determinateness of objects in the world.[8] It is by virtue of assuming that each aspect of real objects implies yet other aspects which are compatible with what is already specified, that the judge is able to flesh out, fill in, and extrapolate the 'more' of the scene in question. The mundane suppositions furnish the formal framework through which mundane reasoners engage in the 'documentary method of interpretation' (Garfinkel 1967; McHugh 1968) in which particulars are given their significance through an imputed underlying pattern. The mundane idealizations establish the formal pattern of relationships which exist among mundane particulars and serve as the skeletal framework around which mundane reasoners construct possible scenarios of the real. They also furnish the background assumptions through which mundane reasoners may accountably credit and discredit claims about concrete reality.

The idealizations and the crediting and discrediting of possible versions of reality

From the point of view of mundane reason, an account of a real state of affairs cannot validate itself. The description of what really happened on the highway does not and cannot guarantee its correspondence to what really happened on the highway. This is a manifestation of mundane inquiry's fundamental paradox, which is initiated because of mundane inquiry's concern with 'reality'. What really and actually happened refers to the state of affairs as it is in and of itself, independent of the mode and manner of its explication. For mundane reason accounts cannot certify their own adequacy because they are representations of the state of affairs and not the states of affairs themselves. While accounts do not validate the actuality of their referent, they do, from the point of view of mundane reason, provide for the *possibly existent character* of their intended referent.[9] That is, insofar as certain relations obtain among the aspects through which an account realizes its object, the object can be qualified or disqualified, as the case may be, with respect to its possibility as an object which could exist in the world. Specifically, the aspects through which an object is realized must not contradict one another. If the scene is to be made observable as one which could exist in the world, the particulars in the account must be mutually compatible and congruent. If the aspects contradict one another, they render their intended referent what Escher (1967: 22) would call an 'impossible object'. The aspects through which the scene is realized 'cancel' (Husserl 1962: 278, 388) one another. The intended scene is nullified for there is no single unified scene which can be the locus of its posited details. We cannot, for example, entertain the possibility of a car travelling simultaneously at sixty *and* seventy miles per hour without sacrificing the primordial idealization of mundane inquiry, the assumption of an essentially objective world.

The constraint imposed by mundane reason as the minimal conditions for mundane existence is manifest in the following excerpt from an arraignment in one of the largest and busiest traffic courts in the United States. Although this court is devoted to traffic arraignments, defendants are permitted to plead 'no contest'. When such a plea is entered, the defendant is allowed to account for the violation; and the officer is, in effect, represented by the court's copy of the original citation. Provision for more than fifty pieces of information is pre-formatted on the face of the citation. Information provided by the citation includes a specification of the violated vehicle code, officer's comments, the observed speed of the vehicle and the posted maximum speed limit. The citation involved in the case in question contained the following information:

> Violation: California Vehicle Code Section 22106
> Description of Violation: 'Heard tires squealing – obs'd [observed] Deft.
>   at Maine and 3rd – excessive speed (med. traf.) Lost traction of tires.'
> Approximate Speed: 15 mph
> Vehicle Speed Limit: 35 mph

It is fairly common practice for officers to specify the 'short title' of the violated vehicle code in their comments, and judges sometimes employ the 'short title' as a specification of the vehicle code subsection under which the defendant is cited. In this case, the judge treats 'excessive speed' as the title of the vehicle code, and it is with respect to the charge of 'excessive speed' that other specified aspects are found lacking.

> Judge: (Name), how do you plead?
> Defendant: Well your honor I wasn't at –
> J: No, no. You can't be guilty on the face of it. He says you were . . .
>   excessive speed, fifteen miles an hour in a thirty-five mile zone. And
>   that's not good enough for me. It's dismissed. You're free to go home.

The scene, which is initially characterized by the feature 'excessive speed' implies further possible aspects which must be fulfilled in certain pre-specified ways to be adequately realized as an instance of what it is purported to be. Specifically, the observed speed must exceed the posted maximum limit. To be sure, there is a latitude with respect to the requirements imposed by the aspect 'excessive speed'. The vehicle may be noted as traveling but a few miles, or a very great number of miles, over the speed limit. But the latitude of these possibilities is bounded by conditions which must be satisfied if the scene as described is to count as a possible mundane existent. Insofar as these conditions have not been satisfied, then a most peculiar object has been realized, one which cannot possibly exist. The possible existence of the scene is nullified on 'the face of it' by its presentation through aspects which cancel one another as possible details of the self-same object.[10]

The anticipations of mundane reason go beyond the absence of contradictions, inconsistencies and incongruities. Certain definite relations of continuance, complementarity and conformance among aspects are anticipated. In assuming the determinateness of the object, it also is assumed that both explicitly noted aspects and those yet-to-be-determined 'continue and complement one another and thus form a system, coherent in itself . . .' (Gurwitsch 1965: 21). There is, thus, the expectation for any accounted ensemble of aspects that not only will the aspects be in logical accord with one another, but, further, that the aspects form a continuous, coherent and, in this sense, 'harmonious' ensemble of aspects of which the intended object is the locus. This is not to say that accounts of reality are necessarily harmonious. But it is because of mundane reason's anticipation of such a harmony and determinateness that the disjunctures, 'gaps' and contradictions are notable in the first place. Mundane reason holds that practicalities notwithstanding, the 'scene on the highway' is *in posse* amenable to a complete specification which would, when completed, reveal itself as harmonious in the previously described sense. Let us consider the ways in which the idealization of non-contradiction and determinateness inform the practices of the judge in an actual arraignment. Because the following transaction involves a clear and direct conflict *between* accounts (whereas the last illustration dealt with a contradiction internal to a single account), a few prefatory remarks are in order.

A single account realizes its referent as a possible mundane existent by virtue of the internal congruency of posited aspects. This criterion of mundane reason holds for two or more accounts insofar as they purport to describe the self-same object. Each account furnishes a constraint for its counterpart in the sense that it comprises a description of the object with which other accounts must be logically compatible, insofar as the accounts are to be regarded as collectively realizing a state of affairs which could exist in the world.[11] Mundane reason attends to multiple accounts of the self-same object as virtual extensions of one another. To the extent that multiple accounts are to realize a jointly intended object, they must present themselves as if they had been uttered by a single speaker who had inspected the object from diverse perspectives. Merleau-Ponty's (1962: 84) description of perception's primordial presupposition that 'monadic and inter-subjective experience is one unbroken text' is an especially cogent characterization of mundane reason's anticipation of the relation between accounts. The presupposed consistency of the object anticipates that all observers will speak, in effect, as one. On the occasion of conflict among accounts, the aspects cancel one another and the intended object is, in Husserl's (1962: 388) terms, 'exploded'.

In the following transaction the citation asserts that the defendant was 'aiding and abetting' a drag race but the defendant states that no drag racing took place.[12] The descriptions contradict one another insofar as they are regarded as intending an identical spatio-temporal referent. Taken jointly as accounts of the self-same scene, they realize a scene which defies recognition as a possible mundane existent. Each account taken in isolation realizes a possible state of affairs – there could be drag racing or not – but when considered in relation to one another, they jointly formulate an event possible only in an absurd world (the features of which we shall have occasion to describe later). Given mundane reason's presuppositions, the accounts formulate a scene which cannot be. How could a scene-in-the-world have transpired of which 'drag racing' and 'no drag racing' are correct reports? That is a mundane problematic *par excellence*. From the point of view of the judge, the conflicting accounts, by virtue of the conflict, render one another mere 'versions' of what really happened. The problem: Of precisely what are the versions versions? At this point, we are afforded a glimpse of the way in which the idealization of determinateness informs the judge's interrogation and the defendant's response.

> Judge: How do you plead?
> Defendant: Could I plead guilty with an explanation?
> J: All right sir.
> D: Well it's true that I was at the scene of this incident, but it's not true that I was guilty of what I was charged of which was aiding and abetting a drag racing contest because there wasn't any drag racing going on. What happened is . . . I saw my mother and a friend parked . . . They were just down there to see what was happening, so I parked my car and I went over and I was inside their car talking for a few minutes and then the police barricaded both ends of the street off so we couldn't leave, then they charged me with aiding and abetting a drag racing contest, and there was no drag racing at all taking place.
> J: Well, the officers appeared at the scene of extensive drag racing and

gave an estimate of three hundred people present. Were there about three hundred people there:

D: No, ma'am, there wasn't.

J: Then, well perhaps –

D: I would say approximately a hundred and fifty and I –

J: Er, what were a hundred and fifty people doing at Riverside and Fletcher Drive?

D: Oh, well maybe there had been drag racing part of the time, but . . . while I was there, there was no drag racing at all, not even anyone driving a car in the street.

J: That'll be twenty-five or five. [Twenty-five dollars or five days in jail.]

The question, 'Were three hundred people there?' may be regarded as part of a search for those features upon which both officer and defendant are in agreement. The size of the crowd is presumedly relevant in that the presence of such a number of persons would require reference to an event which occasioned their presence: a congregation of three hundred persons would be a noteworthy event. The judge's next question, following the defendant's response, illustrates the use of an aspect to retrieve the character of the scene of which it is a coherent detail. The admitted presence of one hundred and fifty people is treated as promissory of a further determinable chain of complementary and harmonious aspects. Because of the presupposed unity and coherence of the object, any aspect serves as the grounds for further inference as to other yet-to-be revealed aspects. The judge's question seemingly searches for further explication of the scene adumbratedly revealed through the admitted presence of a crowd sufficiently large to have an occasioning reason. If not drag racing, then what aspectual ensemble is compatible with the presence of one hundred and fifty persons?

The defendant's response indicates an appreciation of the presupposition latent in the judge's interrogation. In the absence of any definite alternative, drag racing offers itself as a plausible feature of the scene thus far known only by reference to the presence of a crowd. The defendant's response simultaneously admits the viability of the chain of inferences and provides the 'solution' as to how drag racing could be admitted as a further aspectualization of the scene on the one hand and denied as he has already done, on the other. The solution, which in many ways is prototypic of mundane reason's *ad hoc* reconciliation of conflicting accounts, resides in the defendant's proposal that drag racing *might* have taken place prior to his arrival on the scene. The defendant proposes, in effect, that his report and that contained in the citation intend two temporally distinct but compatible phases of an ongoing activity. In this way, the conflict is made to 'disappear', because the two accounts no longer describe an identical referent.

Although neither judge nor defendant specifically articulate their assumptions about the nature of mundane reality, the moves within the transaction are predicated upon the idealizations. The judge's puzzlement regarding the presence of a crowd is predicated upon assumptions pertaining to the harmony or compatibility among the aspects of a real scene. The defendant, in turn, sees the 'puzzlement' and after an initial attempt to reconcile the ostensible incompatibility of 'large crowd' and 'no drag racing' by contesting the size of the crowd, resorts to an alternative reconciliation and so proposes that he and the officer are describing different phases of the scene. The formulability, intelligibility and solution of the puzzles reflect the mundane idealizations.

The world as the Great Object

Until this point we have been concerned exclusively with the ways in which single or multiple accounts are considered for their capacity to realize a possible existent. But mundane reason does not seek the in-itself by reference merely to the internal coherence of an account. Indeed, if it did then there would be no way to distinguish fairy tales from scientific accounts. Mundane reason anticipates not only the relations which obtain among the aspects of an object proper, but also the relation of the object to the encompassing order of which it is a part and which, when extended to its utmost, comprises the world.

We have seen the pre-requisites which mundane reason sets for an account insofar as it is to be regarded as describing a possible mundane existent. These pre-requisites are derived from mundane reason's idealized image of the relations which are exhibited by an absolute thing known to an absolute spectator. As we have also noted, these conditions extend beyond the object proper to include its 'context'. Mundane inquiry anticipates that a particular scene will be internally harmonious *and* that it will be continuous with and complementary to the order of mundane existence in which it is embedded. For example, a defendant's story may be internally coherent, and yet its validity may be disputed because it was known that a storm had demolished the coast highway at the time and place to which the defendant's account refers. All of the anticipations which mundane reason holds for the 'isolated' object are held as well for the object-in-context. In fact, for mundane reason, the object-in-context is but another object proper. And, of course, like any other object, the object-in-context has its context which may be expressed as (the-object-in-context)-in-context, which is itself but another object *ad nauseum, ad infinitum.* For mundane reason, the world and the universe come to comprise what Merleau-Ponty (1968: 15) calls the 'Great Object'. From the viewpoint of mundane reason, the world, as the over-arching context of lesser objects and thus an object itself, is idealized as a 'finished explicit totality in which the relations are those of reciprocal determination'.[13]

The idealization of the world as object means that the actuality of any particular scene depends on its compatibility with every other state of affairs which comprises the world. An account of an event on the highway, insofar as the event is proffered as real, implies a compatibility of the event with its surrounding context, a context which ultimately comprises the universe. The relation between the accounted event and what mundane reasoners treat as given or factual regarding the context provides a resource for establishing or assessing the possibility and plausibility of the accounted event. The assumed compatibility between an event and the context in which it presumably occurred, for example, allows mundane reasoners to mobilize putative knowledge about the context to credit, qualify or discredit claims about what 'really' happened. The sources of knowledge about context are diverse and range from personal observation to commonsense knowledge of particular or typical aspects of social or physical reality. Insofar as they are treated as matters of fact or likelihood, the specifications of context comprise constraints to which an account of a purportedly real event may be held responsible. Thus, a mundane reasoner, though not witness to an actual scene, nevertheless has warrantable ways of assessing the extent to which a claimed version corresponds to what really happened.

In the following arraignment, the defendant's status as a student furnishes a specification of the world with which the accounted scene must be reconciled, insofar as it is to count as a possible mundane existent.

> Judge: You're charged with a university parking violation. Did you hear and understand your rights?
> Defendant: Yes sir.
> J: Do you want to see an attorney?
> D: No.
> J: How do you plead?
> D: Guilty.
> J: Do you want to be heard and sentenced now?
> D: Yes sir.
> J: What have you to say?

> D: Well, there were no signs indicating that there was no parking. There
>   was no sign indicating it was university property, and there was a sign
>   that said – 'Property of Collegeville City, No Dumping' –
> J: Didn't you know this was the University?
> D: No. It was in the – sort of in the sloughs. By the airport.
> J: What do you do?
> D: I'm a student.
> J: Where?
> D: At the University.
> J: And you don't know that this is the marine laboratory area?
> D: Well, I mean you'd have to see – I'd imagine you'd have to see it to
>   understand. It's by the slough. And it's just so –
> J: Whose property did you think it was?
> D: Well, I thought possibly it was the city's. There's a sign there that
>   said, 'Property of Collegeville City, No Dumping'. So –
> J: Well, I'll cut it [the fine] down.

The account realizes an object which, from the point of view of the
judge, could have happened in the world were it not for the fact that the
world in which it presumedly occurred is one which contains the
defendant as a 'student'. The judge in this instance employs what Sacks
(1972a, 1972b) has termed a 'member's categorization device' to warrantably establish what the defendant *qua* incumbent might or ought to
properly know.[14] If one is a 'student at the university', then one
presumedly has some knowledge of the layout of the campus. Insofar as
the relation between categorization and expected knowledge is accepted
as a factual aspect of the world, it contradicts an aspect of the scene
realized in the defendant's account. Insofar as 'what any student knows'
includes the boundaries of the campus, an otherwise coherent story is
made observable as contradictory *vis-à-vis* the order of mundane existence in which the scene is purported to have happened.[15] In proposing
the defendant's status, the judge, in effect, is explicating aspects of a
mundane order in which the accounted scene makes its claims for
membership, and with which it will have to be reconciled, insofar as it is
to be a possible event in that order.

Judges' versions of typical police practice furnish another source of
knowledge of the context of highway events. As part of their workday
circumstances, judges accumulate and construct versions not only of
typical violators and violations (Sudnow, 1965) but of the ways in which
police typically respond. These versions of typical police practice may be
invoked as features of the context with which accounted events must be
compatible insofar as the event is to be counted as having really occurred.
For example, judges know that police use discretion in issuing a citation

and that they may elect not to cite violators given exceptional circumstances. Thus, a judge may question the veracity of a defendant's account
of exceptional circumstances precisely because if the circumstances were
as described they ought not to have resulted in the issuance of a citation.

In the following arraignment, the defendant recounts what he specifically prefaces as an exceptional sequence of events. The very exceptiona-
lity of the sequence set against the assumption about typical police
response to such events, however, precipitates the judge's search for
how the defendant came to receive a citation in the first place.

> Judge: Mr. Flood, uh, handing you a copy of a complaint filed in this
> court that charges you with a violation of 22349, exceeding the
> maximum speed limit and also alleging a prior offense of the same
> type. The effect of the prior offense, uh, has only to do with what
> penalty might be assessed.
> Defendant: I understand.
> J: All right now . . . Are you gonna have a lawyer in this case?
> D: No, your honor.
> J: All right, well, how do you plead?
> D: Guilty, with an explanation.
> J: All right.
> D: Uh, I don't know if you can understand this, your honor, because I
> mean it's not something I imagine that you hear very often.
> J: Well, let's try it anyhow.
> D: Ok. (laughs) I'm a hemophiliac and occasionally I do internal
> bleeding as a result of this. And on this particular evening I was in Los
> Angeles having dinner with my parents, and on the way back to
> Collegeville where I go to school – I'm a senior there . . . On the way
> back to school I realized that I was doing some internal bleeding. And
> it was in my ankle. And the longer that it goes on, the worse that the
> pain gets, and pretty soon you lose all mobility and you're just laid up
> for a lot of days. And what I needed was an immediate transfusion of
> plasma . . . which I keep at school. And the reason that I was speeding
> was so that I could get there as fast as possible so that I can get, get this
> plasma.
> J: Well, do you have any kind of card like, uh . . .
> D: Yes, I have identification.
> J: Well, give it to the mmmm . . .
> D: Oh yeah.
> J: . . . uh, bailiff there, and uh. Well, did you show this to the officer?
> D: No, I didn't and there was a couple of reasons why I didn't. That big
> . . . those cards come out monthly and that's my February one and it
> entitles me to withdraw plasma from the blood bank.
> J: Well, why, why didn't you tell the officer about this?
> D: Well, there was two reasons why. First of all, I was – well you know I
> was guilty of speeding and I figured if I was guilty of speeding, I was

just, you know, guilty of speeding. And secondly the officer was,
mmmm you know, he was kind, but he was also brusk, as far as you
know, the speed which he started to write this ticket. I mean he just
walked up and he says, 'let me see your license', and then he says,
'you were going 80 and I'm gonna give you a citation', and then he
walked back to his vehicle and began to write it, and so, as soon as he
came back to my car, I just, you know, I left again.

J: All right. Awright. It'll be a judgment of the court then, that you pay a
fine and penalty assessment of five dollars, all right?

D: Thank you very much your honor.

J: All right.

Assumptions about typical police practice may affect contextual specification in even more subtle ways. For example, all citations provide
space for the citing officer to describe the nature of the violation. From
the point of view of the judge, the officer's comments are a 'judicious'
selection from among the infinitude of details which might have been
noted. The comments are not regarded as a random or arbitrary selection
of details, but rather are treated as representing features of the scene
which are distinctively relevant to the offense for which the citation was
issued. Further, judges recognize that officers may note details which
serve to aggravate or mollify the severity of the offense. Indeed, at one
time the letters 'HBD' enjoyed a certain currency as officers' *sub rosa*
terminology for informing the judge that the defendant 'had been
drinking'. Judges' knowledge of and assumptions about the construction
of police texts procedure imparts significance to an officer's written
comments and their absence. Not only are the citation particulars
regarded as having been judiciously selected, but the empty lines are
regarded as if the officer had functioned under the rule: when there is
nothing relevant to add, note that by leaving the lines empty.

Needless to say, empty lines represent an infinitude of unmentioned
details. What the citation specifically leaves unsaid – what *this* officer in
writing *this* citation did not note – awaits the defendant's account. The
citation is reviewed for what it does not state under the auspices of what
the defendant claims to have been the case. In the previous excerpt, the
'hemophiliac' arraignment, the judge's interrogation of the defendant
may have been informed by the noted absence of any comments of the
officer which would imply his, the officer's, responsiveness to the
defendant's compelling justification for speeding. Given the defendant's
'strong' excuse, the citation's failure to note any mitigating circumstances
induces the judge to search for how the absence came to be. One
possibility, of course, manifest in the judge's interrogation, is that the

defendant did not tell the officer the justification; and hence the officer could not respond to what he did not know.

In the following excerpt we see how the 'empty lines' are employed to *confirm* the possible adequacy of the defendant's account. The defendant was cited for an improper right-hand turn. He claims that in order to get off the freeway at a particular exit, he had to sweep across several lanes but that he did not interfere with other traffic. The judge notes that the citation does not state what it should not state if the accounted scene is to be regarded as a possible mundane existent.

> Judge: If that's the case, what you should do is just go right on.
> Defendant: I know it. I –
> J: Specially with a freeway.
> D: I know. Right. I made sure I was far enough ahead of the other car, but I didn't think of the other angles.
> J: Well, he didn't note that there was apparently anybody that you blocked off. He also noted you didn't signal. Well, I'll cut it down and make it eight dollars.

The judge's reference to what the ticket does *not* note relies implicitly on knowledge of the ways in which police typically describe scenes. The meaning of the empty lines presupposes knowledge of what an officer would, in fact, note had he observed the conditions which the defendant claims did not obtain. As we noted previously, from the viewpoint of the judge, the empty lines are motivated omissions in the sense that they are regarded as not saying things which need not have been said. The empty lines confirm the defendant's account in this case because they are compatible with the defendant's claims. That is, what the officer did not state is precisely what he should not state if the defendant did not interfere with the flow of traffic.

The significant feature of these arraignments is the way in which the judge's knowlege of police practices constitutes an aspect of the world with which an accounted scene must be harmonious, insofar as it is to be regarded as a possible mundane existent. More generally, they are illustrations of how mundane inquiry's idealization of the world as the Great Object founds the practices through which the judge, in particular, and mundane inquiry, in general, arrive at a determination of potentially correct versions of the 'in-itself'. In each of the analyzed arraignments, a contextual specification was used to discredit or accredit the existential possibility of the accounted scene. And such practices are predicated upon mundane inquiry's anticipation of the world as determinate, non-contradictory, and internally coherent.

Concluding remarks

Mundane inquiry projects its idealizations of the object, and thereby furnishes itself with a formal depiction of the real. The anticipation of the coherency of the object and, more generally, of mundane reality dictates the relations which must obtain both within and between reported experiences of mundane reality. Mundane reasoners, moreover, attempt to achieve these relations over the course of inquiry. They reconcile conflicting or discrepant reports to produce a corpus of accounts which is coherent, determinate and non-contradictory. Through the work of reconciliation – the qualification or discrediting of one or another version – the *a priori* suppositions regarding mundane reality are invariably confirmed by mundane reasoners. In this fashion, mundane reason's assumptions are reproduced as self-evident features of mundane reality.

The idealizations ground the practices of inference which provide for the qualification or disqualification of accounts as possibly correct versions of the scenes upon which they report. Indeed, in the very way in which they specify the relations which obtain among aspects of a real object, the idealizations furnish the possibility of inference *per se*. It is only by reference to the idealizations of coherence and determinateness that the practice of deriving one aspect from the noted presence of another is possible. Similarly, the idealization embodied in the principle of non-contradiction provides for the possibility that given one determination of an object an alternate set of determinations is *prima facie* invalid.

The idealizations are not incidental aspects of the prejudice of an essentially objective world. Rather, they are implicated in the prejudice in the sense that they are formal specifications of the real object as a real object. It is not as though, for example, one could maintain the prejudice while suspending the anticipation of, say, the non-contradiction of an object's aspects. The principle of non-contradiction is, from the point of view of mundane inquiry, a constitutional principle of the real. Indeed, the preceding discussion suffers in that it tends to depict the idealizations as instrumental devices which are more or less arbitrarily invoked in order to furnish mundane inquiry a handhold on the transcendent. In fact, the idealizations are built into mundane inquiry from its outset. In the very ways in which mundane inquiry is constitutionally oriented to an objective order, mundane inquiry projects the idealizations onto the world. But even this formulation misses the mark. It is not that mundaneity 'projects' or 'imposes' its idealizations on the world, but rather that the world – in the way that it is the world – is internally coherent, non-contradictory and determinate. That the idealizations are definitive of the world in this fashion is manifest in the fact that mundane reason is essentially indefeasible by reference to contrary observational reports on what the world is like. As we have seen, for example, a conflict between the report of an officer and that of a defendant does not provide the occasion for questioning the system of mundane reason. It does not provide the occasion for asking if, perhaps, it is possible that there could be both drag-racing and no-drag-racing taking place simultaneously. Instead, the conflict, which is itself a term in the idiom of mundane reason, precipitates a search for which, if either, of the two reports is correct.

From 'outside' the network of distinctions and suppositions comprising mundane reason, episodes of conflicting accounts are of special interest: they are moments at which mundane reason's fundamental prejudices are threatened. Yet mundane reason provides its practitioners with a wide range of explanations which preserve mundane reason's stipulation that reality is coherent, determinate and intersubjectively accessible. The nature of the self-preservation of mundane reason comprises our next concern.

3

The self-preservation of mundane reason

Mundane inquiry presupposes a world, that is, a determinate order which exists independently of the methods of observation and description through which it is considered. Indeed, it is by virtue of the assumption of objectivity that the sense of 'description' or 'observation' is constituted. The assumption of an objective reality is an assumption: one cannot move quite quickly enough to run around consciousness or discourse to ascertain the ultimate or transcendental nature of 'reality'. The end run would only culminate in yet another perception or another description. Thus, the 'thereness' of the world, this most obvious and unremarkable feature of mundane existence, is not empirically given but a prejudice:

The central and most cunning feature of the taken for granted everyday world is that it *is* taken for granted. As common-sense men living in the mundane world, we tacitly assume that, of course, there is this world all of us share as the public domain within which we communicate, work and live our lives. Moreover, we naively assume that this world has a history, a past, that it has a future, and that the rough present in which we find ourselves is epistemically given to all normal men in much the same way . . . Throughout all of the routine elements and forms of existence, we simply assume, presuppose, take it for granted that the daily world in which all of these activities go on is there; it is only on special occasions, if at all, that a serious doubt arises as to the veridical character or philosophical signification of our everyday world (Natanson's introduction to Schutz 1967: xxvi).

The prejudice is so deeply engrained in mundane reason and mundane reasoners that save for very special philosophical moments it is never seriously doubted or seriously threatened. Yet mundane reason is under a veritable siege of events which threaten to subvert or dissolve its primordial prejudices. From within, mundane reasoners may feel 'ontologically secure' to borrow Laing's (1965: 39–61) phrase but from without the security is visible as the product of courses of reasoning through which mundane reason reflexively preserves itself. In this chapter we seek to examine the ways in which the mundane prejudices preserve their integrity in the face of subversive possibilities.

As a prelude to such an examination, we must probe more deeply into the matter which is to be examined. What after all, is meant by 'preservation'? Indeed, what is the nature of the 'threat' against which mundane reason preserves itself? In order to answer these and related questions adequately, we must re-examine and specify the relations which mundane reason anticipates will obtain among observers' reports or descriptions of the 'self-same' object. This is necessary because the 'threat' resides in the conflict among accounts. It is at the moment of conflict or contradiction that mundane reason's founding assumptions are jeopardized. At such moments mundane reason is confronted with the question: Given the presumption of an essentially objective world, how are conflicting reports possible? Is it possible that the founding prejudices of mundane reason regarding the determinate and intersubjective nature of reality are 'invalid'?

Having obtained insight into the potentially subversive nature of conflicting accounts, we shall advance to a specification of mundane reason's reflexive preservation of its founding prejudices. Here again, however, we need to gain distance from mundane reason in order to appreciate the practices of preservation. We do so by examining the self-preservative features of an alien idiom: the reasoning of the Azande as it is manifest in their use of the 'poison oracle' (Evans-Pritchard 1937). As we shall see, what at first appears to be merely a circular albeit ingenious use of reasoning practices among the Azande, turns out to have a parallel among mundane reasoners.

A further specification of the idealizations of mundane reason

The mundane prejudices are anticipations of the relations which obtain among observers' experiences and accounts insofar as they intend the self-same object. Given (a) the presumptive independence of the object or scene from the methods through which it is made observable and, given (b) the idealization of the object as internally coherent, non-contradictory and determinate, then the object in the ways in which it is an object prefigures (Husserl 1961: 347) the relations which obtain among a corpus of determinations of the object's aspects. Specifically, these prejudices found the expectancy that determinations of the object's aspects will be essentially identical and compatible. That is, mundane reason anticipates that the formal properties of the object *qua* object will obtain among determinations of the object's aspects.

The idealization of the object in turn is inextricably wedded to parallel idealizations on the level of experience and the level of accounts or verbal reportage as well. The assumed self-identicality, determinateness, and internal coherence of the object is simultaneously an anticipation of other persons experience of the object. Schutz (1962) called a variant of this anticipation 'the idealization of the interchangeability of standpoints'.

I take it for granted – and assume my fellow man does the same – that if I change places with him so that his 'here' becomes mine, I shall be at the same distance from things and see them with the same typicality as he actually does; moreover, the same things would be in my reach which are actually in his. (The reverse is also true.) (p. 12)

The idealization states in effect that the object (in the ways that it is an object) is that which would be similarly experienced by alter, were she and ego to exchange positions. The object as object makes unavoidable reference to the actual and potential experiences of others. Indeed, mundane reason's anticipations extend beyond the perceptual or exper-iential level. They are tacit expectations of the relations which ought to obtain among observers' reports insofar as they have witnessed the self-same object. As Merleau-Ponty (1963) notes:

I know that by changing place I could see sides which are hidden from me; by occupying the position which was that of my neighbor a moment ago, I could obtain a new perspectual view and give a verbal account which would concur with the description of the object which my neighbor gave a moment ago (p. 213).

The objectivity of the object makes references to a community of corroborating perceptions and accounts. The other – every other – is my perceptual surrogate and complement enjoying the perceptions which I would were I to assume his position, perceptions which are to some extent announced in my contemporary apprehension of the object. To speak of the objectivity of the world is to anticipate the essentially similar or corroborative experiences and reports of an infinity of other actual or imaginable persons.

The mundane idealizations regarding a commonly shared world are more complex than these terse statements might imply. Consider, for example, that the thesis of the interchangeability of standpoints cannot be sustained when the other is deemed 'impaired' or 'incompetent'. Indeed, the anticipation of a community of corroborating experience implicates an indefinitely large and various *ceteris paribus* (Helmer and Rescher 1959) provision regarding the capacities of the community with respect to which experiences are deemed interchangeable. For example, the other must be assumed to be psychically homogeneous with ego. Obviously, to the extent that the other is deemed psychically 'different', ego can no longer anticipate that the other would experience and/or report upon the scene in a corroborative fashion. Thus, the possibility of intersubjective verification presupposes a version of alter's psycho which holds that it is essentially similar to ego's. 'I take for granted until counter evidence appears', Schutz (1967: 327) notes, 'not only the bodily existence of my fellow-man, but also the fact that his conscious life has substantially the same structure as my own'.

In the phenomenological literature these and related theses or assumptions have been largely attended to for the ways in which they infuse and inform our perception of the world and others. In what follows I shall address these suppositions for the ways in which they inform persons' discourse about the world and about others. We are addressed, for the moment, exclusively to the ways in which the suppositions regarding a commonly shared world comprise the basis for a variety of talking activities of which the posing of puzzles and the formulation of solutions are prominent examples.

Mundane idealizations as conditions for posing a puzzle

The mundane assumptions are of such pervasive import in everyday interaction that it is exceedingly difficult to pinpoint their specific functioning. What indeed would it be like to abandon the assumptions of a world shared in common with presumptively competent and psychically homogeneous others? Minimally, it would seem that one is relegated to an unrelieved and unrelievable uncertainty as to what others perceive and, radically, to an autistic domain void of a sense of world, others, and self. But relatively specific usages can be identified, particularly when we conceive of the suppositions as the background understandings presupposed by some very special sorts of language games (Wittgenstein 1951). That is, the suppositions of a commonly shared world provide for the possibility of linguistic moves which, to put the matter grossly, would be virtually unintelligible were the mundane suppositions not invoked as a schema of interpretation. What are those moves? Prominent, if not foremost among the activities made possible by the supposition of a commonly shared world is the intelligible posing of a certain sort of puzzle on the one hand and a class of candidate solutions to those puzzles on the other. As we have already noted, the archetype of the puzzle, made possible by the assumption of a world shared in common with competent similarly constituted others, is the one posed by disjunctive experiences and/or accounts of what is purported to be the same world.

In proposing that the schema provides for the recognition of disjunctures as puzzles, we mean to indicate that there is nothing intrinsically problematic about persons having or reporting contradictory experiences. A possible response to conflicting reports as to, say, whether or not an automobile was parked at a particular place at a particular time could be 'So?' That they are heard and attended as something 'troubling' or 'wrong', as something in need of solution or explanation, requires reference to an understanding and expectancy of the sort of relations which ought to obtain among experiences purportedly intending the same world. It is in attending to conflicting experiences under the auspices of a schema which presupposes a commonly shared public domain and thereby anticipates congruent and compatible experiences that the 'something wrong' is constituted as such.

Presumably, for persons who do not or cannot invoke the schema of suppositions regarding a commonly shared world, disjunctive experiences would not pose a problem. Such a naivete or incapacity may be on the fringes of conceivability for adult Western thinkers inasmuch as the mundane schema seems to be implicated in the very notion of person. One who never grasped the sense of that which was other than and independent of himself – the world – could not grasp himself as a self and would thus be condemned to live his life in an autistic, egocentric fashion (whose character as such would be available only to others). And indeed it is perhaps just those persons who are said to move in such realms – schizophrenics and children – persons who have abandoned or have yet to achieve use of the mundane assumptions who afford a glimpse of the ways in which the constitution of puzzles, posed by disjunctures, is not assured outside of the invocation of the assumptions as a schema of interpretation. For example, Minkowski (cited in Binswanger 1968) speaks of 'desocialized' patients who have earned their title not simply by failing to perceive what other persons perceive but by failing to be surprised by the lack of consensus. Relatedly, Piaget's (1928) description of the egocentric mentality of children emphasizes their non-existent or embryonic grasp of the idea of the ways in which they and others are confronted with a common world. As a consequence, the problems which are problems only under the auspices of such a schematic understanding are not problems for young children or, insofar as a rudimentary recognition obtains, they are problems which are solved in ways that do not comport well with adult solutions.

The problem posed by disjunctures is a contingent problem in that not any one could have it as a problem. Its constitution as a problem requires a competence of which a minimal component is the knowledge and use of a schema of suppositions specifying the relations between the 'real' world, others' experience, and one's own experience. That a community orients to the world as essentially constant and as known and knowable in common with others, provides that community with the warrantable grounds for asking questions of a particular sort of which a prototypical example is: How come he or she sees or claims X and you do not?

Competence as a mundane reasoner consists not only of the capacity to hear a puzzle on the occasion of a disjuncture, but to be able, as well, to formulate and recognize candidate correct solutions. Not any solution will do for as we shall see mundane reason provides implicit guides for how one is to search for an answer and for deciding upon possibly correct ones. But in order to see how a mundane reasoner is in fact guided toward certain solutions we must gain at least an analytic sense of how he or she is guided away from others. Indeed, on the occasion of conflicting accounts mundane reason is threatened with a crisis to its primordial assumptions regarding the presumptively objective and intersubjective nature of reality. The 'crisis' of mundane reason arises on those occasion wherein the presumptively self-same world is described in contradictory or otherwise incongruous accounts. It is at this point that the foundational idealizations and prejudices are in jeopardy, for the unanimity of accounts implicitly predicted by them is not forthcoming. Is it possible, given the conflicting accounts, that the world is not the self-same world for us all? To appreciate the crisis and mundane reason's self-preserving and prejudicial manner of resolving it requires that we contemplate alternative ways of attending to these disjunctive moments of experience and reportage.

Perspectives for making observable the properties of mundane solutions to mundane puzzles

As a means of gaining perspective on the organisation of mundane solutions, it is useful to consider the properties of ostensibly esoteric systems of reasoning. In a memorable section of his book, *Witchcraft,*

Oracles and Magic Among the Azande, Evans-Pritchard (1937) describes Azande reasoning regarding the 'infallible' poison oracle. The poison oracle is a method used by the Azande to gain knowledge of future or otherwise uncertain matters. A ritually prepared poisonous substance is administered to a chicken and the poison, *benge*, is interrogated. The benge responds in an affirmative or negative fashion by either killing the chicken or allowing it to live. The correspondence between the life and death of the chicken and an affirmative or negative response are formulated when the interrogator addresses the benge. A verdict of the oracle is corroborated by asking essentially the same question at a later time with the response alternatives reversed. Thus, if the oracle was initially instructed to kill the chicken if it intended an affirmative reply, it is subsequently instructed to permit the chicken to live if it intends an affirmative (p. 299).

Evans-Pritchard reports that over the course of his field work many of the questions which his European audience subsequently raised had occurred to him in the field.

what happens when the result of one test contradicts the other which it ought to confirm if the verdict be valid; what happens when the findings of oracles are belied by experience; and what happens when two oracles give contrary answers to the same question (p. 313).

Is it not on such occasions that the oracle is most vulnerable to exposure? Would not the failure of the oracle to appropriately confirm an earlier verdict, for example, reveal the oracle to be void of any prophetic or magical power? Evans-Pritchard reports upon the consequences of his attempt to confront the Azande with actual events and experimental possibilities which, from the point of view of a European, would unequivocally demonstrate the fallacious premises upon which oracle reasoning rests. The particulars are too rich and diverse to recount here. At every point, however, Evans-Pritchard's apparently well founded, albeit implicit, indictment of the Azande's belief in the oracle was met and rebuffed by an equally formidable logic.

Azande observe the action of the poison oracle as we observe it, but their observations are always subordinated to their beliefs and made to explain them and justify them. Let the reader consider any argument that would utterly demolish all Zande claims for the power of the oracle. If it were translated into Zande modes of thought it would serve to support their entire structure of belief. For their mystical notions are eminently coherent being interrelated by a network of logical ties, and are so ordered that they never too crudely contradict sensory experience but, instead, experience seems to justify them. The Zande is immersed in a sea of mystical notions, and if he speaks about his poison oracle he must speak in a mystical idiom (pp. 319–20).

Indeed, at times it appears that the Azande are amused by the absurdity of Evans-Pritchard's questions, and regard him with a charity reserved in our own society for recognized cultural incompetents (such as children). Azande are never threatened by Evans-Pritchard's questions or by ostensible contradictions and anomalies.

As we may well imagine, the oracle frequently kills both fowls or spares both fowls, and this would prove to us the futility of the whole proceeding. But it proves the opposite to an Azande. They are not surprised at contradictions; they expect them. Paradox though it be, the errors as well as the valid judgements of the oracle prove to them its infallibility. The fact that the oracle is wrong when it is interfered with by some mystical power shows how accurate are its judgements when these powers are excluded.

Azande is seated opposite his oracle and asks it questions. In answer to a particular question if first says 'Yes' and then says 'No'. He is not bewildered. His culture provides him with a number of ready-made explanations of the oracle's self-contradictions and he chooses the one that seems to fit the circumstances best. He is often aided in his selection by the peculiar behavior of the fowls when under the influence of the poison. The secondary elaborations of belief that explain the failure of the oracle attribute its failure to (1) the wrong variety of poison having been gathered, (2) breach of a taboo, (3) witchcraft, (4) anger of the owners of the forest where the creeper grows, (5) age of the poison, (6) anger of the ghosts, (7) sorcery, (8) use (p. 330).

Other questions which Evans-Pritchard puts to the Azande (and which are quite understandable and potentially devastating to the Azande system if one uses Western science as a frame of reference) are greeted with similarly self-preserving responses. Indeed, the maxims regarding the omniscience of the oracle – the Azande say 'The poison oracle never errs' – may be treated as the warrant for bringing into doubt the validity of one's experience and knowledge. The oracle, for example, is routinely used to identify witches. After an oracle identification is made the accused individual is confronted with the oracle's statement by an emissary of the offended party and requested to 'blow water' and thereby end the witchcraft he is accused of working. In such confrontations (or in private, for it is good form to blow water if one 'knows' he has not bewitched anyone) the oracle's verdict may be disputed by reference to one of the previously mentioned possibilities or by charging the accusers with fraud. On some occasions, however, the accusation served to bring into doubt the accused's perception and knowledge of his own activities.

a man accused of bewitching another may hesitate to deny the accusation and even to convince himself for a short while of its evident untruth. He knows that often witches are asleep when the soul of their witchcraft-substance flits on its errand of destruction. Perhaps when he was asleep and unaware something of the kind happened and his witchcraft led its independent life. In these circumstances a man might well be a witch and yet not know that he is one. In Zande culture witchcraft is so much a daily consideration, is so much taken for granted, and so universal, that a man might easily suppose that since any one may be a witch it is possible that he is one himself (p. 125).

For the Azande, the maxim that the 'poison oracle does not err' functions in the capacity of what has been termed an 'incorrigible proposition' (Gasking 1965). While seemingly formulated as a descriptive assertion, it is in fact a proposition which no 'happenings whatsoever would ever prove false, or cause anyone to withdraw it'. Gasking has considered mathematical propositions as instances of incorrigibles and his remarks are instructive for illuminating the nature of the Azande achievement and, ultimately, the operational structure of mundane reasoning.

A corrigible proposition gives you some information about the world – a completely incorrigible proposition tells you nothing. A corrigible proposition is one that you would withdraw and admit to be false if certain things happened in the world. It therefore gives you the information that those things (i.e. those things which would make you withdraw your proposition if they happened) will not happen. An incorrigible proposition is one which you would never admit to be false whatever happens: it therefore does not tell you what happens. The truth, for example, of the corrigible proposition that Smith is away for the day, is incompatible with certain things happening (e.g. your going to his room and finding him there). It therefore tells you what sort of thing will happen (you will find his room empty) and what sort of thing will not happen (you will not find him in). The truth of an incorrigible proposition, on the other hand, is compatible with any and every conceivable state of affairs. (For example: whatever is your experience on counting, it is still true that $7+5=12$). It therefore does not tell you which events will take place and which will not. That is: the proposition '$7+5=12$' tells you nothing about the world.

If such a proposition tells you nothing about the world, what, then, is the point of it – what does it do? I think that in a sense it is true to say that it prescribes what you are to say – it tells you how to describe certain happenings. Thus the proposition '$7+5=12$' does not tell you that on counting $7+5$ you will not get 11. (This, as we have seen, is false, for you sometimes do get 11.). But it does lay it down, so to speak, that if on counting $7+5$ you do get 11, you are to describe what has happened in some such way as this: Either 'I have made a mistake in my counting' or 'Someone has played a practical joke and abstracted one of the objects when I was not looking' or 'Two of the objects have coalesced' or 'One of the objects has disappeared,' etc. (pp. 432–3: italics deleted).

The Azande maxim 'the poison oracle never errs' functions as an incorrigible proposition. As Evans-Pritchard's description indicates, the maxim is immune to discrediting: it is compatible with every observed and conceivable state of affairs. No matter what is subsequently observed to happen, the oracle retains its infallible character. Further, like the mathematical propositions whose usage as incorrigibles Gasking describes, the doctrine of oracular infallibility serves as guide to the description of certain sorts of events. Specifically, it serves as a device for locating the various ways to accountably explain the unfulfilled verdicts of an oracle that never errs. Thus, on the occasion of an unfulfilled verdict, an accountable solution is selected from candidate possibilities which honor the oracle's infallibility as an unquestioned given.

The ironic perspective afforded by Western scientific understanding of the oracle, reveals the ways in which the incorrigibility of the oracle's infallibility is the gloss (Garfinkel and Sacks 1970) for the practices of the Azande through which the status of incorrigibility is secured and sustained. The incorrigibility of the oracle's infallibility is at once the process, presupposition and product of Azande reasoning practices. It is a process in that the maxim's incorrigibility is assured in no other way than through the artfulness of Azande practices of the formulation of accounts, which explain the discrepancy between oracle verdicts and the actual fall of events. Simultaneously, the doctrine is a presupposition of the Azande practices in that the field of possibilities from which explanations are selected are predicated on the oracle's infallibility. All of the candidate explanations from which the Azande choose are uniform in their respect for the integrity of the oracle: they locate the source of the discrepancy in conditions which leave the oracle's validity unquestioned and intact. Finally, in the ways that the incorrigibility of the oracle's infallibility is a presupposed feature of the concrete reasoning process through which it is sustained and in the ways that the embeddedness of that supposition produces accounts which reflexively preserves its own incorrigibility, the oracle's infallibility presents itself as the given, stable feature, which from the point of view of the Azande it always was.

The operations which comprise mundane reason are analogous to those for which the poison oracle is the gloss. The suppositions regarding objectivity and intersubjectivity are analogous to the doctrine of oracular infallibility at least in the sense that they are the incorrigible theses which promote the search for and constitute the nature of the explanations sought on the occasion of ostensible anomalies. There is, however, a certain transparency to the Azande practices – again made observable by the introduction and use of Western understandings of natural processes – which is not readily available in attempts to discern the structure of mundane reasoning. Indeed, it is difficult to obtain an ironic view because the mundane idiom, whose operational structure we pursue, so deeply permeates scientific and common sense thought. As Evans-Pritchard noted of the Azande, 'they reason excellently in the idiom of their beliefs, but they cannot reason outside, or against, their beliefs because they have no other idiom in which to express their thoughts' (p. 388). And now we find ourselves confronted with the task of having to discover an 'excellency' in our reasonings, which remains opaque precisely because we have no other idiom from which to consider of what its operations might consist.

In order to furnish a sense of the contingency of mundane reason and display its accomplished character, I want to propose a *Gedanken* experiment. It is misleading at certain junctures but its heuristic value is sufficiently great that we may indulge ourselves provided that we are sufficiently mindful of its shortcomings. The *Gedanken* experiment will furnish one aspect of an equivocalness endemic to mundane reasoning, which will stand in lieu of the contingency which is available to Evans-Pritchard by virtue of his use of a Western understanding of natural process as an analytic resource.

Let us for the moment suppose a 'stranger' who suspended his subscription to the assumption of a commonly shared world, at least in its capacity as the foundation of a language game. For the 'presuppositionless' stranger, what we now regard under the auspices of the mundane assumptions as a conflict or discrepancy of experience, might be treated as symptomatic of any one of a number of possibilities other than, say, that someone is lying or mistaken, etc. Specifically, conflicting testimony might be regarded as indicating that the world is how you perceive it and that the 'it' which you perceive exists only in the perception. It is so, to borrow from Pirandello (1952), if you think it is so, and the 'it' which is so is only in the thinking (or saying, or perceiving, etc.). In adopting the radical stance (by relinquishing the mundane stance), matters adjudicated in the courts, disputations in science, disagreements in everyday affairs, and so on can be conceived of as an ever-growing compendium of instances testifying to the fact that there is no 'same world'. The very conflicts which are mundanely regarded as a 'failure' in the perceptual process through which the world is observed and its features brought to formulation may alternatively be regarded as 'evidence' of the absurd and radical subjectivity of the world.

The *Gedanken* experiment, which consisted of the suspension of the tacit commitment to the natural thesis and its ancillary components reveals an alternative interpretation of conflicting accounts. The imaginative contrast begins to provide the irony necessary to see the ways in which the mundane assumptions are in fact special prejudices and the ways in which their incorrigibility is the accomplished product of the artful use of the operations comprising mundane reason. The incorrigibility of the mundane assumptions like that of the doctrine of oracular infallibility is simultaneously presupposition and product of the process through which it is oriented to, reflexively sustained, and thereby accomplished.

A further explication – one which deepens the sense of the accomplished incorrigibility of the natural thesis – is found in Mannheim's (1955) analysis of the historical emergence of the questions which generate a sociology of knowledge.

It is with this clashing of modes of thought, each of which has the same claims to representational validity, that for the first time there is rendered possible the emergence of the question which is so fateful, but also so fundamental in the history of thought, namely, how it is possible that identical human thought-processes concerned with the same world produce divergent conceptions of that world? And from this point it is only a step further to ask: Is it not possible that the thought-processes which are involved here are not at all identical? May it not be found, when one has examined all the possibilities of human thought, that there are numerous alternative paths which can be followed? (p. 9).

If we but treat the reference to 'identical thought processes' as a particular instance of the *ceteris paribus* clause which, as we have proposed, is at least tacitly implied by the assumption of an intersubjective world, then Mannheim's questions specify the essential aspects of the problematic formulated from within mundane reason on the occasion of disjunctive accounts and the reflexively preservative nature of candidate resolutions.

The first question – how is it possible that identical analytical processes concerned with the same world produce divergent conceptions of that world? – betrays the primordial prejudices of mundane reason. The very formulation of the question presupposes the objectivity of the world. The puzzlement regarding variable representations is predicated upon an anticipated harmony among accounts and experiences which, as we have seen, is in turn predicated on the assumption of an essentially objective and intersubjective world. The puzzlement reveals the assumption of an essentially intersubjective world which is to say a world which presents itself in an identical or, at least, corroborative fashion to all those who make it the object of their concern. If the self-same world presents itself to a multiplicity of persons presumedly homogeneous with respect to their perceptual, cognitive, and reportorial abilities, then analyses of that world should be harmonious and compatible with one another.

The second question – is it possible that the analytic processes are not identical? – reveals not only the special prejudice of mundane reasoning, but the method of its own preservation. Note that there are two 'assumptions' embedded in the preceding question – the assumption of the homogeneity of analytic procedures on the one hand and of the invariance or self-sameness of the world on the other. Disjunctive 'representations', as Mannheim calls them, are symptomatic of the invalidity of either assumption. On the one hand, as our *Gedanken* experiment suggested, discrepancies between analyses could be treated as a peculiar sort of evidence for a peculiar sort of inference – the radically relative, radically subjective character of the world. On the other hand, however, the discrepancies may be attended to as evidence that the source of conflict resides in conditions extrinsic to the object proper, conditions which prior to the emergence of the discrepancy were tacitly, i.e. in an unformulated manner, subsumed under the *ceteris paribus* provision. Because either assumption is equally dubitable, the 'prejudi-cial' character of mundane reason's foundational supposition reveals itself as does its accomplished incorrigibility. Specifically the mundane prejudice consists of the commitment to the assumption that there is but 'one single world'. Its incorrigibility consists of the use of an idiom of accounts, which locates the source of conflict not in the world but in the ways the world is observed or described.

The solution of mundane puzzles and the preservation of mundane prejudice

The assumption of a commonly shared world does not function for mundane reasoners as a descriptive assertion. It is not falsifiable. Rather, it functions as an incorrigible specification of the relations which exist, in principle, among a community of perceivers' experiences of what is purported to be the same world. But how is the principled unanimity reconciled to the presence of concrete disjunctures? On the occasion of a disjuncture a mundane reasoner looks to the 'all other things being equal' clause implicated in the anticipation of unanimity. In light of the commonly shared world's incorrigible status, the solutions for disjunctures are selected from the indefinitely varied set of conditions which were previously treated as 'equal' and operational but are not inferentially open to question. In general terms, the anticipated unanimity of experience (or, at least, of accounts of those experiences) presupposes a community of others who are deemed to be observing the same world, who are psychically constructed so as to be capable of veridical experience, who are motivated so as to speak 'truthfully' of their experience, and who speak according to recognizable, shared schemes of expression. On the occasion of a disjuncture, mundane reasoners are prepared to call these and other features into question. For a mundane reasoner, a disjuncture is compelling grounds for asserting that one or another of the conditions otherwise thought to obtain in the anticipation of unanimity, did not. For example, a mundane solution may be generated by reviewing whether or not the other had the capacity for veridical experience. Thus, 'hallucination', 'paranoia', 'bias', 'blindness', 'deafness', 'false consciousness', etc., insofar as they are understood as indicating a faulted or inadequate method of observing the world serve as candidate explanations of disjunctures. The significant feature of these solutions – the feature that renders them intelligible to other mundane reasoners as possibly correct solutions – is that they bring into question not the world's intersubjectivity but the adequacy of the methods through which the world is experienced and reported upon. The application of such designations declares, in effect, that intersubjective validation of the world would obtain were it not for the exceptional methods of observation or perception of the persons identified as employing them. The successful demonstration that a condition which was otherwise assumed to obtain did not, serves to establish that a community of corroborating experiences and accounts would have been produced had it not been for the exceptional circumstances of the particular case. The explanation of a disjuncture by reference to an unsatisfied condition finds members of the experiential community to have been, wittingly or not, in error and thereby reaffirms the essentially intersubjective character of the world.

Reflexive preservation in traffic court

The features which mundane reason renders problematic in preserving the assumption of a real world parallel its projected idealizations. Given that mundane reason anticipates the coherence of the object, experience and accounts, solutions to reality disjunctures may be sought out at each level of idealization. Thus, for example, disparate or conflicting accounts may be reconciled by inferring that observers were not observing the self-same scene, object or event (level of the object), that their experiental or cognitive processes were distorted or impaired (level of experience) or that their accounts are not designed as literal reflections or reports, that is, that one is 'lying', 'joking' or 'speaking metaphorically' (level of accounts). At each level, the objectivity of the world is retained while the processes through which the world is encountered, experienced or described are sources of candidate explanations of contradictory versions.

Let us turn to examples of how mundane reason preserves its foundations in the face of what can ironically be regarded as foundationally subversive possibilities. Actually, we have already encountered several instances of what Polanyi (1964) calls 'epicyclical explanations'. For example, in the drag racing arraignment described in the preceding chapter there was a direct and unequivocal contradiction as to what 'really' happened at Riverside and Fletcher Drive. The court copy of the citation stated that the officer had appeared at the scene of extensive drag racing: the defendant stated that there had been no drag racing whatsoever. How could that be? That is, how could a scene exhibit itself through an aspect and its negation? The defendant's explanation, that there may have been drag racing prior to his arrival, states, in effect, that the officer's account and the defendant's original account were not reports of the self-same world. The accounts report upon temporally differentiated segments of the scene. This explanation renders the initial accounts mutually compatible with one another and provides for the jointly intended scene's possible mundane existence.

In the following excerpt, the conflict is reconciled by an appeal to possibly faulty instrumentation.

> Judge: Mr. Allan. How do you plead?
> Defendant: No contest sir.
> J: What happened?
> D: From the time I got on the freeway until when he pulled me over, I was checking my speedometer constantly and on my speedometer reading I never went over 68 miles an hour. Between six –
> J: You ever have your speedometer checked?
> D: I got another citation two months ago and I also got cited for ten miles an hour over what I thought I was doing. And I had my speedometer – and I went down to San Diego and checked it. And –
> J: Well I'll continue in two weeks. Go have your – see, apparently you might have an error in there son. That's what's giving you the problem. Have it checked and bring me the results back and if your

speedometer's in error, I'll dismiss this. If it isn't, then you'll have to do something else. But I think that's your problem. I just think you're actually going faster than you're indicating . . .

Notice that were the mundane thesis and its ancillary idealizations suspended, conflicting representations of the speed of the defendant's vehicle might be regarded as evidence that the vehicle had travelled simultaneously at two different speeds. That such a possibility sounds absurd is an expression of the extraordinary power of the mundane idiom when it is encountered from 'within'. Under the auspices of mundane reason, such a possibility is unacceptable and, more importantly, inconceivable. It is not merely that mundane reason renders observational processes problematic because to do otherwise would undermine its foundational presuppositions. Mundane reason never conceives of the jeopardizing alternative of bringing into doubt the world's facticity in the first place. From within a mundane idiom, as we shall see, the problem of conflicting accounts in the very ways that it is a problem will admit of solutions which have as their definitive feature the retention of the mundane prejudices. True, there is substantial latitude in terms of the specific reconciliatory mechanism within the idiom – e.g. the officer is 'lying', the defendant is 'lying', or both are 'lying' – but the candidate possibilities are uniform in their respect for the integrity of an objective world.

In the following arraignment, the judge and defendant collaboratively preserve the facticity of the world by specifying the conditions under which it would be possible for an officer to report that the defendant had been obstructing traffic and the defendant to report that he had not. Specifically, they provide for the possibility that the officer was not in a position to properly observe the real obstructing vehicle.

> Judge: Mister Dale, you're charged with violating twenty-one six-fifty-four – driving slower than normal traffic.I take it that you heard and understood my statement concerning your legal rights?
> Defendant: I understand my rights, yes sir.
> J: And having that in mind are you ready for your plea?
> D: I entered the freeway at Lopez and I remember having the thought at that time that since there were several right-hand on-ramps that I would stick to the center lane. And I was proceeding down the center lane, at about the speed. And this is what the officer could not have known. I was going at fifty-five miles an hour and if I had gone sixty-five I would have been following too close, or driving the guy in front of me off the road. Because the speed of fifty-five miles an hour was being set by the person in front of me. The officer didn't take this in consideration. And as he pulled me over, he blamed me for

> obstructing traffic in the central lane and I feel that, well, I'm guilty of
> that I was going fifty-five –
> J: Did you tell him that there was a car in front of you?
> D: I mentioned this to him but he –
> J: What did he say?
> D: He said that he considered that it was my car which is a camper bus
> that was obstructing the traffic, so I feel I was guilty of going at a safe
> speed.
> J: Well of course the difficulty with having a camper bus is that people
> can't see around you very well, can they?
> D: Yes, and people tend to look at this huge thing and say, 'This is really
> obstructing traffic. Everybody else must be held up by him.'
> J: (They) can't see anything in front of you, huh?

In this example, the contested matter turns on whether or not the
defendant's vehicle was obstructing traffic. For mundane reason, the
essential issue is how could two observers of the same scene produce
such disparate accounts. The collaboratively developed solution is that
the individuals were not observing precisely the same scene. The
discrepant accounts are reconciled by reference to the possibility that
the vision of one of the parties, the officer, was restricted such that he
could not properly see the 'real' offender. As with the preceding
excerpt, the proposed reconciliation appeals to features of what we
have broadly defined as processes pertaining to experience and cognition while maintaining profound respect for the foundational assumption of the idiom within which the reconciliation is advanced, the
préjugé du monde.

If we enlist the aid of the previously developed heuristics, then the
preceding transactions, as trivial as they may be in light of the fateful
events which the legal system is capable of generating, are visible as
accomplishments of some moment and ingenuity. In these transactions,
the presumptively intersubjective character of a domain of real events
and objects is preserved in the face of some very strange possibilities.
What are the strange possibilities? Given that both the officer and the
defendant have both observed the 'same' event, and nevertheless
produce discrepant accounts of that event, is it possible that the event in
question did and did not take place? Is it possible that drag racing did and
did not occur at the same time, the same place? After all, we may add,
there is evidence that such is the case: the officer saw drag racing and the
defendant did not. Or, again, is it possible that objects of and in the world
are not the intersubjective events we suppose them to be? The large
number of traffic trials alone furnishes a rather impressive corpus of
instances in which persons who were observing the 'same' scene

experienced the scene in radically conflicting and contradictory ways. It is in contrast to such ostensibly outlandish possibilities that we may gain an initial comprehension of the nature of the accomplishment of mundane reasoners.

In each of the preceding transactions neither judge nor defendant brings the intersubjectivity of highway events into question. Rather, they search for solutions to the disjuncture. In effect, judge and defendant hold that if all of an indefinite number of suppositions regarding the conditions of observation and the adequacy and motives of the observers are correct, or, in other words, if 'all other things are equal', then persons observing the same world will produce corroborating accounts. If corroborating accounts are not forthcoming, then judge and defendant (like all good mundane reasoners) hold that all other things were not equal. Their solutions to the disjunctures consist of conjectures as to which of the suppositions contained in the *ceteris paribus* provision may now be seen to have been inoperative or unsatisfied at the time of the actual event. Thus, for example, the anticipated unanimity of experience presupposes a properly functioning observational apparatus. On the occasion of a disjuncture the presumed adequacy may be brought into question as when the judge proposes that the defendant's speedometer may have been in error. Similarly, an anticipated unanimity of experience regarding the 'same' world presupposes that persons are in fact looking at the same world at the same time. Consequently, a candidate solution to a disjuncture may be developed by proposing that the disjunctive parties were not really looking at the same scene at the same time as when, for example, the defendant proposes that there may have been drag racing prior to his arrival (and, by implication, that it is this earlier phase that the police were experiencing and reporting upon).

In each of the transactions the incorrigibility of the mundane assumptions is simultaneously presupposed and reproduced in the ways that the assumptions are used as a search prescription for candidate explanations of the disjunctures. For mundane reasoners, the *ceteris paribus* provision is an endless and compelling source of explanations of disjunctures. Each explanation preserves the world as an objective and shared order of events by showing how unanimity would have been forthcoming had it not been for the absence, failure or violation of one of the presupposed but previously unformulated conditions necessary for unanimity.

A final illustration may serve to indicate some of the more subtle aspects of the ingenuity of mundane reasoners. The following transaction occurs at the end of a trial of a young man who claimed not to have made the illegal turn which the citing officer claimed he did. The district attorney (DA) recapitulates the police officer's version of the event but the judge decides in favour of the defendant.

> Judge: Any argument?
> DA: No your Honor. Only to the point that the officer testified that he clearly saw the defendant's car making the turn from that lane. That is the lane that's marked with green up there on the chart. And assuming that to be the situation, and based on the sequence of the lights, that would be an illegal left turn. And we believe that was the situation that evening.
> J: Well, I think that at night it would be difficult to tell at that distance away at that intersection. So, not doubting anybody's word or anything like that, – I know Officer Chord's an experienced and reliable officer, – but in this particular case the defendant's not guilty. That's all. All right.

The diversity of idiomatic possibilities which are available as candidate solutions to a disjuncture poses a selection problem for anyone who would attempt a resolution. For example, the preceding disjuncture could be accounted for by the proposal that the officer was 'lying' *or* 'hallucinating'. As these possibilities suggest, however, any particular solution varies in its implications for the moral and mental competencies of persons who are so categorized: to be a 'liar' is to be morally suspect and to be designated a 'hallucinator' is to be open to as profound an indictment of one's general mental bearing as mundane reason is capable of generating (cf. Coulter 1975).

In traffic court, solutions, when they are advanced, are established inferentially. The reasons why one didn't have an adequate 'experience' or produce a correct account of a particular event in the world is not itself an observable event: having decided a version of 'what really happened' does not unequivocally generate an explanation of how a now-to-be-seen erroneous version was produced. Thus, a mundane reasoner can recognize that other mundane reasoners may inferentially develop alternative accounts of how a disjuncture occurred.

It is within this context that the ingenuity and tact of the judge's closing remarks is visible. Specifically, the judge not only advances a solution to the disjuncture, posed by the conflicting accounts of officer and defendant which is in keeping with the general structure of mundane reason, but he explicitly precludes other possibilities which are at least candidate solutions given that the defendant's version has been selected as *the* version. The judge, in noting that he is 'not doubting anybody's word', anticipates and excludes solutions that others might formulate for themselves or take as implied given that the officer claimed to have seen an event in the world that did not take place. The judge's remark that the officer is 'experienced and reliable' further precludes pejorative inferences and also functions to avoid the derogatory implications derivable from the characterization of the officer as one who, minimally, failed to see what was there to be seen and, more specifically, as one who was somehow deceived by night time conditions. Insofar as to be so deceived can be heard as rendering suspect an officer's competency, then the judge is artfully engaged in resolving a disjuncture while keeping a reputation intact.

Concluding remarks

By virtue of their mutual orientation to the assumption of an incorrigibly objective and commonly shared world, mundane reasoners are able to pose, recognize and constitute as a 'puzzling' event the disjunctive experiences and/or accounts of persons looking at what is purported to be the same world. While such puzzles are potentially subversive of the assumptions of a common world, they are ingeniously resolved by mundane reasoners. For a mundane reasoner, the disjuncture is not the occasion for questioning the fundamental intersubjectivity of the world. Rather, it is the occasion for determining which of the conditions, which are tacitly implicated in the anticipation of a unanimity of experiences and accounts, can be inferred to have been inoperative. Thus, it is the methods and motives of observation and reportage which are rendered problematic in the search for a solution to the disjuncture. The posing of a candidate solution serves in effect to declare that the world is the intersubjective order of events it is known to be and that a community of compatible experiences would have been forthcoming had it not been for the exceptional character of the methods, motives or circumstances of one or another of the parties to the disjuncture.

From within mundane reason, by virtue of its prejudice and the depth at which it functions, the foundational threats are never appreciated as such. In this sense, mundane reason is oblivious to the ways in which it is jeopardized. For mundane reason, conflicting accounts represent a problem, but not one which imperils its foundations. For mundane reason, the problem of conflicting reports precipitates the search for how such a conflict would arise, *given* the world's objectivity. The obliviousness to the foundational threat, however, is not a 'failure' on the part of mundane reason. Rather, the obliviousness is integral to mundane

reason's self-preservation and testimony to the artfulness and insidious-
ness of mundane reason's prejudices. We could say, as Evans-Pritchard
said of the Azande, that for mundane reasoners, mundane reason is the
only idiom that they know and they reason excellently within its
confines. And because the idiom is singular in authority, the self-preservative features of the system, when witnessed or practiced from 'within',
do not present themselves as merely defensive rhetoric. Instead, they are
encountered as normal, natural, no-alternatives-to-it talk.[1]

The Azande do not 'defend' or 'sustain' the poison oracle by ingenious
use of oracle wit. The subversiveness of Evans-Pritchard's questions, as
is discernible in his account, are subversive for Evans-Pritchard alone.
The Azande's explanations are not defensive additions intended to
buttress and/or preserve the oracle. Rather, the explanations are integral
features of the 'belief' in the oracle. In a similar fashion, the enumerated
devices for reconciling conflicting accounts with the mundane prejudices
are not superfluous additions to the mundane idiom which they preserve: *they are the idiom which they preserve*. They are not secondary or
epicyclical elaborations or occasional conceits to the idiom, for to be
within the province of mundane reason is to use the mundane idiom
both in the formulation of problems and in their resolution.

4

Mundane puzzles and the politics of experience

Given our mundane assumptions about the world, persons and perceptions, contradictory experiences of the world – reality disjunctures (Laing 1967: 35–6) as we shall call them – are puzzling events. If the world is the 'out there' and perceptually shared domain of objects and events it is commonsensically assumed to be, how does one account for the 'alarming fact that the same world can appear differently to different observers' (Mannheim 1955: 6). Mundane reason, as we have seen, generates a variety of candidate solutions to the puzzles posed by disjunctive experiences of the same world. For practitioners of mundane reason, reality disjunctures are potentially explainable by formulating one or another (and perhaps both) of the competing versions of reality as the product of an exceptional method of observation, experience or reportage. Thus, for example, the puzzle posed by conflicting accounts of the same world may be resolved by identifying one of the versions as the product of a defective sensory apparatus such as poor vision or poor hearing, as the product of an empiricially inadequate or distortive psychological mechanism such as projection, hallucination or imagination, or as the product of a special method of reporting experience such as lying, joking or metaphor. Such solutions declare, in effect, that intersubjective validation of the world would obtain were it not for the exceptional means and methods of observation, experience or reportage of the persons identified as employing them.

The mere availability of possible explanations, however, does not assure a consensual resolution of reality disjunctures. There is a fundamental equivocality inherent in disjunctures which renders problematic the determination of which of the parties to a disjuncture is a deficient witness of reality. I may propose, for example, that you are joking or lying or 'need glasses' when you say that you have not seen what I know any competent person can and ought to see. But, alas, you can do the same to me. That is, you can propose that I am joking or lying or 'seeing things' at the very moment I am telling you what we should both be seeing. Just as ego's experience of the world can be used to dismiss the veridicality of alter's experience, alter can respond to ego in kind. We learn from the presence of these potentially endless equivocalities that resolution of reality disjunctures cannot be achieved simply by 'looking at the world'. Indeed, that is presumably just what parties to a disjuncture have done and that is not the end of their troubles, but the beginning of them. The presence of the equivocalities teaches us to ask a question. If reality disjunctures are infused with potentially endless equivocalities, how are they ever resolved?

In this chapter I shall explore the nature of equivocalities which arise in the resolution of reality disjunctures, the ways in which the disjunctures may be protracted endlessly and the ways in which they may be resolved or dissolved. Resolution often involves a 'politics of experience' (Laing 1967) in which a group's or individual's experiences (or claims) about reality are dismissed or discounted in favor of what will be regarded as the official or accredited version of reality. The point to which I build, and which is of special relevance for our earlier discussion about the embeddedness of the social sciences within mundane reason, is that many social scientific concepts are the product of the politics of experience: concepts ranging from 'false consciousness', to 'repression' to 'interpretation' are constructed through the treatment of the social scientific version as definitive of reality by reference to which the lay member is found to be a deficient or 'subjective' observer. The nature and origins of this constructed deficiency or subjectivity often comprise a significant topic for inquiry. Thus, the social sciences are not merely embedded or constituted through mundane reason in the sense of addressing an exterior and constraining order of natural or social fact: The very fabric of the facts addressed is also produced by mundane puzzle posing and solving.

Ironicizing experience

The dynamics of disjunctures are best appreciated by reference to an operation that we shall term the ironicizing of experience. We can illustrate and describe the operation by examining the way it functions in the activities which yield designations such as 'illusion' and 'delusion'.

Many of the events which are cited as evidence of a profound pathological state consist of a person's actual, claimed or inferred experience of the world. To hallucinate is to hear or to see another; to be paranoid is to know that others are actively conspiring against oneself. But such experiences, of course, are not self-evidently indicative of psychopathology. After all, almost everyone hears and responds to voices and the possibility of conspiratorial action is not *prima facie* absurd. What, then, endows these experiences with their character as possibly pathological, as potential symptoms of a deeply disordered psyche?

In part, to hallucinate is to experientially encounter an event (such as voices) or an object as real, that is, as independent of one's perception when, in fact, it is not. Similarly, to be paranoid is to know that there is a real or objective conspiracy when, in fact, there is none. The diagnostic possibilities of illusion and delusion presuppose an experiential version of the world which is regarded as definitive of what is 'really' available for perception. It is in contrast to a definitive or accredited version of the world that other experiences of the same world may be reviewed, formulated and treated as incorrect and eventually as the product of a perverse subjectivity. These invidious contrasts comprise the ironicizing of experience. The ironicizing of experience occurs when one experience, tacitly claiming to have comprehended the world objectively, is examined from the point of view of another experience which is honored as the definitive version of the world intended by the first. The irony resides in the subsequent appreciation that the initial experience was not the objective representation that it was originally purported or felt to be.

The ironicizing of experience is implicated in the constitution of many varieties of 'subjectivity'.[1] The very possibility of an experience being treated as the product of 'seeing things', 'impaired vision', 'denial', 'rationalization', 'selective (in)attention' (to name but a few of the less subtle possibilities), requires an ironic reference to a definitive experiential version of the world. The latter version is definitive in the sense that it is treated as having comprehended the features of the world more faithfully and objectively than those experiences which are subsequently defined as somehow faulted or erroneous. Thus, that I am 'color blind' awaits the definitive experiential version of what sorts of colors there are to be seen in the world. That I have 'seen a mirage' awaits the definitive experiential version of what the road up ahead is really like.

As might be anticipated from our examples, the ironicizing of experience is not exclusively an interpersonal operation. Persons can and do recognize for themselves and by themselves that their experience of the world may be faulted. They themselves furnish the definitive experiences of the world in terms of which a set of their own experiences is ironically revealed as empirically inadequate. Further, the experiential versions, in light of which other experiences are invidiously reviewed and evaluated, are not necessarily direct or immediate experiences of the world. Definitive versions of what the world is like may be derived from a corpus of knowledge, commonsense or otherwise, regarding the sorts of objects and events which can occur in the real world. Thus, for example, by virtue of the knowledge of the ways in which highway signs are typically painted, the seeing of a fuzzy sign may be rendered grounds for suspecting the inadequacy of one's own vision; the knowledge of the ways in which signs are typically painted serves, in effect, as a version of the sign's actual properties in terms of which the initial experience of a fuzzy sign is reviewed and assessed for its faulted character.

More dramatic (and complex) examples of the use of commonsense versions as the resource for ironicizing experience are encountered in turning to consider the ways in which persons suppose or suspect themselves to be radically incompetent. Consider, for example, the experience of a psychiatrist who decided to live-in on an acute treatment ward:

One night during my second week in the hospital I had difficulty falling asleep – understandable in view of the constant coming and going of a not very quiet staff. As I lay in bed, I became aware of a muffled, distant sound, identified first as a baby's crying. As I made more of an effort to define the sound, I experienced two things. First, the thought that I had really gone off the deep end and was hallucinating struck me, with more than a little associated anxiety; and then, to my great relief, came the realization that the sound in fact was the strange gurgling of pipes in the wall. At this point it became clear to me how easily something like this could be elaborated into a great deal more by an anxious patient (Rockwell 1971: 217).

In some settings, the hearing of a baby's crying is an unremarkable event: new parents are fitfully subjected to such treats. That the hearing of a baby's cry is rendered grounds for the self-imposed label of hallucination requires reference to a contrasting version of an environment's properly hearable sounds. Unless and until some alternate and conflicting version of what is 'in fact' available for hearing is invoked, the hearing of a baby's cries remains unchallenged and hence undoubted. The status of the heard cries as a possible hallucination awaits the intrusion of what William James (1950, vol. 2: 289) called the 'world otherwise known', which, in this case, consists of a version of the ward's putative hearables. The putative hearables serve as a surrogate perception in terms of which the initial experience is endowed with its suspect and ironicized status.[2]

To summarize: The characterization of experiences as faulted reflections of reality is the product of an operation of irony. The experiential version that will be labeled, say, hallucination, presupposes an experience or version of the world that is deemed to have presented the world as it really and actually is. It is in terms of the definitive version that other experiences may be reviewed and named for their faulted character. The definitive version may be furnished by another person or it may be furnished by the same stream of consciousness within which the to-be-discredited experience has occurred.

Irony and choice

The ironicizing of experience requires a choice as to which of several competing experiences of the same world, each of which for an instant tacitly claims to have faithfully reflected the world, will be accredited as *the* version of the world. William James (1950) spoke of the choice and its consequences:

The sense that anything we think of is unreal can only come, then, when that thing is contradicted by some other being of which we think. *Any object which remains uncontradicted is ipso facto believed and posited as absolute reality.*
... That we can at any moment think of the same thing which at any former moment we thought of is the ultimate law of our intellectual constitution. But when we now think of it incompatibly with our other ways of thinking it, then we must choose which way to stand by, for we cannot continue to think in two contradictory ways at once. *The whole distinction of real and unreal, the whole psychology of belief, disbelief, and doubt, is thus grounded on two mental facts – first, that we are liable to think differently of the same; and second, that when we have done so, we can choose which way of thinking to adhere to and which to disregard.*
The subjects adhered to become real subjects, the attributes adhered to real attributes, the existence adhered to real existence; whilst the subjects disregarded become imaginary subjects, the attributes disregarded erroneous attributes, and the existence disregarded an existence in no man's land, in the limbo 'where footless fancies dwell' (pp. 288–91).

The choice referred to by James is the choice between alternate ways of thinking or experiencing the same object. It is by virtue of these alternate ways of thinking or experiencing the same object that the object is rendered problematic as to its existential status, as to whether or not it is the absolute reality it presents itself to be. But at the same time *in posse* the status of the object as otherwise known may be rendered problematic in light of the immediate experience. For the ironic function to move to completion, a choice must be made as to which determination will be adhered to and which will be disregarded.

Because of the artfulness of our commonsense reasoning practices, we need rarely engage in an explicit deliberation in order to choose. We are typically confronted with the products of our tacit choices, with completed ironies. The choices themselves and the practices through which alternate possibilities are reviewed, elected and acted upon often seem so natural, so void of any sense of valid alternative that the problematic potential which inheres in disjunctive situations is hidden from view. We have made a choice, we encounter an ironicized experience, when for example, we characterize the man gesticulating to empty space as 'talking to himself'. We have made a choice, we have encountered an ironicized experience when we characterize as 'overlooking' the course of activity in which we point to the pen on the desk only to hear the searcher say that he does not see it. We have made a choice, we have encountered an ironicized experience when we characterize as 'mistaken' the others' experience of us in Westwood on Saturday night given that we never left the house that evening. In each instance, the characterization requires a choice as to which of several competing experiences or claims is to be honored as definitive of the world. Thus, that you have 'overlooked' the pen (as opposed to say the possibility that I am 'seeing things' or that pens have some hitherto unappreciated properties such as differentially disclosing themselves to selected persons) rests not only on the assumption of object-constancy but on the selection of my experience of the immediate scene as definitive.

What is the nature of the choice? In arriving at a characterization of a portion of another's (or our own) experience as specious, we have to choose between competing experiences each of which purports to have comprehended reality. If we choose alter's experience of the desk as definitive then we may dismiss ego's as specious. If we honor ego's experience as definitive then it can be employed as the unquestioned point of departure for, if not formulating alter as 'seeing things', then at least for questioning the properties of pens. The choice, which culminates in what we earlier termed a completed irony, is a choice among experiences which by virtue of their intending the same world are capable of discrediting one another's tacit claims to objectivity. That is, which experience of the world is to be treated as having grasped reality and which is to be treated as faulted is assured by neither the experience *per se* nor by any of the reasons offered in support of a particular selection. Neither of the competing experiences can authorize themselves as definitive because any competing experience can be used as the grounds for discrediting such an attempt.

As we noted, the radical equivocality which inheres in disjunctures often goes unnoticed. Under some circumstances, however, the mutually discrediting potential of competing experiences of the same world may be a matter of deep and dramatic concern. Dewald (1970), for example, recounts a case in which his patient, having been continually accused of having had relations with other women, decides to 'fabricate' a confession and thereby appease his wife.

During the six months before consultation the patient became increasingly convinced that any outsider would see him as a fool for not 'confessing' the sins of which the wife accused him, and that he might lose her. He felt that confession would be a way of satisfying her demands and of allowing her to reconcile with him, and he increased the fabrication of false 'confessions', filling in women's names, 'fictitious details of times, places, and elaborate fantasised descriptions of his sexual activities. As this continued he became plagued with thoughts that perhaps the confessions were really true, that perhaps he did or wanted to do all of the things that she accused him of, and that he had merely forgotten the reality of having done them. He was no longer sure about fact or fantasy in regard to his own memory and behavior, and was increasingly accepting of his wife's version of his behavior. At the time of consultation he was working in one city during the week, living alone in a motel room, and commuting to his home in another city for weekends with his wife and children.

During the weekend prior to his consultation, he made an unusually lengthy and detailed 'confession', following which he spent 'the best, most satisfying closest, most relaxed and normal times with her that I have had in many, many years.' The wife became increasingly loving, responsive, and accepting of him as the extent and intensity of the confessions increased. But the patient became increasingly anxious, perplexed, unsure of himself, and uncertain of the difference between fact and fantasy, and he was plagued with a mounting need to find out whether or not he really did the things to which he had confessed (pp. 391–2).

The patient's plight illustrates the equivocality latent in all disjunctures.[3] If the ironic function is to move to completion, one among several competing experiences must be chosen as definitive: each of the competing experiences, however, is capable of undercutting its contesting counterpart's claim to veridicality.

Insofar as each of the disputes to a reality disjuncture maintains his or her own experience as the incorrigible grounds of further inference, then potentially endless cycles of mutual discreditation may persist. If the conflicting parties presume themselves to be in possession of the truth and are versed in the rhetoric of mundane reason, each disputant is armed with the diagnostic apparatus to explain away the veridicality of the other's experience of the world. Legal and psychiatric establishments are repositories of protracted disjunctures. Thus, for example, traffic courts are replete with disjunctures in which defendants and citing officers are at least implicitly prepared to explain away one another's version of 'what really happened' on the highway as the product of a deficient sensorium. Similarly, psychiatric texts and institutions are rich with persons who are ingenious and dedicated in their preservation of a particular version of reality. Bleuler's (1950) account of a 'litigious schizophrenic' suggests a compounded and extended disjuncture.

A young woman had charge of a physician's household. Perhaps he really did make some erotic advances to her. In any event, she imagined that he had promised to marry her. She demanded that he fulfill his promise and marry her; she made all sorts of scenes, difficulties, and unpleasantnesses, and he finally had to dismiss her. She carried her complaints to the courts, always of the opinion that she had and could prove all her allegations. Then she lodged a complaint against the judge himself because he had not found in her favor. She became more and more confused, could not work. Lawyers got most of her possessions in the course of the many lawsuits. She was judged to be mentally ill by a board of experts; she filed a complaint against the expert testimony, etc. From time to time, she managed to spend a year outside the hospital although never without difficulty (p. 23).

A dramatic example of the perpetuation of reality disjunctures is found in the account of a transaction between Milton Rokeach (1964), a psychologist, and Leon, a mental patient who claimed he was Jesus Christ and to possess a number of unusual abilities.

Through bilocation he could be in two places at once and through translocation he had the power to go instantaneously from one place to another. Leon also claimed to be able to perform miracles. He had once commanded a table to lift itself off the floor – and it had obeyed. When I expressed disbelief, he volunteered to repeat the miracle for me. He went into the recreation room and picked out a massive table. He then turned his back to it and, in a loud affirmative tone, commanded it to lift itself.
 'I don't see the table lifting.'
 'Sir, that is because you do not see cosmic reality' (p. 75).

The transaction may be regarded as a test to empirically determine the validity of Leon's claim to levitate tables. But the test reiterates the very equivocality it was intended to resolve. Obviously, the table did not rise and Leon perhaps was – or so we may conjecture on Rokeach's behalf – hallucinating or pretending. But it is equally obvious that the table did rise and Rokeach cannot – as Leon specifically notes – perceive 'cosmic reality'. The dispute cannot be reconciled by simply examining whether the table is on the ground or floating above it. Indeed, the actual, i.e. empirical, location of the table is what the dispute is all about. The equivocality is perpetuated by a mode of reasoning in which each of the disputants, treating his version as a given and thereby ironicizing competing experiences, finds the experiential claims of the other to be the product of an inadequate procedure for perceiving the world.[4]

The generality and indefinite extendability of this mode of reasoning can render reality disjunctures quite beyond the pale of consensual resolution. To the extent that each of the protagonists attends to his specific version as an axiomatic point of departure for further inferences, they may render their versions virtually unassailable by what from another's position is irrefutable evidence.

The resolution of reality disjunctures

Parties to a disjuncture may not feel any compelling need to come to an explicit specification of 'what really happened' (or of whose methods for observing the world are in need of repair). The disjuncture, for example, may be of such minor pragmatic consequence and a principled solution of such little use for further action that participants to the disjuncture may be quite willing to leave the disjuncture open and unresolved in any explicit sense. Alternatively, disjunctures may be resolved by being dissolved. A disjuncture exists as long as participants are assumed to have observed the same object, at the same time, from the same place. If these conditions are shown to have been unsatisfied then one has shown that a disjuncture did not really exist. Thus, for example, in a previously considered transaction a defendant in traffic court proposed that the reason he did not see the 'extensive drag racing' observed by the police who cited him for aiding and abetting the drag race, was that while 'maybe there had been drag racing part of the time, but ... while I was there, there was no drag racing at all, not even anyone driving a car in the street'. When such attempts to dissolve a disjuncture are allowed to prevail, parties may ease themselves out of a disjuncture by, in effect, proposing that there really was no disjuncture to ease out of.

Disjunctures may be precluded or curtailed through indicating that one has a version of reality which others would do well to honor as definitive (cf. Pomerantz 1981, 1984; Schegloff *et al.* 1977). In the following transaction, for example, a traffic court judge alerts the defendant through a repetition of a question that he has a different version of whether a specific traffic signal has a button to change the light for pedestrians. The defendant retracts his earlier version and thereby inhibits the further development of a disjuncture.

Judge: Well uh, does it say 'no walking'?

Defendant: It said 'don't walk' but there were no cars coming.

J: Does it have a button thetche press there?

D: No it didn't.

J: They don't have any – button thetchu c'n press t'turn the light a little bit?

D: I don't – I don't remember. But there was – there were no cars coming.

In contrast to these possibilities are what we may term full-fledged reality disjunctures, that is disjunctures that resist being precluded, defused or dissolved. In the full-fledged disjuncture, each participant treats his experience of the world as definitive and, hence, as the grounds for ironicizing his opponent's experience. If consensual resolution is to be achieved, one of the protagonists will have to relinquish the use of his experience as the incorrigible grounds of further inference. Of course, the abandonment cannot be secured on empirical or logical grounds alone. Competitive versions equally satisfy (and, with respect to one another, fail to satisfy) the demands for empirical validation and empirically correct conclusions. Thus, a choice between them cannot be made compelling in empirical or logical terms alone for the choice is between empirically and logically self-validating and self-sustaining systems. Consequently, relinquishing the faith in the validity of one's own experience may have the flavor of an existential leap. It is a leap without logical or empirical foundations because it is a leap from and to such foundations.

The person who relinquishes his commitment to the validity of his initial experience regains foundations only after he has accepted his former protagonist's version of the world. The conversion of commitments serves in effect to render the converted a member of what was once the oppositional community. He is now their experiential colleague. He is collegial in his subscription to their version of 'what really happened' and in its use for exposing and retrospectively characterizing the subjective, specious or otherwise faulted methods upon which his previous claims and experiences were presumptively predicated.

The conversion may occasion a special sort of theoretical problem for the converted: how did he ever come to experience the world in the way that he did in the pre-conversion state given that in an important sense he did not experience the world at all? The problem, of course, is but a variant of the one posed by disjunctures in general, only now the contradiction arises between versions which happen to have been maintained by the same person. The idiom of mundane reason does yeoman service in providing accounts of how a world now 'known' for what it 'really' is could have been experienced in contradictory ways. Of particular interest are the varieties of 'subjectivity' which are advanced as solutions. It is on the occasion of attempting to solve such puzzles that persons may retrospectively construct the 'minded' character of their experiential activities. Thus, for example, the knock heard by no one else and unaccompanied by a visible presence when the door is opened may be formulated as 'the knock I *thought* I heard'. The interposition of a subjective process such as 'thinking' functions, in effect, to signal the subjective origins of the heard knock; the knock was not in the world but in the confused projections of thought.[5]

The following dialogue between a psychiatrist and a young schizo-phrenic illustrates the language of conversion (English *et al.* 1961):

> Doctor: Remember last week you promised you wouldn't lie to me any more when you told me that you weren't nervous about masturbating and that stuff.
> Patient: Yes.
> Dr: But you did lie to me again. The very next lie – you told one of my assistants that when you were brought home from the hospital after you were born you heard a broadcast.
> Pt: I thought I did.
> Dr: You knew that was a lie.
> Pt: I made myself believe it I wanted to . . .
> Dr: Inside of yourself, Gerald?
> Pt: Yes.
> Dr: You knew that was a lie.
> Pt: I couldn't have remembered a broadcast when I was five weeks . . . I can't remember anything that happened when I was five weeks old.
> Dr: Of course not. And yet you lied to my assistant here. You knew your dead Aunt didn't speak to you, that it was a hallucination. You know what a hallucination . . .
> Pt: Yes, it's what I said. I said the first day I came here I was still believing that I heard her voice.
> Dr: Well, how about now? Are you hearing voices now?
> Pt: No.
> Dr: Are you sure?
> Pt: Yes, I'm sure.
> Dr: I hope you're telling me the truth.
> Pt: I am.

The dialogue is of particular interest for the ways in which the hearing of the broadcast and the dead Aunt's voice are accounted for by the interpolation of subjective operations such as 'thinking' and 'believing'. Such interpolation provides for the ways in which broadcasts and voices which could not possibly be heard were nevertheless heard. The patient's account ironicizes his own experiences in terms of the version of possible experiences maintained by the psychiatrist. The ironicization is achieved by treating the experiences as existing only in the (subjective) belief that one had them.

But what happens when such conversations are not effected? How are resolutions achieved in the face of a sustained commitment to the validity of one's own experience and the potentially indefinite disjunctures which may be set in motion? In the absence of conversion, full-fledged disjunctures are assured of closure only in and through the practices through which members successfully promulgate their respective version over and in the face of a contradictory version. Thus, the question of which of the competing versions shall prevail as the grounds for further action and inference is answered by reference to the practices through which members enforceably honor and act upon that version. The practices for sanctionably invoking and sustaining a particular version as adequate empirical grounds for further decision – grounds which from a countervailing point of view are utterly groundless – comprise the politics of reality and experience (Laing 1967).

By 'politics' we mean to indicate the activities whereby a version of reality is used as the grounds of further inference and action give the recognition that the version is rendered empirically equivocal by the counterclaims and counterexperiences of the other. What do these practices consist of? They would include all the activities through which a particular version of the world is supported, reasoned from, and used as the grounds of inference and action. Thus, they would include activities such as the simple insistence that 'I saw what I saw' and the recommendation to the other that he look again. They would include the offering of 'good reasons' for how what the other claims to have experienced as in the world could not be in the world. They would include an appeal to further experiential or reasoned evidence which contradicts the possibility of the disputed experience. They would include the instantaneous recognitions of the other's error and the 'subjective' origin of his claims. They would include, as well, activities which are perhaps more readily regarded as political such as mobilizing support for one's version from relevant segments of the community, such as family members and friends, psychiatrists and police.

What gives these enterprisings their political character are the contentions, claims and experiences of the other. It is by virtue of the other's counterclaims that the commitment to the veridicality of any particular version is constituted as a commitment. It is in his contrariness that the other makes possible a choice which cannot be decided by appeal to the respective versions and their supportive reasonings, for it is exactly those versions which comprise the options of the choice. It is the other who, by virtue of having looked and seen otherwise, renders equivocal the veridicality of the versions of those who are his or her others and thereby assures that simply looking at the world will not be sufficient to establish what is there to be seen. It is because of the flaw posed by the other's claim, a flaw in the sense that his claim breaks the network of unanimity and universality anticipated by a version that purports to have comprehended the world as it really is, that his opponents are rendered political insofar as they nevertheless proceed to use their version as the grounds of inference and action.

In the following section I should like to exhibit the politics of reality as they appear in areas which ought to be quite familiar to sociologists and psychologists – the doing of sociology and psychology.

Social science and the politics of experience

Certain styles of social-scientific research rest heavily on revealing how persons or groups encounter a spurious world, that is, a world which, while it may seem 'real' or 'out there' to some, is analyzable as the artifact of a set of sociological or psychological mechanisms for producing and sustaining the semblance of objective reality. Such research ironicizes subjects' experience and then sets about to explain how the subjects could have experienced a spurious world as real. The ironicizing occurs in the implicit or explicit contrast of the researcher's version of the world with the version entertained by the subject groups: the investigator's version is usually regarded as the objective version, the lay person's version is 'subjective' and the worth and power of social-scientific theorizing is exhibited in formulating psycho-social mechanisms or practices which account for the discrepancy between the two versions. In effect, the researcher and lay person are joined in a reality disjuncture.

In an experimental setting, the disjuncture is produced when subjects' estimates of the values of a stimulus are at odds with what are regarded as its objective properties by the experimenter. In clinical situations, the disjuncture is produced when a patient offers an account which the clinician 'knows' or assumes cannot be true. In field research, the disjuncture is established in the difference between what the field researcher knows about the world and what the observed collectivity claim they have seen and experienced. Consider, for example, Kerckhoff and Back's (1968) interesting study of 'hysterical contagion'. The authors report an incident in which a number of workers at a textile mill claim to have been bitten and infected by insects initially thought to have entered the plant in a shipment of cloth. Yet, when public health officials were brought in they seemed to reach the conclusion, in effect, that it was 'nothing', just anxiety. This, to them, seemed to be the only possible conclusion as they could find no evidence that any kind of insect was present which could have caused the symptoms recorded (p. 7).

Many of the women, however, were not fully persuaded, and some claimed to have actually seen the insect:

I got bit on my finger. It left a stinger in my finger. They said it was all imagination, but they are crazy. I can understand that, though, because it would have been bad for the company if people thought it was an insect (pp. 9–10).

The official version of what really happened is treated by Kerckhoff and Back as the definitive version over and against accounts proffered by some of the mill workers. Thus, it is the mill workers whose experience and claims are rendered the spurious product of 'hysterical contagion'.

When the analyst's version is treated as the privileged version in terms of which alternative accounts and experiences are ironicized, subsequent analysis is often a search for the presumptive sociological and psychological mechanisms through which proponents of the subjective versions are allowed to encounter a spurious world. Typically, the discovered discrepancy is not regarded as a function of a person's playfulness or malice; the discrepancy between (say) the objective value of a stimulus and those estimated by a subject are not explained by proposing that the subject was joking or deliberately lying. Instead, the discrepancies are accounted for by a variety of psycho-social mechanisms which are endowed with the ability to operate unbeknownst to those for whom they produce a spurious world. What professional and lay psychology know as the defense mechanisms furnishes a variety of methods for accounting for 'a lie without a liar' (Sartre 1966). Rationalization, projection, denial – all the operations through which the experience of the real world is purportedly transformed to accord with psychic needs – comprise ways of explaining how persons can sincerely see what was not to be seen.

Sociological encounters with allegedly spurious worlds yield equally creative ways of explaining them away. As Lofland (1966) has noted, sociological analyses of radical or deviant belief systems are often implicitly predicated as 'positivistic common sense' (p. 193). These initial assumptions lead to analyses which portray the organizational features of deviant systems as mechanisms functioning to 'protect the adherents from seeing their gigantic error' (p. 194). The devices by which such control and protection are allegedly achieved include selective attention to facts congruent with the erroneous version, contrivance of supportive situations, confirmative interpretation of ambiguous evidence and so on (as described in Simmons 1964).

In the type of analysis whose features we have sketched, the researcher's version of the world establishes the terms within which alternate versions will be considered. Because the analyst's version is accorded a privileged status, at least by himself and his colleagues, alternate versions are ironically reviewed and inspected for the socio-logical and psychological mechanisms through which they are sustained. It is precisely in assigning his own version a privileged status that the analyst engages in the politics of experience. It is in the use of his version of the world over and in the face of competing versions of 'what's really happening', competing versions which by their very existence render equivocal the empirical support of what ultimately is honored as *the* version, that the analyst elects and acts upon a commitment which is beyond consensual empirical support.

Note that the political character of the analyst's work cannot be mitigated by proposals that his versions are likely to be more authorita-tive or objective by virtue of (say) his professional competence and judiciousness or his reliance upon scientific method. The politics of such analyses cannot be mitigated by appeals to the preceding sorts of considerations because they themselves can be brought into question by the presence of contrary experience of the world. Thus, for example, the claim of dispassionateness as a means of warranting the validity of a particular version about the world may be critically reviewed and attacked by persons who have looked at the world and seen otherwise.

Of course, consensual confirmation can be achieved. The proletariat can transcend and thereby recognize their 'false consciousness', the neurotic can be brought to recognize his own 'rationalizations', the psychotic can find himself 'hallucinating' just as some of the factory workers studied by Kerckhoff and Back, even some who were bitten, became sceptical of the 'real cause' of the epidemic. Whether a version of reality is consensually analyzable as the product of psychological and sociological mechanisms (as opposed to being regarded as the product of having looked at the world and seen what is there to be seen) is, like other conversions, contingent upon the analyzed subjects' abandonment of the commitment to the veridicality of their version. In the absence of such conversions, the election of a definitive version may be settled by the simple fact that the analyst writes and publishes the analysis beyond reading and responding range of his subjects.

In the few instances where analysts report their sociologizing and psychologizing efforts to their subjects, subjects may be capable of analyzing their analyzers, discrediting their discreditors. The subject's own experience of the world may serve as the version in terms of which the analyst's attempts at sociological and psychological ironicizing are dismissed. An interesting illustration of such table-turning is found in the research of the anthropologist Carlos Castaneda. Castaneda (1968) became an apprentice to a Yaqui Indian sorcerer. The sorcerer, don Juan, attempted to impart an esoteric system of knowledge and way of 'seeing' to Castaneda with the aid of hallucinogenic drugs. For example, under the influence of peyote Castaneda encountered an 'ally', Mescalito. After a several-year lapse in the apprenticeship, Castaneda (1971) returned to don Juan armed with a more or less academic analysis of how certain dramatic effects were achieved.[6]

As soon as I woke up in the morning, and without any preliminaries, I told don Juan that I had constructed a system to explain what took place at a peyote meeting, a mitote. I took my notes and read to him what I had done. He listened patiently while I struggled to eludicate my schemata.

I said that I believe a covert leader was necessary in order to cue the participants so they could arrive at any pertinent agreement. I pointed out that people attend a mitote to seek the presence of Mescalito and his lessons about the right way to live; and that those persons never exchange a word or a gesture among them, yet they agree about the presence of Mescalito and his specific lessons. At least that was what they purportedly did in the mitotes I had attended: they agreed that Mescalito had appeared to them individually and had given them a lesson. In my personal experience I had found that the form of the individual visit of Mescalito and his consequent lesson were strikingly homogeneous, although varying in content from person to person. I could not explain this homogeneity except as a result of a subtle and complex system of cueing.

It took me close to two hours to read and explain to don Juan the scheme I had constructed. I ended by begging him to tell me in his own words what were the exact procedures for reaching agreement.

... 'You're deranged!' he exclaimed. 'Why should anyone be bothered with cueing at such an important time as a mitote? Do you think one ever fools around with Mescalito?'

I thought for a moment that he was being evasive: he was not really answering my question.

'Why should anyone cue?' don Juan asked stubbornly. 'You have been in mitotes. You should know that no one told you how to feel, or what to do; no one except Mescalito himself.'

I insisted that such an explanation was not possible and begged him again to tell me how the agreement was reached.

'I know why you have come,' don Juan said in a mysterious tone. 'I can't help you in your endeavour because there is no system of cueing.'

'But how can all those persons agree about Mescalito's presence?'

'They agree because they see,' don Juan said dramatically, and then added casually, 'Why don't you attend another mitote and see for yourself?' (37–8; italics deleted).

Concluding remarks

There is a fundamental equivocality inherent in reality disjunctures which renders problematic the determination of which of the parties to a disjuncture is a faulted witness of the world. A conflict as to the objective presence of (say) 'voices' can be resolved by proposing that one of the disputants is 'hard of hearing', or that the other is 'hearing things'. Which of these alternate solutions is appropriate, however, turns on whether or not the voices were 'really' available for the hearing. But of course, whether or not the voices are actually present is precisely the problematic which precipitates the search for a resolution in the first place. The solution of the puzzle posed by the disjuncture hearings requires a decision as to whether there was a voice to be heard. Yet whether there was a voice to be heard is the very issue comprising the disjuncture. There is, then, a rather nasty and potentially endless vicious circle embedded in reality disjunctures.

The presence of the vicious circle does not mean that reality disjunctures are beyond the pale of resolution. If by resolution we mean the selection of one version as definitive of 'what really happened' and its use as the grounds of further inference and action (e.g. designating the proponent of some alternate version as 'hallucinating'), then reality disjunctures are resolved frequently and with extraordinary dispatch. The presence of the vicious circle does however suggest that the ways in which resolutions are brought about is not quite as simple as they might appear at first glance.

We began our inquiry by deepening the analysis of the potentially endless equivocalities which permeate reality disjunctures. Specifically, we indicated some of the ways in which any version of 'what really happened' can be rendered empirically and rationally irrefutable and the ways in which that irrefutability may be perpetuated indefinitely. Having established how experiential versions of the world can sustain themselves against all manners of seemingly contradictory evidence, we proposed that the resolution of full-fledged disjunctures implicates what, for lack, of a better word, we chose to call a politics.

The very nature of reality disjunctures, the fact that the other has looked at the world and experienced it in contrary ways, assures that the choice of a particular version as definitive of 'what really happened' receives less than universal support. The decision to nevertheless act upon a particular version as the grounds of further inference and action (over and against competing possibilities) comprises the politics. Because the decision to act upon a disputed version of the world typically includes as one of its consequences the discrediting of the other's ability to properly perceive reality, the politics of which we speak is, often, a 'politics of experience'.[7]

5

Mundane autobiography

Mundane inquiry depicts itself as responding to entities, events and relations which are independently established facticities – be they pulsars, psyches, class structures, causal sequences or, as in this investigation, the 'properties of mundane reason'. Mundane inquiry does not understand itself as creating these entities but as discovering or reflecting their real properties (which may include the property 'all properties are created'). And, indeed, mundane practitioners pursue, discuss and experience these domains and the relations and entities of which they are composed as 'real', 'objective' or 'natural' orders of fact. Reflections and analyses from outside the particular system of inquiry suggest, however, that the nature and structure of what is 'out there' is in varying ways and to varying degrees constituted or constructed through the very acts in which a domain is conceptualized, addressed and engaged. The contrast between the 'inside' ontology and epistemology of mundane practitioners and the 'outside' ontology and epistemology of analysts can be turned to analytic advantage in highlighting the inner work of mundaneity. Specifically, the contrast affords the opportunity to ask how mundane reasoners 'construct' a domain, as the outside view would have it, while nevertheless pursuing, discussing and experiencing the domain as 'absolute', 'out there', or 'real' (cf. Stolzenberg 1984).

The issue is deepened by the appreciation that a radical grasp of the constitutive nature of mundane activity may obliterate an entire order of mundane inquiry as when, for example, the ascendance of secular versions of reality make it impossible or absurd to be a witch-hunter or to consider the correspondence between witchcraft accusations and witchcraft reality. Insofar as the ontology from within is replaced by the ontology from without, the issue of correspondence collapses and questions of truth and falsehood are no longer formulated or formulable (although mundane discourse may be reconstituted at another level).[1] Insofar as mundane inquiry gains a radical grasp of the contingency of its domain or world it is threatened with an *ontologically fatal insight*. Depending upon the depth and scope of mundane inquiry's appreciation of the alternative or outside ontological stance available to it, any particular system of mundane inquiry is threatened with what may appear to its practitioners to be complete dissolution of themselves and the world over, against and within which they stand. Thus, in juxtaposing 'inside' and 'outside' ontologies we seek to discover the ways in which mundane inquiry is able to sustain what Laing (1965) has called 'ontological security', mundane inquiry's faith, as it were, in the thereness of its world and of itself, and the validity of its primordial prejudices. One feature of the accomplishment of ontological security is mundane inquiry's seemingly endless capacity to reiteratively formulate itself as a subject confronting an object, to provide as it were a *mundane autobiography* of itself which casts itself in the role of representing, reflecting, discerning or judging the properties or nature of what is already 'there'.

In this chapter I wish to highlight the nature of mundane autobiography in traffic court through use of one of the more interesting and important efforts to describe the constitutive character of legal and judicial processing: labeling theory, especially Howard Becker's (1963) seminal formulation. Becker's work affords an 'outsiders' or constitutive view of deviance: for labeling theory, the deviant is not someone who has behaved in an inherently immoral fashion but rather one to whom the label 'deviant' has been successfully applied. From a point of view outside the discourse and practices of courts, the labeling theory view is cogent and insightful: the only feature common to acts and individuals designated as deviant (when viewed broadly and cross culturally) is indeed that they have been labeled as such. From within the enforcement and judicial establishment, however, labeling theory's portrayal of the constitutive role of judgment seems absurd and threatens fundamental idiomatic distinctions and operations which comprise the very substance of enforcement and judicial discourse (cf. Hund 1985). If, for example, the deviant is one who is labeled as such then it is impossible to make or even consider the possibility of a 'true' or 'false' judgment about an individual: from the labeling perspective, after all, the individual is no more and no less than what he or she is taken to be. I seek to capitalize on the tension between the cogency of the labeling formulation as an 'outside' view and its absurdity when considered from the 'inside'. Just as Evans-Pritchard's Western perspective highlights the idiomatic ingenuity of Azande in reproducing poison oracle discourse, labeling theory will allow us to highlight a comparable ingenuity of mundane reasoning within the court as it reproduces itself and the idiomatic space within which distinctions of *really* guilty or *really* innocent and mistaken or accurate judgment are intelligible possibilities. Given the cogency of the 'outside view', the issue put to traffic court (as an example of mundane inquiry) is how do mundane reasoners nevertheless manage to represent themselves as reacting to or attempting to discover the nature of a pre-given, independently defined or 'objective' state of affairs.[2]

The matter is more complicated. As powerful and provocative as Becker's early formulation proved to be, it was not entirely an 'outside' or 'constitutive' model: Becker's early statement, which was meant to establish the ways in which deviance and deviants were constructed through the response of the community, did not fully purge itself of the mundane elements from within the field of discourse it had intended to transcend. Thus, in order to use labeling theory as an outside ontology to juxtapose to the inside ontology of traffic court, we shall have to specify and then clarify the nature of labeling theory's confounding. An unfortunate complication in one regard, it presents us with an opportunity in another, for we are able to gain a glimpse of how sociological efforts to deconstruct a mundane point of view and attain a constitutive, outside or 'radical' perspective may nevertheless become ensnared within mundane autobiography.[3]

Mundane and constitutive versions of deviance

Becker (1963) proposes a sociological view of deviance which stands in contrast to the ways in which deviance has typically been conceived by scientists as well as laymen. The essentials of the distinction are specified in statements such as the following:

What laymen want to know about deviants is: Why do they do it: How can we account for their rule-breaking? What is there about them that leads them to do forbidden things? Scientific research has tried to find answers to these questions. In doing so it has accepted the commonsense premise that there is something inherently deviant (qualitatively distinct) about acts that break (or seem to break) social rules. It has also accepted the commonsense assumption that the deviant act occurs because some characteristic of the person who commits it makes it necessary or inevitable that he should. Scientists do not ordinarily question the label 'deviant' when it is applied to particular acts or people but rather take it as given. In so doing, they accept the values of the group making the judgment.

It is easily observable that different groups judge different things to be deviant. This should alert us to the possibility that the person making the judgment of deviance, the process by which that judgment is arrived at, and the situation in which it is made may all be intimately involved in the phenomenon of deviance. To the degree that the commonsense view of deviance and the scientific theories that begin with its premises assume that acts that break rules are inherently deviant and thus take for granted the situations and processes of judgment, they may leave out an important variable. If scientists ignore the variable character of the process of judgment, they may by that omission limit the kinds of theories that can be developed and the kind of understanding that can be achieved (pp. 3–4).

Social groups create deviance by making the rules whose infraction constitutes deviance, and by applying those rules to particular people and labeling them as outsiders. From this point of view, deviance is not a quality of the act the person commits, but rather a consequence of the application by others of rules and sanctions to an 'offender'. The deviant is one to whom that label has successfully been applied; deviant behavior is behavior that people so label (p. 9).

[Deviance] is the product of a process which involves responses of other people to the behavior. The same behavior may be an infraction of the rules at one time and not at another; may be an infraction when committed by one person, but not when committed by another; some rules are broken with impunity, others are not. In short, whether a given act is deviant or not depends in part on the nature of the act (that is, whether or not it violates some rule) and in part on what other people do about it (p. 14).

If we take as the object of our attention behavior which comes to be labeled as deviant, we must recognize that we cannot know whether a given act will be categorized as deviant until the response of others has occurred. Deviance is not a quality that lies in behavior itself, but in the interaction between the person who commits an act and those who respond to it (p. 14).

If 'deviance' is regarded by the commonsense actor as somehow inhering in the acts so designated, then the proposal that deviance is behavior which persons so label seems to stand the commonsense attitude on its head. That is, from the point of view of the commonsense actor deviance is an 'objective' feature of the environment which invites and in some sense precipitates an appropriate response from the community. Deviance is presumedly 'discovered' not 'manufactured' by the various legal institutions. From the viewpoint of the commonsense actor, deviance is the pre-existent cause of his response to it. Yet as Becker's observation that different groups judge different acts to be deviant suggests, there is a sense in which 'deviance' exists in and by virtue of the response of the relevant community. Viewed sociologically, the deviant character of the act is not intrinsic to the act but depends on or, more emphatically, is constituted by the subsequent response of the community. If one were concerned to know if a particular act was or was not deviant, then nothing would be gained by examining the act *per se*. Nothing would be gained according to Becker, because the properties with which the act is seemingly endowed are created by the community's response to the act.

In contrast to the absolutist proclivities allegedly characteristic of the commonsense actor, then, the labeling theorist advances a relativistic model. Seen from the 'inside' of an already established symoblic universe, 'deviance' presents itself as a property inhering in the acts so characterized. Yet, when viewed from the 'outside', the deviance that such acts are deemed to possess is assured only by virtue of a community's orientation to them as wrong, immoral, evil, etc. From within, deviance is an objective property of an act, or at least constituted by some method other than the immediate response to the act: from without, deviance is brought into the world by the communal response.

Let us call the model of relations presupposed by and implicated in commonsense experience of deviance the mundane model of deviance. The mundane model conceptualizes the deviance of an act as existing independently of a community's response. It implicitly posits that certain acts are (or ought to be) responded to in particular ways because they are 'deviant', that is, their 'deviance' is defined by criteria other than the fact that you or I happen to regard or experience the act as deviant. Let us call the model of relations, advanced in at least some of Becker's statements, the constitutive model of deviance. This model conceptualizes deviance as a property which is created and sustained by a community's response to an act as deviant. It proposes in effect that while the commonsense actor may regard deviance as a pre-existent cause of his action toward a particular act or person, deviance is being constituted by those very actions.

The mundane model is an 'insider's' ontology, a member's ontology. The constitutive model is an 'outsider's' ontology, one that the sociologist might use when he turns to the phenomenon of deviance. Unfortunately, there are aspects of Becker's presentation which allow for a possible confusion of the relation between the two models which blunts the potentially radical and useful thrust of the distinction. The ambiguity is particularly acute in the observations and reflections which are mobilized to specify what is to be understood by the maxim 'the deviant is one to whom that label has been successfully applied; deviant behavior is behavior that people so label' (Becker 1963: 9). In several ways the observations and reflections which interpret the maxim are derived from a mundane model understanding of deviance: the resultant conceptualization of the labeling process is then but a variant of common-sense recognitions of the sorts of relations which can exist between, say, law enforcement officials and the judiciary on the one hand and 'real' deviance on the other.[4] In order to precisely specify the confusion it is necessary to specify the ways in which each model conceptualizes the labeling process.

Mundane and constitutive understandings of the labeling process

One understanding of the maxim, 'The deviant is one to whom that label has been successfully applied; deviant behavior is behavior that people so label', is derived from the demonstrable inadequacies and variability of the detection and categorization of rule violations. The maxim takes its mandate from the observation that not all those who violate rules are categorized as deviant and not all of those who are categorized as deviant have violated a rule. Presumedly, if the classes of deviance and non-deviance were properly assembled (i.e. in perfect conformity with the criterion of rule violation), if all the faults of police and judicial processing were removed so as to provide for homogeneous categories, then labeling would be superfluous. Rule violation and application of the label 'deviant' would coincide and the deviant would in effect be he or she who has violated a rule and only incidentally he or she who has been labeled deviant.

Insofar as Becker endorses the notion of 'real deviance' – the evidence is admittedly equivocal – then the labeling maxim is predicated upon and motivated by a modified version of the 'constancy hypothesis' (Gurwitsch 1966: 4–5). The constancy hypothesis anticipates certain uniform relations between objective stimuli and sensation. Any anomalous relations are accounted for by reference to various supervening processes such as judgment and interpetation (Gurwitsch 1966: 5). The mundane model version of labeling theory is based on a parallel model of the social actor. Specifically, it is based on the assumption that identical objective stimuli, i.e. rule violation or non-rule violation, should yield identical responses from law enforcement and judicial personnel, etc., i.e. categorization as deviant or non-deviant, respectively. Under the auspices of the constancy hypothesis, rule violation is accorded the status of an objective stimulus. Categorizing or not categorizing the act in question, marks off the range of possible reactions from the relevant community. Given the model of the actor (or community) and its relation to the world, there is an anticipated (perfect) correlation between the properties of the act and subsequent categorization. Rule violation, the constancy model implicitly predicts, should be categorized 'deviant'; rule compliance should be categorized, minimally, 'non-deviant' or conforming. Given these expectancies specified by the constancy model, discrepancies between the objective properties of a particular act and ultimate categorization are anomalies. Under the mundane model, the labeling process is the theoretical construct through which the anomaly is accounted for. That is, the labeling process serves to account for the disparity between expected and observed categorizations. It represents, in effect, an appeal to a process which intervenes between detection of the objective property of rule violation and ultimate categorization. Certain rule violators are not categorized as deviant because of the variable exigencies of the process. Thus, for example, a disparity between rule violation and applied label may be accounted for by an appeal to factors which are roughly the analogue of the psychological notion of 'attention'.[5]

A person believed to have committed a given 'deviant' act may at one time be responded to much more leniently than he would be at some other time. The occurrence of 'drives' against various kinds of deviance illustrates this clearly. At various times, enforcement officials may decide to make an all-out attack on some particular kind of deviance, such as gambling, drug addiction, or homosexuality. It is obviously much more dangerous to engage in one of these activities when a drive is on than at any other time (Becker 1963: 12).

In this passage, the differential concern of legal officials expressed in the notion of 'drives' provides an implicit answer to the question: how is it possible that a person may violate the law and yet not be regarded as deviant while being nevertheless 'deviant'? This is a characteristic mundane problem and a characteristic mundane solution. The mundane model formulation of labeling provides a means for resolving the mundane anomaly of the fact that the commonsense actor (or sociologist) can propose that an act really and actually is deviant while other members of the society seemingly do not concur. That is, the 'judgmental activities' collected under the heading of the labeling process serve as a source of solutions to the puzzle posed by the fact that a person identified as deviant and, consequently, a candidate for certain prescribed treatment is not accorded that treatment. As we shall see, the mundane model conception of the role of the labeling process is not so much a unique sociological conception of deviance, as it is a member of the society's way of conceiving of the relation between the activities of the legal system and the violation of the law.

In the constitutive model's version of the maxim 'The deviant is one to whom that label has been successfully applied', the labeling process is constitutive not only of particular determinations of deviance, in the sense that certain acts are 'labeled' as deviant while other deviant acts are not so labeled, but of the very possibility of any determination of deviance or rule violation in the first place. From the constitutive viewpoint there is no deviance apart from the response; for deviance is in effect the gloss (Garfinkel and Sacks 1970) for the processes through which it is realized as such. The 'characters', to borrow Mead's (1938) words, of the 'objective' stimuli or rule infraction are assured of in no other way than in and through the definitional response of the individual or relevant community. The properties of the stimuli, when seen from the perspective of the constitutive model, are not built into the stimulus. Rather, they are the accomplished creation, so to speak, of the response to them. Thus the labeling process is not merely an intervening process between the 'real' stimulus and its ultimate categorization – as it is regarded under the mundane model – but, instead, is constitutive of deviance and includes every aspect of the communal response, from the formulation of rules through to their situated application to particular cases.

Confusion between mundane and constitutive models

The mundane and constitutive models develop very different understandings of the role and nature of the labeling process. Indiscriminate intercourse between the two spawns an internally contradictory theoretical formulation. One such contradiction manifests itself with dramatic lucidity in Becker's classification or typology of deviant behaviors. The typology presented in Table 1, is produced by the cross classification of whether or not an act did in fact violate a rule and whether or not the actor is perceived as deviant:

Table 1

Types of deviant behavior[a]

	Obedient behavior	Rule-breaking behavior
Perceived as deviant	falsely accused	pure deviant
Not perceived as deviant	conforming	secret deviant

[a] Becker (1963: 20).

While the typology may have been developed by Becker to illustrate certain features of the constitutive model, it is, in fact, a schematic portrayal of how the mundane model views the relation between community perceptions and deviance. Indeed, given the constitutive model's presuppositions, the categories 'secret deviant' and the 'falsely accused' are conceptual anomalies (at least insofar as Becker presents the types as 'sociological' observations). If deviant behavior is behavior that persons so label, then 'secret deviance' wherein 'an improper act is committed, yet no one notices it or reacts to it as a violation of the rules' (Becker 1963: 20) is a theoretical *non sequitur*. If the labeling is constitutive of deviance, then the fact that no one reacts to an act as deviant means that it is not deviant.[6] Similarly, the notion of 'false accusation' is anomalous with respect to the constitutive model: if the label is constitutive of deviance, then there can be no 'error'.

The typology is not an adequate expression of an outside conceptualization of the phenomenon of deviance. In fact it is a schematic representation of possible relations that a mundane or inside reasoner can envision as existing between the response of a community and real deviance (where the latter is treated as a property defined by some method other than the actual, immediate response of the community). For example, the typology is isomorphic with the major features of a traffic court judge's conception of the possibilities which derive from the interaction between law enforcement officials and violators/non-violators of the law. What Becker calls 'types of deviant behavior' represents judges' more or less explicit conception of the possible outcomes of judicial and police activities.

Judges 'know' that there is not a one-to-one correspondence between citations and offenses which warrant a citation. Offenses, i.e., traffic code violations, are regarded as occurring with increasing frequency and because of the limited size of the available police force, laxity, etc., some violations go undetected. From the point of view of judges, these 'real' but undetected violations constitute a population of 'secret deviants'. They are in effect a collection of acts which, had the police or the highway patrol been present to observe them, would perhaps have been citable. Relatedly, judges 'know' that the police may for one reason or another erroneously cite an individual for an infraction she has never committed. Such persons would presumedly fall in the category labeled the 'falsely accused'.

There are a number of relatively subtle variants of these categories, but they are all dependent upon the assumption of objective deviance. That is, the idiomatic variations assume that the deviance of a particular act is independent of the processes through which it is displayed and detected as deviant. Judges and others know that police discretion, for example, may produce a category of persons who have committed a deviant act and who are perceived as committing a deviant act, but because of some situational exigency are not cited. From the point of view of judges, these are persons who, but for the grace of the officer, would be counted as 'pure deviants'.

The conceivable outcomes produced by the presumption of police discretion (and a host of other contingencies of response) presuppose the independence of the deviant character of the defendant's act from the process through which it is labeled by the officer. Judges are aware of the contingencies of the identification process. In a sense, conventional (mundane) labeling theory provides the mandate for judges' verdicts. If, for example, deviance were equated with labeling, then the defendant would, having been labeled, be deviant. There would in effect be no need for adjudication of the label. It is precisely because the identification of deviance is presumed to stand in some variable and contingent relation to 'real' deviance that the judgment of the judge is required.

With appropriate terminological modifications, Becker's typology characterizes the possible outcomes of adjudication as they are envisioned by the judge and the legal system in general. Table 2 portrays the relations between judges' assessments and violations of the law as the relations are formulated by judges.

Table 2

Defendants' actual status		
	Complied with law	Violated law
Judge finds defendant guilty	falsely convicted	correctly convicted
Judge finds defendant innocent	correctly acquitted	falsely acquitted

From the point of view of the judges, the upper right and lower left categories define 'justice'. The coincidence of actual and assessed guilt defines a correct decision. The remaining categories are varieties of error and injustice. For judges, a particular determination may be right or wrong because the determinations of guilt are presumed to vary independently of actual guilt. Indeed, the presupposed independence of the defendant's guilt provides for the sensible character of interrogation in order to find out 'what really happened'. Without such an assumption, the sense of the correctness of a determination dissipates – as does the very sense of a determination. If the existential belief in an independent and objective state of guilt or innocence (i.e. the defendant did or did not violate a rule) is suspended, then a judge's determination could neither correspond nor fail to correspond to the actual state of affairs, for there would be no actual state of affairs apart from their determination.

The mundane model's conception of deviance is a constituent feature of the process through which 'deviance' is realized as such. Thus, insofar as Becker's typology is intended as a constitutive or outside characterization of deviance it is inadequate because it is in fact a schematic representation of a mundane or insider's version. The typology of possible deviant acts and the dimensions along which the typology is assembled – reactions of the police and judge on the one hand and the status of the act as a rule violation on the other – comprise part of court discourse as do the 'types' produced by variation in the two dimensions. Thus, to attain a fully outside ontology, these ways of representing the relation between rule violation and reaction have to be purged as a feature of labeling theory's analytic characterization of deviance. Insofar as they are retained, labeling theory is ensnared in an insider's version of labeling theory which is not very different from the version of deviance labeling theory set about to make problematic. If an insider's version informs labeling theory, then labeling theory's questions are reduced to the various factors or contingencies which affect the response of the police or judiciary to acts which have the same 'objective' properties in relation to the law. These are questions of the order: Why do social control agents treat some of the guilty as though they were innocent, and treat some of the innocent as though they were guilty? These are questions from within: the idiom from which they derive is part and parcel of how the judge, defendants and police represent and describe *their* relation to deviance.

Yet, if labeling theory must purge itself of inside discourse in order to fully realize an outside version, it cannot remain indifferent to inside discourse. Inside discourse is not to be debunked or superceded for it is a constituent feature of what after all is to be understood. Indeed without returning to consider the role and nature of inside discourse, a 'radical' labeling theory – one which equated deviance solely and exclusively with the immediate response of, say, police – would appear to be an absurd rendering of judicial processing. Thus, a comprehensive outside version of labeling theory returns to inside discourse to consider it, not as an analytic resource, but as part of the phenomenon. Insiders, though they constitute or construct deviance, nevertheless discursively cast their accomplishment so as to mask their achievement: insiders talk about, reflect upon and even experience their talk, reflections and experience as mirroring in greater or lesser degrees of verisimilitude an independent or pre-given facticity. A fully outside version returns to and addresses the discourse of members as inside, or, what I term on the most general level, mundane autobiography. While the outside version alerts us to the constitutive nature of insiders' work, it highlights as well that members do not see, talk or experience matters in that fashion and that they do not comprises an integral feature of the constitutive effort.

Mundane autobiography

The nature of mundane autobiography is thrown into relief by considering a typology constructed from a constitutive model of labeling purged entirely of 'inside' or mundane elements. Table 3 presents a typology of the relations between reaction and deviance constructed in accord with a pure constitutive model. Insofar as deviance is equated solely and exclusively with the reaction of the community then there are neither 'secret deviants', nor 'falsely accused'.

Table 3

Constitutive typology of deviant behavior

Responded to as deviant	Deviant
Not responded to as deviant	Not deviant

While the typology captures the relativistic thrust of a pure constitutive understanding of the phenomenon of deviance, it precludes a variety of inside or mundane recognitions. After all, for example, as inside reasoners we 'know' that some persons who are perceived as deviant are not 'really' deviant – they have been 'falsely accused'. We know further that some persons who have not been perceived as deviant – really are. However, insofar as deviance is radically equated with the response of a particular community, a vast array of commonsense or mundane recognitions are denied their possibility. For example:

1   A defendant is deviant (or guilty) simply by virtue of the fact that he or she is responded to as deviant. He is what he is taken to be.
2   Given that the defendant's status is constituted by or consists of the individual or collective response, the defendant is all things to all persons. That is, there as many statuses as there are determinations of that status, each of which is equally valid and equally correct even though they may directly and unequivocally contradict one another.
3   The equation of 'deviance' with response, moreover, means that given a multiplicity of (contradictory) determinations, there is no appeal nor any

concern with an appeal to whether the defendant 'really' is or 'really' is not guilty. The notion of 'real' deviant loses its sense and possibility. In a world where 'deviance' is equated with the processes through which it is realized as deviance, the idea of a status which stands independent of the response is an alien conception. It is also, parenthetically, a world in which there is no possibility of a 'mistake'.

4 The very sense of terms such as 'determination' ('taken to be', 'perceived as', 'judged', etc.) disintegrates. These are terms derived from the idiom founded upon the duality which is implicitly dissolved in a world where the constitutive model is somehow a 'lived' epistemology. The conception of the judge's 'determining' or 'assessing' the guilt of the defendant is derived from a model which presupposes an inquirer confronting an essentially objective world. These terms are specifications of the possible explicative acts which an inquirer may make with respect to the world and, as such, have currency only within a model which is predicated upon the subject-object duality.

The cherished terms of the deviant-making enterprise such as 'truth', 'bias' and others such as 'perception' and 'judgment' are predicated upon the duality of 'response' and 'real deviance', and, more generally, between subject and object. The disintegration of the duality between the subject and object (or any of the synonyms and variants of that dichotomy) deprives these terms of their sense and possibility. A Pirandellian (1952) world where 'it is so if you think it's so' is a world in which – insofar as its inhabitants are 'aware' of their predicament – the possibility of truth (and error) has ceased, for there is no 'reality' apart from the perception of it. Issues of veridicality and verisimilitude can no longer be formulated, for their sense as issues presupposes an independent facticity with respect to which perceptions, descriptions and responses may be compared.[7]

A narrow reading of the labeling stance and of the constitutive model then seems to have no conceptual room for the idiom of commonsense possibilities which informs commonsense talk about deviance. Indeed from within, the constitutive model seems to be an epistemology of the absurd. How is the relativism recommended by the sociological attitude to be reconciled with the absolutism of the talk of parties to the deviant-making enterprise?

The reconciliation is achieved through the (analyst's) recognition that while a community creates deviance, it may simultaneously mask its creative work from itself. Even though deviance is created by the response of the community, an integral feature of that response is the autobiographical conception of itself as confronting an order of events whose character as deviant is presupposed as independent of the immediate response of the community. Thus, for example, while the community creates the possibility of traffic violations in the sense of making the rules which can be violated and developing the agencies for their detection, from within the court the rules may be treated as definitive of 'real' deviance, as establishing that class of acts that are deviant whether or not they are concretely noticed or responded to as such. A consequence of such treatment is that the community can conceive of itself as 'responding' to deviance in a restricted sense: it conceives of its response as an effort to correlate its discovery, suppressing and judging activities with the 'real' properties of acts. In so conceiving of its relation to deviance, the community produces for itself all of the commonsense recognitions which turn on the distinction between 'real' deviance and a community's 'assessment' or 'judgment' of deviance.

A fully realized outside version of deviance understands that inside work involved in the constitution of deviance includes the inversion, masking or hiding of that work. The ways in which both praxis and perception organize and constitute world, while simultaneously masking the organizational work so as to provide for the appearance of determinate and objective or absolute entities, have been indicated by a variety of titles. Merleau-Ponty (1964), for example, writes of the 'retrospective illusion' whereby 'we take the perceived object constituted by our perceiving consciousness as a pre-existent cause of our perception' (p. xiii). Similarly, Berger and Luckman (1966) write of 'reification':

Reification is the apprehension of human phenomena as if they were things, that is, in non-human or possibly super-human terms. Another way of saying this is that reification is the apprehension of the products of human activity as if they were something else than human products – such as facts of nature, results of cosmic laws, or manifestations of divine will. Reification implies that man is capable of forgetting his own authorship of the human world, and further, that the dialectic between man, the producer, and his products is lost to consciousness ...

It must be emphasised that reification is a modality of consciousness, more precisely, a modality of man's objectivation of the human world. Even while apprehending the world in reified terms, man continues to produce it, that is, man is capable paradoxically of producing a reality that denies him (pp. 82–3).

The concept of mundane autobiography, however, directs us to consider the *discourse* through which insiders portray their relation as a response to exterior and constraining structures. Mundane autobiography as a discourse is both reproduced and presupposed in remarks which formulate officers, judges, or defendants as potentially 'right' or 'wrong' in their assessments of what really happened or in the deviance of a particular act. Thus, the judges' opening statement is a powerful statement of the mundane autobiography of the court.

and if I say dismissed, that means not guilty. You are free to go. Now, we are going to dismiss if we are satisfied that the explanation is a good defense and it raises a reasonable doubt, or too, if we are reading the officer's notes, we come to the conclusion that he has made a mistake, either in applying the law or in his judgment and he should not have issued the citation. Now before anybody takes that as a – my remark about the officer's – criticism of these officers, please don't put that emphasis on it. Because that's not my intention at all. Particularly to you young people that are visiting. I'm not criticizing the officers but I have been in this court for two years, and during that time they tell me they've issued two million citations. Now, I review them at the rate of 25,000 a month. That means I've looked at 600,000 samples, and I can't honestly represent to you that officers are infallible, and that they never make mistakes and that they are always right, and that the public is always wrong. Because that is an incorrect statement. You see, officers are very human, and they do make mistakes – they make mistakes, just like, oh, doctors and lawyers and accountants, and mechanics, and students and teachers, professional ballplayers, housewives, and judges. I'm told that I make more mistakes than any judge on the bench, and I guess that is right. But I'll see more people today through on to 10 tonight to night court than most judges will see in a year. So I'm bound to make more mistakes. See, we recognize the officers' mistakes, and they are dismissed.

The judge creates the discursive space of his judgments and advances a mundane conception of the relation between an officer and deviance. They are not creating deviance but attempting to discern violators and, as a consequence, they may 'make mistakes' either through 'applying the law' or 'judgment'. The application of the law or judgment should reflect an act's actual properties and insofar as a defendant's explanation or the officer's notes indicate they do not, the citation will be dismissed and the defendant is 'free to go'. Not only is the officer cast as responding to an independent field, but the judge casts his own activities in a similar fashion. The relation between an act and the officer's response is itself an objective relation to which the judge responds in an attempt to determine whether officers have made 'mistakes'. The judge does not create the officer's error or deviance, but assesses it. The judge then formulates that he, like officers, may also make 'mistakes'. Thus, the judge offers a mundane version of both the work of officers and the work of judges. In so doing he both presupposes and reproduces mundane autobiography.

In the formulation of a real domain of rules and infractions, the judge (and other mundane reasoners) create the dimensions within which 'deviance' can be treated in terms analogous to concrete events. Thus, for example, once the deviant character of an event is established as a taken-for-granted feature, it is possible to raise typical mundane issues: how can persons differentially perceive, describe or respond to the 'same' act? And, it is possible, indeed necessary, to formulate typical mundane solutions: the differential response is a function of a failure to appropriately apply or interpret the law, perceive the offense, incompetence and so forth. Thus, for example, given the deviant character of excessive speed, a defendant may formulate the puzzle of why such speeds are treated as deviant at one time, but not at another.

> Defendant: . . . On the speeding violation, I violated the law . . . there's no argument about that, but 70 miles an hour, on an open freeway . . . there were essentially no other cars . . . I've seen the Highway Patrol cruise, with cars . . . 70 miles an hour, cruise with me, for that matter, at 70 miles an hour, at 3:00, when the freeway was absolutely jam-packed . . .
> Judge: Well, but still the law is sixty-five and that's it . . . They cite a lot of people, if it makes you feel any better, at 70 miles an hour.
> D: I agree . . . I find the Highway Patrol being slightly capricious on this though, your honor. I do agree it's a violation of the law, there's no question about that. I wish they would be a little bit more consistent though. That's all I have to say.

It is not invariably the formal rules (e.g. the traffic code) which are invoked as defining an act's actual properties. Indeed, the rules themselves may be formulated for their conventional, capricious or relative character. But a significant feature of such formulations is that the success and, in fact, the possibility of such claims requires a method for determining an act's actual properties in terms of which the appropriateness of the rule may be considered. In effect, the mundane version is invoked at a second-order level wherein the formal rules themselves are conceived as integral features of the response to acts whose properties are defined and understood by reference to yet another method of assessment such as *ad hoc* reasoning about what constitutes the warranting circumstances for the application of rules.

There may be conflict or negotiation as to which of several competing methods will prevail: *ad hoc* commonsense criteria and reasoning may be juxtaposed against the law and legal reasoning. Consider the following exchange for the ways in which the defendant's argument that a citation was 'invalid' is established and countered over the course of an arraignment.

> Judge: Yer charged with violating section twenty-one-four-sixty-one – traffic uh- traffic signs.
> Defendant: Uh. I'd like to say that the plane – the claim was invalid.

J: Well I'm not saying it's valid 'r invalid. I take it thetchu'd like tu plead not guilty tuh this matter? Is that right?

D: No I plead guilty, but I'd like to say that there were no cars coming in either direction 'n I was very careful.

J: Show me on the board what happened huh? – C'n you draw a little sketch for me?

D: Sure.

D: This Club. I was right here? There was a police car parked right here.

J: Uh huh.

D: I saw 'im, when I crossed. There was not one car coming in either direction an' I crossed, here. After looking for about two seconds in either direction.

J: You were walking?

D: Yes.

J: What –

D: An' I walked, at least fifty feet. Before the police car turned.

J: Well of course if there's any cars coming 'r not isn't really the determining factor is it.

D: Uh.

J: Th' law says yer not tuh go against the, the light. Zat right?

D: Here's City – City college right there.

J: Uh huh.

D: Uh during class time, people are coming tuh school, an' they cross here. Not at the cross sign. Hunnerds of people every day. Not using the uh cross light at all.

J: Oh yeh.

D: And I was, I was at the cross light 'n I made a point of looking in either direction an' being very careful about it.

J: Course yuh know, at's what – at – lotta people get killed very year, because they look an' they don't see. They don't have as good eyes as you have him? What-time a' day was it?

D: Well – It was – it was at night time, lights 'r very easy tuh see.

J: Okay.

In the exchange the defendant and the judge are proposing alternative methods for establishing the deviance of walking across the street against the traffic light. The defendant invokes the actual dangerousness of the act as a method for establishing its significance: there were no cars coming, he was cautious, and many persons routinely perform the same act. The judge invokes the law as a method for defining the act's relevant properties: 'Th' law says yer not tuh go against the, the light.' The judge also attempts to counter the defendant's 'safety' criterion by noting that many people are killed every year because they 'look an' they don't see'. Although the substance of the criteria is different, the arguments are uniform in their appeal to features other than the immediate reaction of officer, defendant, or judge as a means of establishing the act's 'real' properties.

Thus, mundane autobiography does not simply consist (even within the court) of treating the vehicle code as an objective or independent criterion of correct or incorrect, appropriate or inappropriate actions. Indeed, the rules themselves or their application may be made problematic and may come to be seen as a construction or an arbitrary imposition. The very demonstration of such features although it suspends mundane autobiography on one level nevertheless reproduces it on another. More specifically, even when the law is contested and argued to have been applied inappropriately, there is reference to the independent properties of the event or circumstances against which the inappropriateness is established. Indeed, the very demonstration that the 'law is a construction' or that it has been inappropriately applied occurs within a context in which some independent method of assessing what is (or is not) objective, appropriate or inherently so is implied or invoked with regard to which the properties of rules or their application are made visible.

Concluding remarks

I have suggested that one practice through which mundaneity reproduces itself is the development of an autobiographical version of itself which casts mundane inquiry as addressing a field which is 'out there', pre-given or defined by criteria other than the immediate response or discourse. In this fashion, mundaneity masks the extent to which the field to which mundane inquiry turns is an accomplishment or achievement.[8] In understanding itself as an inquirer confronting nature – be it a judge confronting the range of deviant or non-deviant acts, or most abstractly, a subject confronting an object – mundaneity secures an ontological and epistemological version of itself which allows it to be concerned with a field of events, entities and relations but systematically deflects attention from the ways in which the very field of which it is concerned is constituted.[9] To be sure, mundane inquiry can always take a step-back to reflect upon, and analyze its own organization but after even the most abstract contemplations of mundane inquiry, reflective discourse reiterates the same mundane structures as the original inquiry.[10] Thus, for example, jurisprudents or sociologists or appellate courts may review the nature of legal discourse striving to illuminate its relevant structures – but in so doing the fundamental subject-object duality is reproduced as is the attendant concern with truth and error and the entire mundane idiom. In the reiteration of mundane space, mundane inquiry naively dwells within that space, utilizes it, understands itself through it but misses the phenomenon of the spacing. The 'missing of the spacing', however, is one way in which the mundane space is produced and reproduced.

6

Mundane reflection

Witnessed from the 'inside' of a particular system of mundane inquiry the world offers itself as the 'always already there' or 'pre-given' theater of circumstances within and toward which particular acts of inquiry and explication are directed. Examined from the 'outside', however, that self-same pre-given world is visible as the creative accomplishment of the very activities which presuppose its essentially objective character. A constituent feature of mundane inquiry's accomplishment of its world includes mundane inquiry's *in*capacity to appreciate its circumstances as witnessed from the 'outside'. If mundane inquiry is to find itself directed to a world, then it must remain oblivious to its accomplishment by conceiving of itself in a mundane relation to the world, the maintenance of that mundane autobiography being part of the accomplishment to which mundane inquiry is oblivious.

Depending on the proximity, depth and scope of its ontologically fatal insight into the creative accomplishment of the world over and against which mundane inquiry conceives itself to stand, mundane inquiry encounters a range of consequences. These consequences include simple recognition of what Polanyi (1964: 264–8) calls the 'fiduciary commitment' implicit in all mundane concern to the 'vertigo of relativity' (Berger and Luckman 1966: 5) to complete dissolution of the duality. For persons within a system of mundane inquiry, the recognition of the components of the creative accomplishment may involve 'mere' appreciation that one is 'pretending' or 'playing', or it may involve a loss of the sense of self, being and the real world. The latter possibility is epitomized in psychotic experience.

Psychotic experience goes beyond the horizons of our common, that is, our communal sense. What regions of experience does this lead to? It entails a loss of the usual foundations of the 'sense' of the world that we share with one another. Old purposes no longer seem viable; old meanings are less; the distinctions between imagination, dream, external perceptions often seem no longer to apply in the old way. External events may seem magically conjured up. Dreams may seem to be direct communications from others; imagination may seem to be objective reality. But most radical of all, the very ontological foundations are shaken. The being of phenomena and the phenomena of being may no longer present itself to us as before ... No one who has not experienced how insubstantial the pageant of external reality can be, how it may fade, can fully realize the sublime and grotesque presences that can replace it, or that can exist alongside (Laing 1967: 132–3).[1]

Given that an ontologically fatal insight into mundane inquiry's reflexive constitution of itself and the world can dissolve mundane inquiry, how does mundane inquiry avoid or suppress a radical appreciation of its constitutive work? If mundane inquiry constitutes itself and its world by remaining oblivious to its constitutive work, and if part of that constitutive work includes that very obliviousness, how is this vital incomprehension perpetuated? The ways in which this vital incapacity is sustained constitutes the problematic of mundaneity.

Mundane inquiry renders itself oblivious *not* through failing to reflect upon itself. On the contrary, mundane inquiry may reflect powerfully and deeply upon itself. The reflections, however, are so patterned by the mundane idiom that no matter how deeply, abstractly, or 'transcenden-tally' mundane inquiry strives to move beyond the idiom, it reproduces an 'ontological space' (Spencer 1981) in which mundane inquiry once again finds itself addressing, exploring and describing objective struc-tures. Wherever it rests or is frozen – in considering psyches, societies, or the practices and properties of mundane reason – mundane reflection will 'mundanize' its referent and regard it as an 'already there' entity, which it strives to mirror.

In this chapter I shall consider the processes through which mundane inquiry's reflective concerns are shaped and patterned by the mundane idiom. These processes preclude or inhibit radical reflection (Schrag 1980) by deflecting attention away from mundaneity. Though I shall consider a pot-pourri of forms of mundane inquiry, I will be especially concerned with the more abstract, 'reflexive' forms of discourse including those which seek to focus on the constitutive process in the most comprehen-sive sense, such as the sociology of knowledge and ethnomethodology. Even they, in the very ways in which they set about to show the constitutive dimension of discourse and practice, nevertheless, neces-sarily and irremediably reproduce and organize their efforts within a mundane idiom. Indeed, if I am not mistaken, 'constructionism', 'prac-tices' and 'mundane reason', while they afford a wedge of sorts into the ways in which mundaneity organizes and hides its work, are also the product of just such work.

The retrospective illusion and naivete of mundane inquiry

Merleau-Ponty (1964b) writes of the 'retrospective illusion' through which perception or consciousness permits itself to confront an objective, determinate world, i.e. a world which stands apart from and independent of the particular acts in which it is taken up. The 'illusion' resides in the fact that 'we take the perceived objects constituted by our perceiving consciousness as a pre-existent cause of our perception' (Merleau-Ponty 1964b: xiii). By forgetting its essential contribution to the object, perception allows the world to manifest itself as object. Perception allows itself, by virtue of its 'ruse', to witness the independent being of entities. Mundane inquiry 'illudes' itself in an analogous fashion. While mundane inquiry is constitutive of the field which it explicates, mundane inquiry necessarily regards its accomplishment as the *a priori* cause, motivation and even invitation to act toward its world in the way that it does. From the point of view of judges, for example, the determination of a defendant's guilt is not regarded as constituted by the judgment. Instead, the fact that the defendant is or is not guilty is encountered as the incentive for an assessment. Similarly, while the activities of the Azande are constitutive of the properties of the poison oracle *qua* oracle, the poison oracle from the point of view of the Azande is the *a priori* invitation for Azande to act toward it in the way that they do, i.e. to 'consult' the oracle. To regard the oracle as constituted by the activities directed toward it, or as consisting of those actions, is to reduce the oracle to the status of an object which exists only in a 'playful' or 'pretending' fashion.[2]

Recent studies highlight the nature of the retrospective illusion as it occurs within the social and natural sciences. Spencer (1981) suggests that from the point of view of philosophy, the world encountered by the sciences is a 'construct of human thought' (p. 123). When one steps outside the 'cognitive space' of working scientists it is possible to observe the ways in which the entities and relations which are researched and theorized are reified constructions. This view comprises what Spencer calls a 'philosophical', or, as we would say, outside ontology. From the viewpoint of scientists in their actual work, however, the constructed entities and relations are treated as real: working scientists are 'inexorably captured by the ontologies of these spaces and lose sight of the fact that their constructs are reifications' (p. 138). This working attitude comprises what Spencer calls an 'operational' or 'theoretical' (or what we would call an inside) ontology.

An important example of the distinction, according to Spencer, is found in the work of Kuhn (1970). 'Normal science' consists of 'puzzle-solving' activity in which the 'paradigm' that organizes scientific knowledge is 'taken for granted'. The paradigm (which Kuhn will argue and show is an historical construct) is itself not regarded by practitioners as a hypothesis to test against reality 'but *as the reality* from which normal science proceeds' (Spencer 1981: 123; italics in original). As Kuhn notes:

Normal science, the activity in which most scientists inevitably spend almost all their time, is predicated on the assumption that the scientific community knows what the world is like. Much of the success of the enterprise derives from the community's willingness to defend that assumption, if necessary, at considerable cost (Kuhn 1970: 5).

This attitude is an expression of the operational ontology: for practitioners, the paradigm is regarded as 'what the world is like', not as a mere construct. Yet Kuhn himself adopts a philosophical (or 'outside' perspective): the paradigms are not 'truth' but 'constructs that dominate scientific thought at certain moments in the history of science' (Spencer 1981: 123).

Spencer suggests that while social scientists may appreciate the constructed character of their concepts and paradigms in reflective moments, this knowledge is of no avail when they return to their ordinary preoccupations as social scientists:

They will go about their business talking in the abstractions of the cognitive space of theory – of 'stratification', 'revolution', 'political system', 'productive relations', 'capitalism' – as if these abstractions corresponded to something real, and as if the metaphysics of universal rules was indubitably true, i.e. as if theory were possible (p. 140; italics deleted).

Spencer suggests that his analysis ought not be heard as a critique: as currently constituted the social sciences may have no choice but to reify the cognitive space which they construct. In order to talk about anything, most especially past or remote events of large-scale structures, social scientists may be compelled to treat their constructs in a reified mode and to regularly lose sight of the fact of reification (p. 139).

While Spencer focuses on the disparity of inside and outside ontologies with regard to the social sciences, Garfinkel, Livingston and Lynch (1981) suggest a similar disparity in the actual hands-on work of the natural sciences. In their analysis of the activities through which astronomers at the Steward Observatory discovered an optical pulsar, Garfinkel *et al.* suggest that the 'independent Galilean pulsar' is a 'cultural object' constructed through the embodied practices through which its existence is determined. The relation between the pulsar and the activities through which it is detected is akin to the relation between the potter's hand and the pot it shapes (p. 137): the worldly object is deeply 'intertwined' with the embodied practices through which it is addressed and sought out. Although the pulsar and its discovery are 'intertwined' with the actual practices employed by the astronomers (which include the assumption of a pulsar waiting to be discovered), these practices are disattended over the course of discovery and in journal accounts of the discovery. The disattending of these 'primordial embodied practices' allows what Garfinkel *et al.* construe as a 'cultural' (or, as I would say, constructed) object to be grasped as a 'transcendental, natural object', that is, to be grasped as a real, 'out there' entity.

Theorizing practices in the social sciences as described by Spencer and discovery practices in the natural sciences as described by Garfinkel *et al.* each involve an operation whereby the work through which a domain of objects is constructed is disattended. The effect of the disattention is that practitioners encounter the domain as an independent facticity to be described and discovered. Mundane inquiry performs the retrospective illusion by ignoring or 'glossing' (Garfinkel and Sacks 1970) the suppositional, discursive and embodied work through which its world is constituted. The result of the ignoring is two fold: on the one hand, mundane inquiry becomes naive with regard to the constitution of the entities and processes which comprise its world; on the other hand, the very naivete is part of the process which allows mundane inquirers to explore, describe and theorize about those very entities and processes. Through the retrospective illusion, mundane inquirers find themselves confronting a world which may be problematic in its particulars: Are the observed patterns really a pulsar or the artifacts of telemetric procedures?; Does social class have a major or minor impact on worldview?; In exactly what ways does the retrospective illusion operate in the construction of reality? But it is a world in which the entities and the possible relations among them are treated and encountered as pregiven and as precipitating the theoretical investigative efforts to determine the properties of the entities and the nature of the relations.

The net result of the retrospective illusion is to render mundane inquiry *naive* to the facticity of its world. By virtue of the retrospective illusion, mundane inquiry is forever confronting a world whose facticity is essentially non-problematic. To be sure, the retrospective illusion may be recognized with respect to particular aspects of the world – Becker's (1963) work on deviance may be considered as an example of the de-reification or 'disillusioning' of deviance – but the retrospective illusion is reiterated at a meta-level. The 'labeling process' as a theoretical construct presumptively makes observable and stands in correspondence to some 'real' structure in the world which is 'always already there'. Becker has presumedly discovered, rather than manufactured, a feature of the world. Thus, labeling theory, even though it escapes a naivete on one substantive level, succumbs to it on yet another and, indeed, does so as a condition of having a world to theorize about and inquire into.

Historically, there have been several major attempts to transcend and explicate the naivete of mundane inquiry. Husserl (1962), for example, saw phenomenological investigations as the propaedeutic to the natural sciences. For Husserl, phenomenology was the culmination of a radicalism heralded in the meditations of Descartes. The phenomenological program, which radicalized Cartesian doubt was to be a 'first science' or a 'first philosophy'. The primacy of the phenomenological program, in relation to the already established sciences and philosophies, resided, in part, in its addressing the foundations of natural inquiry in a manner which the sciences and the various 'house philosophies' were unable, because of their obliviousness to the problematic implicit in the very availability of the world as an object of scientific concern. For Husserl, the sciences operated from within the 'natural attitude'. The sciences addressed a pre-given world, a world which, to borrow Merleau-Ponty's phrase, was 'always-already-there' (Merleau-Ponty 1962: viii). The sciences address a world which is essentially non-problematic as to its primordial availability as an object of inquiry. For Husserl, the unexplicated *giveness* of the world to experience was symptomatic of the natural science's naivete with respect to its own point of departure. Moreover, it seemed to be a naivete which the natural sciences themselves could not eliminate.

If certain riddles are, generally speaking, inherent in principle to natural science, then it is self-evident that the solution of these riddles according to premises and conclusions in principle transcends natural science. To expect from natural science itself the solution of any one of the problems inherent in it as such – thus inhering through and through, from beginning to end – or even merely to suppose that it could contribute to the solution of such a problem any premises whatsoever, is to be involved in a vicious circle (Husserl 1962: 88–9).

The foundations of natural inquiry will not yield to the technical apparatus which they support. The explication of the primordial foundations of the natural disciplines required the development of a 'procedure' which was itself not predicated on what it was to render problematic. The procedure which Husserl constructed, and which lies at the heart of the phenomenological program, was the phenomenological reduction. The reduction consisted of suspending the central presupposition of natural inquiry – the natural thesis. The bracketing of the natural thesis – which is in no way a 'refutation' of the presupposition or a solipsistic recommendation – yields consciousness as a primary and privileged domain. That is to say, by virtue of the reduction, the phenomenon of concern is no longer a natural world *per se*, but rather, the objects of the experienced world in the ways, and only in the ways, in which they are presented in consciousness, and the acts of consciousness in which they are grasped. The world is thus rendered '*perceptum qua perceptum*' (Gurwitsch 1966: 96).

As radical as phenomenological investigations may be, they are nevertheless investigations into real structures, that is, structures presumed to be independent of the discourse through which they are described. The noetic and noematic structures of consciousness, for example, are presumedly not the fabrication or invention of investigation. True, these structures are not of the world as conceived by the natural sciences, but they are assumed to have a being independent of the method through which they are made observable. But in the very way that phenomenology attends to structures to be described and which, moreover, can be explicated correctly or incorrectly, with greater or lesser clarity, and so on, phenomenology renders available to itself a second order world *per se* exhibiting all of the formal features of the world prior to the bracketing. In short, the phenomenological bracketing is a first order suspension of the natural thesis which is reiteratively reinstated once the 'residue' yielded by the initial bracketing is taken up as an object of inquiry. It is precisely at this point – the point at which phenomenology takes itself to have surpassed the naivete peculiar to mundane disciplines – that phenomenology becomes 'naive' as a condition of its being able to talk about *anything*.

The remedial self-concern of mundane inquiry

Mundane inquiries are reflective. They do analyze themselves. They articulate their procedures and assumptions, scrutinize themselves for efficacy and objectivity and so on. Indeed, the social sciences have reached the point where they themselves constitute a not insignificant segment of their own subject matter. The 'social psychology of psychology,' the 'sociology of sociology' and, more generally, the sociology of knowledge, are perhaps the leading instances wherein a discipline's own procedural activity is rendered part of the world which that discipline addresses. Is there not a sense, then, in which the naivete which we have proposed is so vital to mundane inquiry is progressively dispelled – at least for the social sciences? If the discipline is rendered in-the-world and explicated, does that not penetrate the vital lies of mundaneity? The answer is 'no'. Mundane disciplines consider and explicate their own procedures under the aegis of a mundane concern, which precludes the radicalization of reflection. In examining itself, mundane inquiry does not exceed itself. Put positively, mundane inquiry exhibits an *essentially practical or remedial* concern with itself which not only assures the perpetuation of the vital gloss, but relies upon it in the very course of its self-scrutiny.[3]

In speaking of mundane inquiry's remedial self-concern, I refer to the fact that for any particular course of mundane inquiry, the course of inquiry examines itself for the extent to which it adequately retrieves the real structures of the domain with which it is confronted. That is, mundane inquiry's self-scrutiny is formulated in light of its presumption of an essentially objective world. It asks of itself how 'true' are its formulations, how valid and reliable its methodology, and so on. The prototype of remedial self-concern is found, of course, in the concern of the sciences with the adequacy of their theoretical and technical practices. Mundane inquiry's self-investigative efforts are from the outset predicated upon the autobiographical version which it maintains of itself, namely, a course of activity directed to the explication of a real world. The questions which it puts to itself are carried out under the auspices of the idiom for which such a model is the architectonic principle.

The remedial self concern of the social sciences may seem belied by inquiries which attend to the organization and perspective of the social sciences as phenomena. Reflexive inquiries such as the sociology of science, the sociology of knowledge and the social psychology of the experiment, suggest that mundane inquiry can turn in on itself in a relatively radical fashion or, at least, in other than remedial ways. To cite them as possible counter instances, however, is to have missed the point. Mundane inquiry can, to be sure, take up mundane inquiry as a possible topic. But it is precisely at the point that the sciences are rendered a topic that the course of inquiry which attends to them as such, on the occasion when it turns in on *itself*, turns with an eye to *its* adequacy for explicating the structure of the sciences. Thus, for example, the social psychology of the experiment employs experiments to analyze the social psychological dynamics of experimentation (e.g. Rosenthal 1966). Although experimentation becomes a topic or phenomenon on one level, it is excluded as a phenomenon on the metal-level: in reflecting upon its own experimental methods, the social psychology of the experiment considers the extent to which *its* experimental procedures might have provided a biased, distorted or limited view of the social psychological dynamics of the experiment. Meta-inquiry in considering itself in this remedial fashion presupposes and reproduces mundane space.

Mundane inquiry's concern with itself is essentially remedial because mundane inquiry conceives of itself as a course of activity directed toward the existence of structures whose objectivity is essentially non-problematic. Given this autobiographical version, mundane inquiry, in turning to itself, finds that that which is of greatest interest to and in itself is the extent to which it can properly, correctly, or objectively explicate objective structures. In this way, mundaneity perpetuates the vital gloss. Mundane inquiry's own constitutive work in the production and maintenance of the domain to which it is directed is never allowed to appear as a phenomenon and, in fact, never suggests itself as that which could or could not appear as a phenomenon. The vital gloss is itself glossed.

Mundane inquiry's remedial self-concern stands in contrast to what might be termed *radical self-concern*. In addressing itself in a remedial fashion, mundane inquiry reviews itself to remedy or enhance its capacity to observe, describe or explain 'reality'. Were mundaneity to make itself available in a radical fashion, then mundane inquiry would be of interest as a phenomenon in its own right without regard to corrective or irony. It would address the remediality of mundane inquiry's self-concern as a constituent feature of mundane inquiry. That is, the very way in which mundaneity formulates and addresses itself as a phenomenon would, under the auspices of a radical concern with mundaneity, be included as a constituent feature of mundaneity's accomplishment of an objective world.

The contrast between a remedial or corrective concern with mundane inquiry, on the one hand, as opposed to a radical concern, on the other hand, is partly visible in the difference between the Azande's interest and Evans-Pritchard's (1937) interest in the poison oracle. As Evans-Pritchard notes, the 'Azande have little theory about their oracles and do not feel the need for doctrines' (p. 314). The absence of a theoretical attitude toward their own affairs is evident when Evans-Pritchard approaches the Azande with questions and problems premised on the poisonous character of *benge* as opposed to its mystical properties (which are central to its functioning within the Azande system). The absence of a theoretical or experimental interest in their own affairs is most visible at those moments when Evans-Pritchard confronts the Azande with hypothetical situations and possibilities which are utterly alien to the Azande idiom and which presuppose a willingness to put an entire moral order of perceivedly natural fact into doubt.

to ask Azande . . . what would happen if they were to administer oracle poison to a fowl without delivering an address or, if they were to administer an extra portion of poison to a fowl which has recovered from the usual doses, or, if they were to place some of the poison in a man's food, is to ask silly questions. The Azande does not know what would happen, he is not interested in what would happen, and no one has ever been fool enough to waste good oracle poison in making such pointless experiments, experiments which only a European could imagine (p. 314).

But the Azande are not totally devoid of a reflective attitude toward the oracle. It is simply that which can be speculated about and reflected upon is formulated from within the Azande idiom. Thus, the reflections do not transcend the idiom: they are shaped and guided by the idiom. For example, as we noted earlier, Azande theorize about the source of inconsistent oracular responses. They provide explanations for what, to a Westerner, appear·as anomalous inconsistencies. Similarly, the Azande are concerned with the quality of the *benge*, its preparation and the conditions attendant to its administration. The Azande may even employ a validity procedure in which the oracle is asked questions whose answers are obvious. A contrary response is regarded as evidence that the oracle is under the control of sorcery. In each of these instances, the Azande's reflective concern with procedures for addressing the oracle consists of a concern for proper and efficacious consultation. It is as if the idiom dictates the terms in which it is prepared to consider itself, and these terms formulate the phenomenon under an abiding respect for the fundamental or ontological validity of oracle responses. In reflexively considering itself, the idiom orients practitioners to the correctness of procedure, that is, the capacity of the poison oracle to retrieve objective as opposed to specious results. As Evans-Pritchard notes:

Azande act experimentally within the cadre of their mystical notions. They act as we would have to act if we had no means of making chemical and physiological analyses and we wanted to obtain the same results as they want to obtain . . . if their mystical notions allowed them to generalize their observations they would perceive, as we do, that their faith is without foundations. They themselves provide all the proof necessary (p. 336).

. . . And yet Azande do not see that their oracles tell them nothing! Their blindness is not due to stupidity, for they display great ingenuity in explaining away the failures and inequalities of the poison oracle and experimental keenness in testing it. It is due rather to the fact that their intellectual ingenuity and experimental keenness are conditioned by patterns of ritual behavior and mystical belief. Within the limits set by these patterns they show great intelligence, but it cannot operate beyond these limits. Or, to put it another way: they reason excellently in the idiom of their beliefs, but they cannot reason outside, or against, their beliefs because they have no other idiom in which to express their thoughts (p. 338).

The Azande, in other words, cannot address their own activities in a radical fashion. In fact, it is the outsider, Evans-Pritchard, who furnishes a 'radical' consideration of the poison oracle. For Evans-Pritchard, the oracle is the gloss for the entire range of activities through which it is addressed and thereby accomplished. For him, the Azande self-concern with propitious use of the oracle and the reconciliation of inconsistent oracle responses are constituent features of the work through which the essential facticity of the oracle is sustained. The Azande do not and cannot have a similar grasp of their own affairs without forfeiting the objectivity of oracle responses. Acquisition of a radical as opposed to remedial comprehension of the procedures for attending to the oracle – and, more generally, the world – is tantamount to depriving the oracle responses of their perceived objectivity and significance. The remediality of reflexive concern assures that the essentially constitutive character of activities directed toward the oracle will remain masked to itself and thereby permit the oracle responses to present themselves as independent and objective answers.

The remediality of mundane inquiry's concern with itself, however, should not be given a functional interpretation. It is not the case, for example, that the Azande exhibit a pragmatic interest in their own affairs because to do otherwise would open an existential abyss. The 'otherwise' is simply not available as a competing alternative. Consequently, the pragmatic or remedial concern is not one among a number of modes for turning to one's own affairs. If mundane inquiry is oblivious to its accomplishment, then the reflective concern of mundane inquiry is oblivious to the obliviousness. That is, mundane inquiry does not deliberately turn away from a reflective consideration of its radical character: it does not know that it has a radical character to turn away from. Mundane inquiry does not find itself walking along a precipice. It does not find itself about to dissolve into the absurd. Because mundane inquiry cannot exceed its own presuppositions in examining itself, for they are the presuppositions which allow mundane inquiry to examine in the first place, mundane inquiry does not know itself in ways other than those in which mundane inquiry will permit itself to be known. Because mundane inquiry rests primordially on the essential objectivity of its domain, it sees itself only in terms of its adequacy to explicate reality.

The privileged self-exemption of mundane inquiry

A structure closely related to mundane inquiry's remedial self-concern is the privileged self-exemption which mundane inquiry tacitly and necessarily accords itself. The definitive features of the privileged self-exemption is that mundane inquiry's investigative efforts are given sanctuary from the world with which the particular course of inquiry is pre-occupied. This structure is recursively reiterated for any and all courses of mundane inquiry, in the very ways in which they are mundane, i.e. addressed to a real world. The 'suspension' of the privileged self-exemption entails dissolution of the mundane idiom and the foundational duality upon which mundane inquiry is predicated. Some examples may illustrate the point.

Homans' 'exchange theory' (1958, 1961), like many other social scientific formulations, can be treated as a product of the processes described by the theory. That is, Homans' formulation might be brought to bear on itself to account for its own production. Thus, a theoretical account of Homans' assertion, that behavior is a function of the rewards and costs of emitting the behavior in question, might be that the rewards of Homans' saying what he said exceeded the costs . . . etc. Were Homans' theory not given asylum from itself, Homans' theory might explain Homans' theory. Note the consequences of an admission of that reflexive possibility. Among other things, the conventional possibility of truth disappears. Any attempted verification of the theory could itself be similarly accounted for by reference to the exchange postulate, e.g. 'He said he verified it empirically because of the rewards in saying so'. In this instance, insofar as the course of mundane inquiry treats itself as an instance of what it is talking about, then it confronts paradoxes and regresses which may deliver fateful blows to its capacity to sustain an objective domain and the possibility of true and false descriptions.

The privileged exemption is often dramatically visible in forms of mundane inquiry which attempt to analyze or account for knowledge of reality. Almost invariably, the formulations of the analyst are exempted from the domain of analysis. The analysis of the 'existential determination' of perspectives on reality (Mannheim 1955) is not itself treated as merely another existentially determined perspective; the analysis of the social construction of reality (Berger and Luckmann 1966) is not treated as merely another social construction. Despite the fact that the analysis is an instance of the class of statements or analyses under consideration, it is delivered as though it derived from a vantage point immune to or exempt from the processes affecting every *other* representation or analysis of reality.

As might be expected, the privileged exemption is especially prominent in the sociology of knowledge. In discussing the evolution of the 'simple theory of ideology' into a full-fledged sociology of knowledge, Mannheim (1955: 78) proposes two critical stages: a movement from the 'particular' to the 'total' conception of ideology and, subsequently, a movement from the 'special' formulation of total ideology to a 'general' formulation of ideology. The particular conception of ideology refers to a skepticism with regard to an opponent's *particular* ideas and representations. The ideas are regarded as 'more or less conscious disguises of the real nature of a situation, the true recognition of which would not be in accord with his interests' (p. 55). The 'total conception' of ideology, on the other hand, brings into question 'the opponent's total *weltanschauung* (including his conceptual apparatus), and attempts to understand these concepts as an outgrowth of the collective life of which he partakes' (p. 57).

Initially, the total conception of ideology yields a relatively restricted critique in that it is concerned exclusively with the structure of an *opponent's* conceptional apparatus. One's own apparatus is exempt from being treated as a mere function of social position and is regarded as absolute. This restricted version is the 'special formulation of the total conception of ideology' (p. 77). In contrast, the 'general form' of the total conception of ideology occurs when one's own position as well as that of one's adversary is subject to analysis: 'what was once the intellectual armament of a party is transformed into a method of research in social and intellectual history generally' (p. 78). The transformation eliminates sanctuary for any and all points of view. No position is privileged: All are equally regarded as existentially determined.

Mannheim's proposals are indeed radical in that they programmatically subjugate any and all points of view to an ideological analysis. Yet, precisely to the degree that the program is successfully executed, one 'point of view' must remain exempt from analysis, and that is the 'point of view' under whose auspices the ideological structure of points of view are being considered. Insofar as other points of view or conceptual structures are regarded as objects for analysis, the analyst's point of view must be accorded an Archimedean status *vis-à-vis* all of the others which it now treats as component elements of the data field. Precisely to the degree that Mannheim's analysis is subject to itself, it negates itself and plummets toward the silence characteristic of an appreciation of the profoundly absurd.[4]

True, one's initial point of view may be relativized. For example, whereas sociology is able to treat of the social determination of intellectual structures, sociology itself may be rendered another 'merely socio-histori-cal' perspective which is examined by a meta-sociology. And it is perfectly conceivable that the meta-sociological framework can be relegated to the field of data by the adoption of a meta-meta-sociological framework *ad infinitum*. In this linear fashion, any particular position can be rendered an object of analysis. But at each level of inquiry, insofar as there is to be inquiry, the position from which all other positions are viewed is accorded asylum from its own programmatic formulations in order to produce the distinction between analysis and object. Precisely insofar as there is to be, say, a sociology of knowledge, sociology exempts itself as merely a per-spective among perspectives. If there is to be inquiry into the social struc-ture of knowledge, the inquiring enterprise must engage in the ruse of all mundane inquiry – which is to forget itself in ways other than in a rem-edial sense, in order thereby to have an objective domain.

The domain of the 'sociology of knowledge' depends vitally on there being that which is other than itself, specifically the inquiring concern under which it is considered. When the inquiry itself is incorporated into the field of data, then not only does the inquiry 'disappear' in a dialectical sense, but the field into which it has been absorbed 'disappears' as well. It is not merely that subject and object merge, but rather that – since they are each constituted by virtue of their relation to one another – the merger obliterates them. The privileged self-exemption allows mundane inquiry to distance itself from its world, and thereby sustain the duality and the mundane idiom upon which it is founded. Insofar as mundane concern is regarded as 'merely' another instance of the world with which it is concerned, then there is, in effect, no distinction between knower and known, and the ontological structure derived from that dichotomy is dissolved.

The consideration of one's own position paradoxically requires that one's own position be exempt from analysis. Analysis cannot comprehend itself and continue to retain an autobiographical sense of itself as analysis. But the privileged self-exemption is not so much a limit or constraint on mundane inquiry as it is definitive of mundane inquiry itself. Mundane inquiry, in being what it is, accords itself a privileged self-exemption. Indeed, it is not even the case that it accords itself a privileged self-exemption, for it cannot proceed in any way other than in and through the self-exemption. The self-exemption is implicit in every act of inquiry in the very ways that it is an act of inquiry.

In the light of our discussion of mundane inquiry's privileged self-exemption, we may now return to briefly reconsider mundane inquiry's remedial self-consideration. We have seen how mundane inquiry, in seeming contradiction to our earlier observations, can render mundane inquiry a phenomenon in its own right. The option of assuming a meta-position *vis-à-vis* its own activities, is, at least, a programmatic option available to a course of mundane inquiry. It can, as it were, consider itself without corrective or irony. But, as we have tried to show, that reflexive consideration is of necessity exempted from the order of affairs it takes up in concern, and *that* concern – insofar as it continues to have its object – can make itself available to itself only in an essentially remedial fashion. These features reiterate themselves for every domain which mundane inquiry makes available to itself. For example, 'labeling theory', at its most general level, would render every feature of the world the gloss (Garfinkel and Sacks 1970) for the course of activity through which it is accomplished, except for the processes through which the meaningful features of the world-as-accomplished are accomplished. The processes for which, say, deviance is the gloss, are presumptively real, objective processes. Yet, in principle, the labeling process may itself be treated as the accomplishment of the theoretical and technical practices through which it is intended although this formulation, insofar as it finds itself describing an objective process, grants asylum to itself.

The pretentiousness of mundane inquiry

These investigations have attempted to formulate and examine what might be termed the 'essential conservatism' of mundane inquiry. Depending upon the perspective from which it is viewed, the conservatism presents itself variously as a naivete, a forgetfulness, a prejudgment, and even as a profound sort of stupidity. Yet, as ostensibly pejorative as these terms may be, the conservatism of mundane inquiry is not the sort from which mundane inquiry can purge or free itself. It can relinquish its conservatism only at the expense of itself. It is through its conservatism that mundane inquiry sustains or conserves itself from dissolution into what, from mundane reason's point of view, is utter absurdity. The conservatism founds mundane inquiry's sense of ontological security or, put negatively, allows mundane inquiry to avoid an ontologically fatal insight.

The exhibition of the conservatism is an extraordinarily complex undertaking. It requires a 'pre-interrogative familiarity' (Sartre 1966: 35) of the radical potential with respect to which the conservatism makes its presence known. As we have seen, the difficulty of the task is compounded in that mundane inquiry does not comprehend its own conservatism, and the lack of comprehension is a constituent feature of the very conservatism it does not comprehend.

The investigations proper began with a consideration of what was alternatively and synonymously called the prejudices, idealizations and, most simply, the presuppositions of mundane reason. These presuppositions found the inferential operations which comprise mundane reason. The mundane 'prejudices' are *a priori* anticipations and constraints upon the relations which obtain among accounts of the world insofar as they are to be regarded as collectively realizing a possible mundane existent.

A significant feature of these primordial prejudices is that while they found mundane reason, they themselves are unfounded and unfoundable. That is, one could not demonstrate their 'validity' by appeal to either empirical or logical procedures for such procedures presuppose the very prejudices to be demonstrated. Given their essentially indemonstrable character, we examined how the prejudices nevertheless maintained their integrity in the face of what might otherwise be conceived as thoroughly subversive and discrediting evidence. Through the preposterous fiction of the transcendental stranger and, later, through Evans-Pritchard's encounter with the Azande, we were able to gain some grasp of the way in which the foundations of mundane reason stood in continual jeopardy. It was possible, for example, to conceive of a contradiction in accounts of the 'self-same scene' as evidence of the radically subjective character of the world. Against the background of these absurd, imagined possibilities, we gained insight into the conservative or, as we then called it, preservative nature of mundane reason. On occasions of conflict, mundane reason preserves its foundational prejudice, the natural thesis, by rendering problematic not the facticity of the world which is implicitly challenged by the conflict, but the method through which the world is experienced or described. Thus, the very conflict which might be regarded as evidence, say, that a particular aspect of a particular scene at a particular time could be both itself and its negation is regarded as evidence of, a 'mistake', 'poor vision', or 'lying'. It is in this manner that the foundational prejudices conserve themselves.

Because the 'conservatism' implicit in the mundane idiom was revealed through an ironic juxtaposition of an essentially preposterous fiction, it was necessary to qualify the preceding analysis. Specifically, it was necessary to point out that, from the point of view of mundane reason, mundane solutions to reality disjunctures are not 'defensive'. Mundane reason never conceives of its founding presupposition as jeopardized. The threat is visible only insofar as mundane inquiry attains an 'outside' view of itself: it is precisely this 'outside' view, however, which mundane reason precludes. The fact that mundane reason is essentially oblivious to the ironically revealed threat points to a still profounder conservatism. Mundane reason conserves itself in ways which are unrecognized to itself – that obliviousness being, in fact, precisely the way in which mundane reason conserves itself.

The conservatism of mundane inquiry was examined subsequently in a somewhat broader perspective. Specifically, we described two seemingly irreconcilable epistemic positions, each of which characterized mundane inquiry's relation to its world. The mundane model advances the model of an actor confronting an objective, pre-given, 'out there' world. The mundane model, we proposed, coincides substantially with mundane inquiry's reflexive or autobiographical conception of its relation to the world with which it is concerned. The constitutive model by contrast conceives of mundane inquiry as constructing its world. From 'within' any particular system of mundane inquiry, the constitutive characterization is absurd; and yet when examined from 'without' – as in, say, the case of the Azande – mundane inquiry can be seen as constitutive of the world it subsequently treats as 'always already there' and by reflexive reference to which mundane inquiry knows itself as such.

Yet, as we have pointed out, an insight from the 'outside' threatens the duality upon which mundane inquiry is founded. Mundane inquiry is threatened with the absurd and with ultimate dissolution, depending upon the depth and degree to which mundane inquiry discovers the radical relativity of its circumstances. These possibilities suggest that mundane inquiry's conservatism consists of the ways in which mundane inquiry prevents itself from achieving what we have termed an ontologically fatal insight. Put another way, part of the creative accomplishment of mundane inquiry consists of the hiding of its own organizational work from itself so as to thereby encounter a world and, indirectly, itself. Specifically, mundane inquiry is conceived as accomplishing itself and its world wherein part of that accomplishment is the sustenance of a mundane autobiography. The ways in which mundane inquiry sustains that autobiographical conception and thereby avoids an ontologically fatal insight comprises the problematic of mundaneity.

We have attempted to gain some grasp of the nature of mundaneity. In some instances, our specification of the ways in which mundane inquiry glosses its accomplishment (as a constituent feature of that accomplishment) is hardly more than a restatement of the problematic itself. Nevertheless, mundane autobiography, retrospective illusion, the privileged self-exemption, remedial self-concern and mundanizing pretentions are suggestive as first approximations of the ways in which mundane inquiry perpetuates the incomprehension vital to its sense of world and sense of itself. As we suggested, these processes are indefinitely reiterated for every world to which mundane inquiry turns its attention, in the very ways that mundane inquiry has a world to turn its attention to. In fact, these structures characterize the work through which they themselves are discovered.

As we have seen, the investigation of mundaneity is characterized by what Jaspers (1955: 145) calls a 'vexatious antinomical structure'. There is a relentless intrusion of paradoxes and regresses, many of which we have had to ignore in order to keep talking. Nevertheless, it is often these overwhelmingly reflexive structures which constitute the phenomenon. That is, the vicious circles which had to be suppressed as a condition of being able to pursue our investigations are the very circles (and the very suppression) which are being investigated.

The problematic of mundaneity is more perplexing than these remarks would suggest. Mundaneity consists of the structures through which mundane inquiry preserves the duality upon which it is founded. Consequently, mundaneity is not merely another object, thing or event in the world. It is not 'merely another' natural structure or process to be examined and described. In fact, mundaneity is not an 'it'. To be sure, mundaneity is implicated in the sense and possibility of all objects; but mundaneity cannot be counted as one more among the multitude of objects. To treat mundaneity as an object, therefore, is to pervert its essential nature. To treat it as an object which can be explicated in so many words is to assure from the outset that mundaneity will be explicated in ways which obliterate its essential character.

Consider, however, that the techniques of 'constructive analysis' (Garfinkel and Sacks 1970) are prepared to examine mundaneity only as an object. As a vehicle for the explication of mundaneity, 'talk about' endows mundaneity with an objective structure. This is because 'talk' exerts its own *a priori* constraints on the nature of that which it takes as its referent object. The 'constraint' consists of the fact that talk can treat its object in no way other than as an object, and an object is precisely what the structure of mundaneity is not. To submit mundaneity to 'talk' is, in effect, to pre-legislate or preconceive its structure in advance of any particular investigation. Indeed, as paradoxical as it may sound, to investigate mundaneity is to preconceive the character of mundaneity as, minimally that which will expose itself to investigation. Thus, as 'pre-suppositionless' as any investigative activity may be by conventional criteria, the very fact that investigation has begun means that the phenomenon has already been implicitly pre-interpreted. Specifically, it has been tacitly assessed as to its amenability to explication through investigation *per se*.

These considerations may be addressed in a more technical manner. Specifically, we may note that analysis or investigation is an intentional (Husserl 1962: 107–11) activity, that is, it is always an analysis of *something*, be it the social structure, the physical world or mundaneity. Analysis, which for the moment I shall treat as synonymous with 'talking-about', by virtue of its intentional character, automatically renders that which it analyzes the *object* of analysis. This, of course, is a blatant truism, and yet it is a truism with a significant implication for the investigation of mundaneity. Given that analysis or 'talk-about' is intentional, then 'talk-about' endows its referent with a structure which derives exclusively from the fact that the referent is explicated through talk-about. Again, that structure consists of talk's referent being rendered an object. Indeed, an immediate example is our current effort to proclaim that mundaneity does not have an objective structure, wherein we talk about mundaneity as if, in fact, it were an object.

Whether or not other ways of explicating mundaneity are available must, for the moment, remain a moot point. The fact that 'talk-about' is possessed of an intentional structure and that the intentional structure pre-interprets mundaneity in essentially alien ways, illuminates what may be termed the *mundanizing pretentiousness* of discourse. In speaking of the mundanizing pretentiousness of discourse, I refer to the fact that discourse or 'talk-about' is concerned only with that of which it can speak about and that it remains silent and essentially unconcerned with that which it cannot speak about. I feel slightly apologetic in articulating such a patently obvious dictum, but it is of great import when we realize that whatever talk talks about is rendered subservient to the capacity of talk-about. That is, not only is talk-about intentional, but it intentional izes. It is not merely that talk explicates its object – as mundane inquiry would autobiographically conceive of talk's work – but rather, that talk-about makes of whatever it attempts to explicate, that which can be explicated in the way in which talk-about is prepared to explicate. Talk-about is pretentious in the sense that once it has begun, it tacitly assumes the always already there structure of that which the talk-about reveals. Talk-about, by virtue of its intentional and intentionalizing (or objectivating) structures pre-delineates the nature of the domain to which it turns in that it renders the domain one which can, in fact, be talked about.

From the 'inside' of analytic disciplines, talk-about is hardly regarded as a constraint, for no phenomenon with regard to which talking and constructive analysis in general would be inadequate is formulable. As we have proposed, not only is talk-about an intentional activity, but it intentionalizes or objectivates the world which it takes up in concern. Thus, so long as one stays within talk, one continually finds it adequate or rather, never discovers structures which might suggest its inadequacy.

The mundanizing character of talk-about and constructive analysis extends to all of mundane inquiry. That is, mundane inquiry, in the ways that it is inquiry, mundanizes its referent. Mundane inquiry pre-establishes its world in such a manner that its world is amenable to examination through the objectivating techniques which mundane inquiry has at its disposal. Because mundane inquiry concerns itself only with what it can be concerned with, and because mundane inquiry's concern mundanizes or intentionalizes, mundane inquiry assures itself that it will never comprehend mundaneity. Yet, what is seemingly a boundary condition or limit from one point of view, is but another aspect of the conservatism through which mundane inquiry maintains itself from another point of view. In the very ways in which mundane inquiry can concern itself only with objects, it precludes the possibility of its ever gaining the ontologically fatal insight into its own foundations. Thus, the ostensible limits of mundane inquiry are precisely what allow mundane inquiry to be what it is.

Concluding remarks

The retrospective illusion or naivete, the privileged self-exemption, remedial self-concern and mundanizing pretention are structures which are reiterated for every world to which mundane inquiry turns. They are reiterated insofar as, and in the very ways that, mundane inquiry has a world to turn to in the first place. They allow mundane inquiry to have a sense of world (and, indirectly, a sense of itself) by assuring that mundane inquiry perpetually fails to comprehend its primordial organization which, in turn, includes, as a constituent feature, the inability to comprehend and the structures which assure the perpetuation of that lack of comprehension.

The discovered structures characterize the process of their discovery.[5] In explicating the retrospective illusion, for example, we implicitly treat it as the pre-existent determinant of our analysis. Yet, it is precisely this attitude, implicit in the talk through which the retrospective illusion is made observable as a structure of mundaneity, which comprises the retrospective illusion. Similarly, our attempt to explicate the nature of the naivete which accompanies the retrospective illusion partakes of the very naivete it explicates precisely insofar as the analysis treats mundane naivete as a structure available for explication. Like the retrospective illusion, 'the naivete' is attended to as an already present, albeit latent, facticity upon which mundane inquiry incidentally stumbles and attempts to elucidate. Of course, our endeavor has been implicitly self-concerned in an essentially remedial or practical fashion. In discerning the structures of mundaneity, after all, we have not been immediately preoccupied with examining our-procedures-for-elucidating-mundaneity as phenomena in their own right but with mundaneity *per se*. Procedural concerns are of interest only in terms of their adequacy to retrieve the presumptive structures of mundaneity. And, indeed, precisely to the degree that our procedures of elucidation and explication were specifically disregarded as phenomena in their own right, they were accorded a privileged self-exemption or asylum from the world which they conceived themselves as analyzing. To 'suspend' the self-exemption would have involved going silent or the presentation of a text which consisted exclusively and endlessly of an analysis of its own production.

7

The social construction of mundane reason

Mundane reasoners always represent themselves as confronting a real world. Whether it is a world of concrete events such as 'what really happened on the highway', a world of symbolic events such as 'deviance' or a world of abstract theoretical properties such as 'the practices through which social reality is constructed', mundane reasoners reflect upon, experience and describe that world as independent of the reflecting, experiencing and describing. We have referred to mundane reasoners' assumption about reality and their relation to it as a prejudice but as we have seen it is also an accomplishment and a condemnation. Mundane reasoners exercise an unwitting ingenuity in their capacity to preserve mundane reason from incipient threats. In this sense mundane auto-biography is a continually reproduced achievement. But to some extent mundane reasoners have no choice for, once within the confines of mundane reason, reflective operations seem to 'automatically' reiterate mundane autobiography. Even as a reasoner strives to 'transcend' mundane reason, he or she continues to dwell within it (albeit on a different floor). In this sense the reproduction of mundane auto-biography is a condemnation.

Given the reiterative power of mundane reason it becomes ever more important to develop the resources for exploring its inner structure as well as the historical and structural forces which cultivate and promote its use as an idiom for representing ourselves to ourselves. Indeed, the reiterative capacity of mundane reason, coupled to processes which extend its province, may eventually make it difficult to conceive of an alternative to mundane reason. It will disappear as a possible phenom-enon because we will be unable to envision or perhaps even imagine alternative idioms. In this final chapter, then, I would like to consider resources for highlighting the contingency of mundane reason and for exploring the socio-historical processes which promote mundane reason's power in society, discourse and consciousness. I shall then take us full circle back to the Student and Mentor whose dialogue initiated our inquiry and consider the question which the mentor hesitated to answer.

Prior to reviewing resources for pursuing mundane reason it is useful to correct a distortion or skew, as it were, in our portrayal of mundane reason. At the outset we proposed that mundane reason was founded on a prejudice of a 'real' or 'objective' order of events. On the occasion of reality disjunctures, it was argued, a mundane reasoner might invoke the subjectivity of the observer as a source of solutions. This implies that conceptions of subjectivity are adjuncts to or secondary elaborations of the mundane idiom, i.e. as though in their desperation to save the real world mundane reasoners grasped for subjectivity ('you *imagined* it') as an account. The varieties of subjectivity, however, are not superfluous or secondary elaborations of mundane reason. They are constituent features of the grammar within which the 'real', the 'objective' and the 'out there' are formulable as intelligible possibilities. The grasp of terms such as 'perception', 'imagination', and 'remembering' presupposes the possibility of the 'real', 'objective', and 'out there' which in turn require reference to the range of subjective modalities for their specification. Thus mundane reason is not simply an idiom founded on the assumption of an objective world. Rather, it is an idiom which is composed of a network of interrelated, mutually defining terms for specifying both subject and object: it includes all of the terms whose meaning implicates and is implied by an objective world. Thus the mundane idiom includes not only the variants for the real world such as 'reality', 'out there', and the 'object' but the variants of the subjectivity which is deemed to stand over and against (and within) the world such as the 'subject', 'person' or 'knower'. And the idiom also includes the modalities which mediate, deflect or separate the 'subject' from the 'object': 'perception', 'experience', 'consciousness', 'dreaming' and 'memory' are but a few terms from the immense and ever-growing mundane idiom of subjectivity.

To be mundane is to use the mundane idiom as a fundamental resource for conceiving of oneself, others, and the collective relation to reality: to be mundane is to construe oneself and others as 'persons' who 'experience' an 'outer world'. As overwhelmingly obvious as the mundane idiom may appear – how might we otherwise construe ourselves? – the elements for the deconstruction (Norris 1985) of the idiom begin to gather. They allow us to understand that although the mundane idiom often seems to lack any alternative, it is the product of historical and cultural processes which have implanted the idiom deep within discourse and consciousness.

The resources for highlighting the contingency of mundane reason come from a wide range of perspectives: philosophy, history, anthropology and, of course, sociology. Despite the fact that each of these disciplines is inevitably mundane, as must indeed be any discipline which takes as its task worldly explication, they yield a body of materials which examine not the world *per se*, nor its relations to an observer, knower or subject, but the very idiom through which these entities, distinctions and relations are constructed. These resources permit one to move toward and perhaps a bit beyond the edge of mundane reason. Within philosophy, for example, critiques of the 'Cartesian heritage' (Rorty 1979; Guignon 1983) take issue with a tradition that according to some has deeply shaped both everyday and scientific conceptions of mind, body and reality. Relatedly, historical and cultural studies of variations in the discourse of mind, body and reality throw the mundane idiom into relief. In presenting idioms of experience so different that seemingly natural categories including 'mind', 'body' and 'reason' and even the distinction between 'inner' and 'outer' are blurred or absent, these studies make visible the socially constructed nature of mundane reason. Moreover, from within the human sciences themselves there is a deepening recognition of the historicity of mundane discourse accompanied by efforts to identify the forms of life and socio-historical processes which contribute to and intensify the categories of mundane reason. They begin to highlight the ways in which what Husserl termed the 'natural attitude,' our more or less taken for granted sense of self, other and world, is hardly a universal given but a socio-historical construction.[1]

Philosophical critiques of mundane reason

We may begin with what is perhaps the most comprehensive but also the most esoteric critique of the mundane idiom. From the point of view of Eastern spiritual disciplines, the subject-object duality is not the precondition of knowledge but a form of illusion or ignorance which curtails enlightened awareness (O'Flaherty 1984). The 'belief' that we are or have 'egos' separated from 'objects' must be suspended or transcended in order to attain a state in which perceiver and perceived are merged or overcome the illusion that they were separated. Almost by definition the transcendence cannot be achieved intellectually for the 'intellect' or 'mind' is precisely that process which reproduces and reflects the duality. Transcendence is a matter of direct experience and often involves techniques in which either the body or the intellect is subject to unusual, intense or rhythmic regimes designed to inhibit a mundane reasoner's reiterative capacity to preserve the mundane distinctions and reproduce a mundane biography (Watts 1957; Ornstein 1975; Tulku 1977). Thus, the moment of insight may be profoundly traumatic, involving both elements of confusion and clarity as the conventional mundane distinctions of self/reality, thought/thing, subject/object collapse. The experiences of Eugen Herrigel (1964a, 1964b), a German philosopher who pursued a program of 'Zen archery' in Japan, are interesting and illustrative in this regard. Zen archery is not an athletic form but a spiritual discipline which moves the archer to a state of 'actionless activity'. As described by the Japanese Masters, the goal of Zen archery sounds enigmatic and contradictory to the mundane ear:

For them the contest consists in the archer aiming at himself – and yet not at himself, in hitting himself – and yet not himself, and thus becoming simultaneously the aimer and the aim, the hitter and the hit. Or, to use some expressions which are nearest the heart of the Masters, it is necessary for the archer to become, in spite of himself, an unmoved center. Then comes the supreme and ultimate miracle: art becomes 'artless', shooting becomes not-shooting, a shooting without bow and arrow; the teacher becomes a pupil again, the Master a beginner, the end a beginning, and the beginning perfection (1964a: 20).

Perhaps even more enigmatic is Herrigel's Master's insistence that it is not Herrigel who has to shoot the arrow but 'It'. An episode in which 'It shoots' occurred about four years into Herrigel's training and was marked by confusion at one level, clarity at another. The confusion consists in Herrigel's inability to compose himself in mundane terms, to provide himself with a mundane autobiography: the clarity is the insight into a mode of being which does not require mundane autobiography.

During these weeks and months I passed through the hardest schooling of my life, and though the discipline was not always easy for me to accept, I gradually came to see how much I was indebted to it. It destroyed the last traces of any preoccupation with myself and fluctuations of my mood. 'Do you now understand,' the Master asked me one day after a particularly good shot, 'what I mean by "It shoots", "It hits"?'

'I'm afraid I don't understand anything more at all,' I answered, 'even the simplest things have got in a muddle. Is it "I" who draw the bow, or is it the bow that draws me into the state of highest tension? Do "I" hit the goal, or does the goal hit me? Is "It" spiritual when seen by the eyes of the body, and corporeal when seen by the eyes of the spirit – or both or neither? Bow, arrow, goal and ego, all melt into one another, so that I can no longer separate them. And even the need to separate has gone. For as soon as I take the bow and shoot, everything becomes so clear and straightforward and so ridiculously simple ...'

'Now at last,' the Master broke in, 'the bowstring has cut right through you' (1964a: 88).

The recurrent use of bodily techniques to produce an ontologically fatal insight also suggests that the mundane distinctions are not simply an idiom or discourse, but a bodily practice as well. The ways in which mundane reasoners are composed in terms of subject-object duality is no doubt deeply tied to language but also to the ways in which the body is organized. The notion of mundane autobiography suggests a 'cognitive' or 'interpretive' construction. It may well be, however, that mundane autobiography is also lodged within and expressed through a bodily *praxis*. It is of interest to note in this regard the nature of the gestures through which a Master discerns a student's level of attainment. Herrigel states:

it is quite certain that one who has experienced *satori* not only sees things differently but 'grasps' them differently, in the most literal sense of the word. But in what way does he 'grasp' them? Not, because he is in the presence of the Master, awkwardly and self-consciously. Not admiring their form, appreciating their value. Not even, in the case of the bowl, *qua* bowl: the importance of the bowl depends on what is in it. Not, on the other hand, *not* noticing it, as if he were sunk in thought. But rather as a potter would grasp it, feeling how it came into being – for it tells of a master's forming hand; he grasps it as though his hands were one with the bowl, so that they themselves become like a bowl and, when he withdraws them, still seem to bear its impress. He even drinks the tea differently from other people. He drinks it in such a way that he no longer knows whether he is the drinker or the drink, completely forgetful of himself, lost to himself: the drinker one with the drink, the drink one with the drinker (1964b: 59–60).

The range of practices employed, the length of time required to effect a change and the problematic nature of the results produced by Eastern disciplines indicate how deeply the mundane idiom is entrenched. The depth and persistence of these disciplines and traditions, however, suggest the contingency of the mundane idiom, and that there are modes of being which do not understand themselves in terms of a 'subject' standing over against an 'object'. I am not proposing in the slightest that one ought to adopt whatever it is that waits beyond or beneath mundane duality as ontologically definitive. I am suggesting, however, that insofar as one grasps the nature of aduality one has a resource with which to question the dynamics through which mundaneity is reproduced.

Eastern critiques are doubly enigmatic to a Western mundane ear. On the one hand they attempt to critique, indeed, crack mundane reason from the outside. The individual may be confronted with demands and exhortations borne of an insight into adualism which for that reason seem virtually unintelligible. Interpeted from within the very mundane hermeneutic which the tasks and talk are intended to dissolve, the latter may appear absurd or obscure. Moreover, originating within a distinctive cultural context, the Eastern critique of mundaneity involves cultural understandings not readily available to a Westerner (cf. Caputo 1978).

Less esoteric critiques of aspects of mundane reason are available within Western philosophical discourse. They are more accessible precisely because they are developed within a Western tradition (although they might seek to question or dissolve the tradition) and because they begin from within mundane reason. One of the more powerful and provocative analyses is Rorty's (1979) critique of philosophy's captivation by a 'picture' of mind, in which mind is regarded as a mirror which 'reflects' reality. This depiction of mind derives from mundane reason and thus Rorty's attack is tantamount to an exegesis of the way mundane reason penetrates philosophical discourse and philosophical projects.

Without the notion of the mind as mirror, the notion of knowledge as accuracy of representation would not have suggested itself. Without this latter notion, the strategy common to Descartes and Kant – getting more accurate representations by inspecting, repairing, and polishing the mirror, so to speak – would not have made sense. Without this strategy in mind, recent claims that philosophy could consist of 'conceptual analysis' or 'phenomenological analysis' or 'explication of meanings' or examination of 'the logic of our language' or of 'the structure of the constituting activity of consciousness' would not have made sense (p. 12).

Rorty (1979) argues that the image of mind as mirror is a historical and philosophical construction. In accepting and contributing to this construction, philosophy unwittingly commits itself to a pretentious and fruitless task of 'getting more accurate representations by inspecting, repairing and polishing the mirror' (p. 12). Not all of philosophy however (and from Rorty's point of view, fortunately) has been captured. In contrast to those whom Rorty refers to as 'systematic philosophers' and who seek to establish 'a proper epistemological understanding of man's ability accurately to represent nature' (p. 367), are 'edifying philosophers'. This latter group, among whom Rorty numbers Kirkegaard, William James, Dewey, and most prominently and interestingly for our interests the later Wittgenstein and the later Heidegger, do not attempt to construct but deconstruct. Moreover, the edifying philosophers do not wish to put a new system in place of that which has been dissolved or destroyed. They position themselves on the periphery of the dominant systems of the day. They are skeptical and what they are skeptical about is systematic philosophy, its pretentions to finality, and the very tradition and supposition which fuel systematic philosophy.

Rorty's commentary on mind as mirror is itself a contribution to the critique of mundaneity. The mind as mirror is a sophisticated though widely shared image which is a variant of the mundane subject/object distinction. Thus, Rorty's sketchy though suggestive discussion of the philosophical-historical 'invention of mind' contributes to an appreciation of the contingency of at least an aspect of mundane reason. Rorty also highlights the value of the edifying philosophers for understanding mundaneity. In precisely the ways they bring into question the imagery of mind as mirror and the processes which cultivate its prominence, they contribute to understanding mundane reason as a phenomenon.

Wittgenstein, Heidegger, and Dewey are in agreement that the notion of knowledge as accurate representation, made possible by special mental processes, and intelligible through a general theory of representation, needs to be abandoned. For all three, the notions of 'foundations of knowledge' and of philosophy as revolving around the Cartesian attempt to answer the epistemological skeptic are set aside. Further, they set aside the notion of 'the mind' common to Descartes, Locke, and Kant – as a special subject of study, located in inner space, containing elements or processes which make knowledge possible (p. 6).

How might the 'edifying philosophers' be of specific use in approaching mundane reason as a phenomenon? An example will have to suffice. Part of Wittgenstein's 'edification' involved undermining certain pervasive aspects of discourse which postulate 'inner' or 'mental' processes. Wittgenstein suggested that many of the terms which are treated as referring to inner, hidden mental processes have no inner essences which correspond to them. Thus, for example, the utterance 'I understand' does not refer to an inner mental process but is an indication that one can proceed.

Try not to think of understanding as a 'mental process' at all. For *that* is the expression which confuses you. But ask yourself: in what sort of case, in what kind of circumstances, do we say, 'Now I know how to go on,' when, that is, the formula *has* occurred to me?
In the sense in which there are processes (including mental processes) which are characteristic of understanding, understanding is not a mental process (Wittgenstein 1951: 61).

As conventional and philosophical conceptions of mind are dereified, a wedge is created for examining the historical and interactional processes through which the reification of mind is produced and reproduced.

Mundane reasoners regard the notion of an inner subjective world as a central feature of their everyday lives and the point of sociological interest would not be to dispell them of their notions but to inquire into the ways in which the mundane distinctions of 'inner' and 'outer' and the myriad derivatives are constructed. Thus, insofar as Wittgenstein exposes conventional hypostatizations of subjectivity and we are allowed to see the ways in which terms such as 'understanding', 'intention' and 'belief' do not have an inner essence, we gain distance from conventional versions of subjectivity. The analytic distance, in turn, allows us to ask how these terms originate and how they are used to produce what mundane reasoners regard as appropriate and competent attributions.[2]

As the nature of mundane reason is plumbed and conventional versions of subjectivity become analytically problematic, the notion of the 'self' or 'agent' or 'ego' which possesses, regulates or comprises subjectivity will also become problematic. Mundane reason in its fullest sense includes conventional notions of 'person', 'ego', and 'individual'. To explore mundane reason is to abandon as comprehensively as possible the analytic use of 'person', 'ego' and 'individual'. These are constructions to be accounted for and as such cannot comprise part of the explanation. The radical exploration of mundane reason does not allow statements such as 'We construe our relation to reality in mundane terms'. Mundane reason *is* the 'construal' of 'construing "ourselves" in relation to "reality"'. I do not construe mundane reason: mundane reason construes 'I'. The notion of the subject, however, is so deeply enmeshed in mundane discourse that we almost boggle at conceiving of action as description without reference to an 'individual' or 'person'. If persons are constructions what does the constructing? Put in terms I have already employed, if mundane autobiography establishes a subject over and against an object, what casts itself in this fashion?

If the notion of the 'agent', 'ego' or 'individual' is not an analytic term but a constituent feature of the mundane idiom, it will be necessary to conceive an alternative way of grasping that which formulates itself in and through mundane reason. The alternative understanding might well be provided by Heidegger. For Heidegger (1962), the sciences proceed within an *ontical* framework within which the subject and object are presupposed as non-problematic (p. 31 *et passim*). While they may bring into question particular aspects of objects and subjects they do not inquire into the nature of Being. Even the primordial subject, what Heidegger refers to as *Dasein* (and which I interpret as that which lies beyond the subject-object duality) may understand itself ontically, that is, in terms of the subject-object dichotomy. *Dasein* has a 'choice' to make regarding how it will understand itself (p. 42). *Dasein* often comes to accept or 'fall' into ontic understandings of its own Being and thereby limits its comprehension of itself. In my terms *Dasein* comes to represent itself through mundane autobiography. For Heidegger, the explication of Being and *Dasein* can only be accomplished by a 'fundamental ontology' (p. 13) which goes beyond the ontic inquiry and understanding characteristic of traditional positivist investigations and conventional philosophical ontology. The Heideggerian notion of *Dasein* may well prove useful as an alternative to analytic conceptions of the actor which suffer from a naive commitment to mundaneity's autobiographical conception of itself.

When mundane discourse and experience is juxtaposed against the radical alternatives raised by Eastern or Western critiques of mundaneity, the nature of that discourse and experience as a construction is illuminated. Terms, distinctions and assumptions which otherwise present themselves as ontologically definitive are visible as the product of deep immersion in the mundane idiom. The insight into the contingency of mundaneity, however, is not an answer to anything so much as it is the beginning of a way of questioning and the formulation of a sociological problem.

Socio-cultural variation of mundane reason

Eastern and Western critiques highlight the contingency of mundane reason. Historical and cultural studies which indicate variation in the primordial distinctions and suppositions which are made about self, others, experience and reality serve a similar function. In displaying the variation of seemingly universal categories, these studies contribute to a dereification of mundane reason. Put somewhat differently, they suggest that mundane autobiography is but one way to construe self, other, reality and experience.

A suggestive example in this regard is Maurice Leenhardt's (1979) rendering of 'socio-mythic' patterns of thought among the Melanesians of New Caledonia, known in French as the Canaque. Leenhardt's intriguing account does not allow easy distillation but what emerges is a portrait of an idiom which emphasizes the consubstantiality 'person' and 'nature'. For the Canaque, what mundane reasoners refer to as a 'person' is an exceptionally diffuse mode of being. A central notion of the Canaque idiom is *Kamo* which literally translated means 'the living one'.

Used with no distinction of gender, *Kamo* is a predicate indicating life (or as Leenhardt's discussion suggests 'human'), but implies no particular form or quality. 'Animals, plants, and mythic beings', Leenhardt writes, 'have the same claim men have to being considered *Kamo*, if circumstances cause them to assume a certain humanity' (p. 24). Thus, the 'human' transcends the division between man and nature, and, more specifically, man's physical body and that which is outside it.

The Canaque do not regard the body in a mundane fashion. While they can represent, analyze and describe the body surface, they have no term for the body as such. The word *Karo* used to refer to the body signifies the supporting element of a structure. The different conceptualization of the body expresses itself most dramatically in the Canaques' inability to distinguish the body from nature or to conceive of it as the site of the self or ego.

The Melanesian is unaware that the body is an element which he himself possesses. For this reason, he finds it impossible to disengage it. He cannot externalize it from his natural, social and mythic environment. He cannot isolate it. He cannot see it as one of the elements of the individual (p. 22).

In a more phenomenological vein, Leenhardt suggests that the Canaque experience their bodies as permeated by nature: 'he does not flow into it, he is invaded by it' (p. 20) and, he continues, 'because the native is filled with the world's pulse, he does not distinguish the world from his body' (p. 21).

Kamo may become invested in a particular form or relation, constituting what Leenhardt refers to as a 'personage'. The personage exists only in and through 'social relationships and the regard it receives from others'. Apparently the Canaque has a different 'name' for the personage as it realizes itself in each relation. A Canaque cannot collect his various relational identities into a single person. He is, as Leenhardt writes, 'unaware of himself' and cannot experience himself as an enclosed and bounded individual standing apart from his relationships.

Given the relational dependence of the personage, the loss or disturbance of a relation may precipitate an existential crisis in which the individual is threatened with non-being. Canaque are unable to cast themselves as autonomous agents who enter and leave social relations, and thus the disruption of a relation may produce the experience of 'acting *bwiri*' or randomly, and the complaint, 'I am a lost personage'.

If a man has a curse laid on him by an angry maternal uncle and is driven out of the society, he feels 'in perdition'. Having been obliged to flee, he no longer has any relationship through which to find himself again. Not even his speech manifests his being, because his being has no correspondence in society and answers to no recognizable personage. He suffers from losing his role in which he felt himself to be specifically a personage. He no longer exists socially. Feeling he is nothing other than a social being, he suffers from not being. He needs to be able to be summoned; he must have a role and a name. This is the price of his existence (p. 155).

The diffuse sense of self or ego among the Canaque affects their sense of location in linear space and time. For Canaque, the mundane null point of 'I am here now' is not as obvious as it might be to mundane reasoners. A Canaque's psychological 'me', such as it is, and the physical body do not necessarily correspond to one another (p. 84). Thus it is difficult for a Canaque to 'take a position and announce, "This is here, ahead, behind, there"' (p. 84).

The difficulty of spatio-temporal location is expressed in the telling of legends. A Canaque may be reluctant to tell a story, because he has forgotten a relevant topographical name. From a Canaque point of view, the absence of such a detail may be thoroughly disorienting because the teller so deeply participates in the narrated events, that to use Leenhardt's words, he can become 'really lost in the geographical area of the story' (p. 84). While the nature of ethnographic accounts generally, and the discursive style of Leenhardt's especially precludes its use as a strong illustration of the way 'description' depends on an idiom in which subject-object are taken for granted, the danger antici-pated or experienced by the Canaque in the recounting of a legend is suggestive. The weak distinction between subject and object and the accompanying transformation of space and time means that a 'legend' is not simply 'about' an event but reconstitutive of the event. The separation between 'event', 'story' and 'teller' is not as sharply defined among the Canaques as among mundane reasoners. Thus (I venture to suggest), the distinction between event/story/teller may collapse more readily: the story may reconstitute the event of which it is about and the teller may enter into the narratively constituted event and become 'lost'.

In Canaque socio-mythic thought and discourse, we find evidence of a very different way of providing an autobiography of being. The Canaque idiom does not partition experience in the same way as mundane reason; the boundary between self and nature is extremely permeable. The very notion of an autonomous self possessing, and more or less sited within, a body is alien to the Canaque. Indeed, the notion of the body as a site in which the relational identities assumed by *Kamo* might be collated and crystallized, appears to be a European import. At least that is how Boesoou, one of Leenhardt's informants, put the matter:

Once, waiting to assess the mental progress of Canaques I had taught for many years, I risked the following suggestion: 'In short, we introduced the notion of spirit to your way of thinking?'

And he objected, 'Spirit? Bah! You didn't bring us the spirit. We already knew the spirit existed. We have always acted in accord with the spirit. What you've brought us is the body.'

An unexpected reply. True, the kò, the mind or spirit affirmed here, is the mythic and magical ancestral ebb and flow, but this does not diminish the significance of the response. This elusive person required firm delimitation, something prevented by its diffusion in the sociomythic domain. Boesoou, in a single word, defined the new outline: the body (p. 164).

The Western body is demarcated from outer nature and certainly from the supernatural forces which ripple through the Canaque *karo*. The construction of the body as a relatively autonomous biological entity, as the locus of organic and psychological processes, allows the Canaque to collect himself as a 'person'.

The person is no longer diffuse. It disengages itself from the sociomythic domain in which it was caught. The body ceases to be the old social costume smothering the person. The personage, having no further role to play, disappears. The person locates itself within man himself. The psychological self we saw wandering everywhere, far from the body, is finally fixed: I have a body. The Canaque perceives the independence of his corporal existence and at the same time enriches his language by filling an old word, karo, with the meaning of a new concept: body (p. 165).

Leenhardt's account is suggestive in several respects. Firstly, it furnishes a radical variation on mundane autobiography. The distinction between inner and outer, self and reality, subject and object is not developed to the same degree as it is for Western or westernized mundane reasoners. Of course, no sooner is the difference framed in this fashion than one becomes aware of mundane ethnocentrism through which the mundane distinction of subject and object is proffered as the ontologically correct state of being by reference to which the Canaque are found deficient. The Canaque are *different* and seem to become more mundane as their vocabulary for formulating what Heidegger would call *Dasein* is infiltrated by mundane concepts, most especially, the notion of a circumscribed 'body'. Secondly, the kind of difficulties the Canaque may experience in 'describing' is suggestive with regard to our earlier observations about the ways in which the possibility of 'description' turns on the assumption of an objective world. Insofar as the mundane distinctions between subject and object have not been constructed then 'description' may be problematic as a conceivable speech act. Without the mundane distinctions there is neither a subject to do the describing nor an object to be described. We might also speculate, and we can do no more since Leenhardt is silent on this matter, that the entire idiom of subjectivity is transformed as mundane distinctions are modified. As mundane notions of 'imagination', 'dream', 'perception', 'memory' and 'mind' require at least indirect reference to an independent, objective reality, modifications of the sense of the latter might be expected to reverberate throughout the entire idiom of subjectivity. The extent of variation in idioms of subjectivity ought not to be underestimated. Observations of the Dinka, for example, suggest that idioms of subjectivity may be so profoundly different that they do not include concepts of mind, subjectivity or interiority.

The Dinka have no conception which at all closely corresponds to our popular modern conception of the 'mind', as mediating and, as it were, storing up the experiences of the self. There is for them no such entity to appear, on reflection, to stand between the experiencing self at any given moment and what is or has been an exterior influence upon the self. So it seems that what we should call in some cases the 'memories' of experiences, and regard therefore as in some way intrinsic and interior to the remembering person and modified in their effect upon him by that interiority, appear to the Dinka as exteriorly acting upon him, as were the sources from which they derived. Hence it would be impossible to suggest to Dinka that a powerful dream was 'only' a dream, and might for that reason be dismissed as relatively unimportant in the light of day, or that a state of possession was grounded 'merely' in the psychology of the person possessed. They do not make the kind of distinction between the psyche and the world which would make such interpretations significant for them (Leenhardt 1961: 149).

In addition to cross-cultural variations in constructions of mind, self and reality, a large and suggestive (e.g. Onians 1954; Barfield 1965) literature points to comparable variations in the history of the West. The terms through which contemporary mundane reasoners designate the sensorium, the mind and the body, for example, either do not appear in the discourse of the ancient Greeks (such as it is available to scholars) or else the terms have a meaning very different from contemporary usage. 'We find it difficult to conceive of a mentality' writes Snell (1960: 6) 'which made no provision for the body as such.' Yet, for the ancient Greeks the sense of the body as a unified whole did not exist. The early Greeks comprehended and portrayed the body not as a unit, but as an ensemble of 'independent parts variously put together': (Snell 1960: 6).

Homer, for example, never refers to the body as such but to 'fleet legs' and 'sinewy arms' (p. 8).

Terms which ostensibly refer to what we would regard today as 'subjective' processes are used in their original contexts to refer to bodily or objective processes. In the Homeric epics, for example, a man's *thumos*, located in the chest or midriff, speaks to him, advises him and he may consult with it. 'A man's *thumos*' writes Dodds (1951: 16) 'tells him that he must now eat or drink or slay an enemy, it advises him on his course of action, it puts words into his mouth.' The *thumos*, however, is not part of the self. Rather it is akin to an organ of feeling experienced, or at least described as peculiarly autonomous. Relatedly, the term *psyche* has no connection to thinking or feeling. As Jaynes (1977: 271) puts it, 'No character in the *Iliad* ever sees, decides, thinks, knows, fears, or remembers anything in his *psyche*.' For Homer, the *psyche* is akin to the 'breath of life' which 'leaves its owner when he is dying, or when he loses consciousness' (Snell 1960: 8). The Homeric Greeks had no unified concept of what we call 'soul' or 'personality' (Dodds, 1951: 15). The ancients had yet to acquire (or construct) what Havelock (1967) refers to as the 'doctrine of the autonomous psyche.' Thus, the Greek idiom for representing reality does not accept 'the premise that there is a "me", a "self", a "soul", a consciousness which is self-governing and which discovers the reason for action in itself' (p. 200). In what is perhaps the most provocative and controversial claim about the ancient Greeks, Jaynes (1977) argues that Greeks (and other ancient peoples) were bereft of any 'subjectivity' whatsoever. 'The characters of the *Iliad* do not sit down and think out what to do. They have no conscious minds such as we say we have, and certainly no introspections. It is impossible for us with our subjectivity to appreciate what it was like' (p. 72).

An awareness of historical variation of seemingly invariant and immutable categories is of inestimable value in developing a sensitivity to the contingent and constructed character of mundane reason. It is important to realize that concepts of body, reality, and subjectivity do not necessarily evolve in a linear or a continuous fashion. Changes in concepts may occur as part of, and, in turn, may contribute to, qualitative transformations of more comprehensive idioms. Reiss (1982), for example, following Foucault, argues that there have been major transformations in 'discourses' for 'enunciating' the relation between individuals, language and reality. The comparatively diffuse conception of the individual (and the very different notion of 'will') characteristic of the early Greeks contributed to a discourse in which the individual, language and reality were regarded as of a piece (p. 58). In the discourse which Reiss designates as 'patterning' (and which was dominant as late as the sixteenth century): 'name and object are themselves part of an order of which the enunciator is also a part . . . Such a class of discourse places the enunciator within the same structure as englobes name and object as well' (p. 32).

Borrowing from Lévi-Strauss, Reiss suggests that 'patterning' is a discourse which 'refuses the ontological and epistemological distinction between an interior and an exterior . . . It assumes that discourse is part of the "world" and not distinct from it. It gives no special privilege either to the enunciator of discourse or to the act of enunciation' (p. 30). Aspects of the attitude cultivated by a patterning discourse are intimated in Reiss's comments on Kepler, who participated in both the discourse of patterning and the analytic discourse which was to displace it.

Emphasizing a lack of accountability in terms of some *real* or of some *truth*, the discourse of patterning, at least as it appears in Kepler's work, is able even to indicate the ludic nature of all 'choices' . . . All phenomena are subject to an unlimited series of interpretations, and any 'explanation' to a limitless series of variations (pp. 141–2).

The sixteenth century sees the ascendance of a radically different conception of the relation of speaker, language and world, an idiom which in certain respects overlaps with what we have referred to as mundane reason. Analytico-referential discourse, as Reiss refers to this emergent network of assumptions and concepts:

assumes that the world, as it can be and is to be known represents a fixed object of analysis quite separate from the forms of discourse by which men speak of it and by which they represent their thoughts. This is the case whether the difficulties of analysis then be posed in terms of the world which is to be seized (idealism) or in those of its representation (empiricism) (p. 41).

The assumptions at the heart of analytico-referential discourse, Reiss argues, are implicated in such notions as those of truth and valid experiment, referential language and representation, and common-sense and the very concept of concept (p. 13).

Reiss suggests that works ranging from Wittgenstein's *Philosophical Investigations* to Lewis Carroll's *Alice in Wonderland* question the limits of analytico-referential discourse.[3] They may even prefigure a new discourse though it has yet to emerge with any clarity. Perhaps, Reiss conjectures, there will be a new discourse in which notions such as 'fixity, discrete denotated objects of knowledge, analytic knowledge itself, discursive transparency, objective grasp, absence of the "subject" would all be strangers' (p. 382). If a new discourse does emerge, it will appear 'non-sensical' within analytico-referential discourse 'because what it could signify (were it able to do so) could never "fit" the other signifieds of the discourse, or *how* it would signify could not do so' (p. 382). For those who continue within analytico-referentiality, the new discourse 'can never be more than the *possibility* of meanings beyond the exclusive space of analytico-referential discourse' (p. 383). The sense of 'possibility' is precisely the heuristic value of anthropological and historical variations. The juxtaposition of mundane reason to alternative discourses, not necessarily expressible within mundane reason, marks out the mundane idiom as one among radically diverse idioms. In learning of the possibility of alternatives, the mundane idiom gains insight into the possibility of itself.

The socio-historical analysis of mundane reason should be able to cast light on the significance of certain forms of pathological experience. The rise of mundane reason creates the possibility of non- or extra-mundane reasoning. Insofar as mundane reason is an idiom which individuals use to construe and construct their relation to reality, the possibility arises that some individuals cannot or will not be mundane. Young children, for example, have yet to acquire the capacity to formulate themselves mundanely. Practitioners of Eastern disciplines, as we have indicated, strive to transcend or suspend mundane reason. Certain forms of 'psychotic' experience suggest that individuals may be ejected, as it were, from mundane reason: they can no longer compose themselves in mundane terms or account for their experiences within the mundane idiom. In contemporary Western society such experiences include and are perhaps epitomized by the unaccountable 'loss of ego boundaries' in which the individual is no longer capable of distinguishing himself or herself from 'others' or from 'reality'. In such circumstances the mundane distinctions between inner/outer, subject/object, thought/topic, description/described explode or fuse: individuals may find that they and their worlds, including the very distinction between the two, are deeply threatened. By contrast, in contexts where the mundane idiom is either unknown or suspended, the 'same' experiences may be unremarkable. Thus, among the Canaque, for example, the diffusely located and defined 'I' and the experience of being 'invaded by nature', as Leenhardt put it, is not experienced as a pathological alteration for it is a feature of their everyday experience.

Consider the following account by an individual of his experience of psychological and physical disintegration:

When I am melting I have no hands, I go into a doorway in order not to be trampled on. Everything is flying away from me. In the doorway I can gather together the pieces of my body. It is as if something is thrown in me, bursts me asunder. Why do I divide myself in different pieces? I feel that I am without poise, that my personality is melting and that my ego disappears and that I do not exist anymore. Everything pulls me apart ... The skin is the only possible means of keeping the different pieces together. There is no connection between the different parts of my body (Schilder 1935: 159, cited in Jaynes 1977: 425).

The description of pathological experience is remarkably resonant with classicists' description of the ancient Greek conception of the body and self. Recall that there was no concept for the body as a whole: the body was conceived and described as an ensemble of limbs and parts. Relatedly, the notion of person and the sense of personality were diffuse. The similarity suggests that episodes which are experienced as profound 'disorganization' by mundane reasoners are everyday experiences in a society where mundane autobiography is not dominant. As mundane reason becomes the dominant form through which individuals compose their mundane autobiographies, the sudden intrusion of phenomeno-logical features which were previously commonplace and unremark-able may be experienced as a profound loss of ontological security.[4]

Mundane reason as a socio-historic product

The historical and anthropological variation in idioms delineates a sociological task. The task is the description of the structural and cultural processes through which the mundane idiom is organized, achieves hegemony as mundane autobiography and is reproduced as a hegemonic method within discourse and consciousness. Without pretending to even a partial overview of the dimensions of an adequate socio-historical explication of the origin of mundane reasoning, I should like to indicate a perspicuous resource for the work.

In his provocative work *The Civilizing Process*, Norbert Elias (1978) proposes that the image of the individual as a being more or less bounded by and contained within the skin and possessing an 'inner' psychological life demarcated from the 'outer' world is deeply problematic. To be sure the image has an extraordinary presence in sociological and philosophi-cal discourse:

The idea of the 'self in a case', ... is one of the recurrent *leitmotifs* of a modern philosophy, from the thinking subject of Descartes, Leibniz's windowless nomads and the Kantian subject of knowledge (who from his aprioristic shell can never quite break through to the 'thing in itself' to the more recent extension of the same basic idea of the entirely self-sufficient individual. (pp. 252–3).

The image pervades far more than scholarly discourse: it forms the basis of the way in which individuals experience themselves in everyday life. It is virtually self-evident and taken for granted within European societies that the individual's self, their true identity, is 'something locked away "inside" them, severed from all other people and things "outside"' (p. 253). The image may attain such a hold that it is difficult for those who move in its sway to conceive of alternative constructions. Thus, the image of the contained ego and more generally the subject-object distinction may seem to be inherent in the human condition.

If one grows up in the midst of such a group, one cannot easily imagine that there could be people who do not experience themselves in this way as entirely self-sufficient individuals cut off from all other beings and things. This kind of self-perception appears as obvious, a symptom of an eternal human state, simply the normal, natural, and universal self-perception of all human beings. The conception of the individual as *homo clausus*, a little world in himself who ultimately exists quite independently of the great world outside, determines the image of man in general. Every other human being is likewise seen as a homo clausus; his core, his being, his true self appears likewise as something divided within him by an invisible wall from everything outside, including every other human being (p. 249).

As ubiquitous and self-evident as the experience of the distinction between 'inner' and 'outer' may be, however, there is no 'inner' self or ego as such. The 'inner' life, Elias argues, is the product of a metaphor of the relation of physical objects applied to human beings. While 'there is good reason for saying that the human brain is situated within the skull and the heart within the rib cage', no aspect of the human psyche is literally inside any other aspect (p. 258). Given that the distinction of 'inside' and 'outside' is not inherent in the structure of the human psyche and that it is nevertheless a pervasive and virtually self-evident perception of ourselves, Elias turns to consider the origins of *homo clausus*.

What provides for the experience of ourselves as shut in and sharply separated from others by a 'wall'? Elias' answer is multileveled. On the most immediate level, the *homo clausus* experience is the product of a slowly evolving but ever more pervasive and intensifying process of control over spontaneous, impulsive or effective behavior, especially with regard to the orifices. What Elias refers to as the 'civilizing process' is the increasingly comprehensive and deeply ingrained constraints on spontaneous or effective behavior. Behavior in various aspects of every-day life, especially as it involves bodily functions, is normatively defined and regulated. Elias traces the process through a survey of manuals of courtesy and manners from the thirteenth century onward. The early manuals are stunning in the explicitness of advice to adults which we would suppose that a child of five or even less need not be told. Thus, advice from a thirteenth-century manual asserts:

A number of people gnaw a bone and then put it back in the dish – this is a serious offense (p. 85).

A fifteenth-century manual cautions:

It is unseemly to blow your nose in the tablecloth (p. 144).

From the Middle Ages:

Do not spit on the table (p. 153).

As one moves toward the present day, the advice and admonitions are more subtle and differentiated. Restraints which had to be explicitly formulated to adults in an earlier era are now inculcated during child-hood. They are so well and deeply internalized that they are regarded as inherent in human nature; violations are viewed with shame and disgust; failure to comport oneself appropriately is viewed as an indication of pathology or perversion. For Elias these heightened self-controls are the basis of individuals' sense of themselves as bounded persons. The constraints on spontaneous impulses are:

experienced as the capsule, the invisible wall dividing the 'inner world' of the individual from the 'external' world or in different versions, the subject of cognition from its object, the 'ego' from the 'other', the 'individual' from 'society' (p. 258).

The increasing number and intensity of constraints on impulsive behavior is tied to the differentiation of society and the increasing interdependence among individuals. As differentiation increases, 'the individual is compelled to regulate his conduct in an increasingly differentiated, more even and more stable manner' (Elias 1982: 232). More complex controls are developed at an earlier age: 'self control' and 'correct' behavior become virtually automatic and present themselves as 'second nature'.

The differentiation of social functions contributes to the replacement of the 'centrifugal' feudal organization by a comparatively stable central organization which is able to exercise a monopoly over physical force. The reduction of the likelihood of 'the free use of physical force by those who are physically stronger' (Elias 1982: 235) and the creation of 'pacified social spaces', yields a further modulation of emotions and affects. The reduction of the fear and terror that others pose for individuals produces a corresponding pressure on individuals to inhibit their own threatening affective outbursts. The division of labor and the establishment of a relatively strong state thus ultimately work to produce a transformation in the entire psychic organization of individuals and, indeed, to organize them as 'individuals'.[5]

Elias' work is significant in several respects. First, he succeeds in making problematic a central component of the mundane idiom, the sense of an enclosed self over and against an outer reality. Second, he intimates that the philosophy of mind and philosophical epistemology do not stand outside the civilizing process and the mundane structures thus created, but are in an important sense embedded within those structures. The very question of how the 'mind', 'subject' or 'knower' can gain knowledge of 'objective' or 'outer' reality presupposes an idiom in which such distinctions and the potential relations among them are formulable. Third, Elias' analysis connects the organization of the duality of 'inner' and 'outer' to social structure: the construction of mundaneity is grasped as a process which involves transformations, at the 'configurational level' (such as the division of labor), which radiate throughout the society and affect ostensibly trivial or intimate behaviors (e.g. manners at the dinner table) which in turn affect an individual's innermost sense of self (which includes the very sense of 'inner').

I have but intimated some of the resources through which mundane reason might be addressed as a social construction. I have suggested that there are useful resources in Eastern and Western philosophical critiques of aspects of mundane reason. The use of philosophy is not intended as a way in which philosophy may usurp sociology but a way in which sociology may appropriate as a topic an idiom and practice in which it is deeply immersed and employs as a resource. The contingency of the mundane idiom is further highlighted by cultural and historical materials which suggest that individuals in other socio-cultural contexts do not necessarily construct mundane autobiographies in which they cast themselves as knowers, agents or subjects standing over and against an 'objective' world. Indeed, in other contexts, there may be an extremely diffuse sense of personhood and a correspondingly tenuous sense of the distinction between 'subject' and 'object'. The contingency of the mundane idiom made visible through philosophical commentary and socio-cultural variation marks out the distinctive macro-level sociological question – what are the socio-historical processes through which the mundane idiom originates and is reproduced? Elias' analysis is hardly the last word but it is an interesting first and initiates a dialogue between mundaneity and major issues of sociological theory.[6]

The concern with mundaneity can lead back to central issues within sociology. The socio-historic rise of mundane reasoning might well be viewed as yet another topic which sociology could take up in relatively familiar ways. Yet if sociology takes up mundaneity, it is also true that mundaneity takes up sociology. For in addressing the social structure of mundane reason, we return to conventional mundane discourse about a real process, the social structuring of the mundane. This brings us full circle to the issues raised at the very beginning of our inquiry.

The Mentor and the Student once again

From the point of view of the Mentor, the Student's naivete consists of the eagerness to appropriate and use assumptions or practices from 'the world'. The Mentor warns his student that these practices and assumptions are not resources for the study of the world, so much as they are integral features of the world. The practices and presuppositions comprising science and sciencing are bound up in the fabric of the social world in a fashion analogous to the ways Azande truth-seeking (and truth-providing) practices are part and parcel of Azande life. Just as an anthropologist would not appropriate and use oracular methods to produce his or her description of Azande life, but rather would, as Evans-Pritchard did so well, describe the suppositions and practice of the oracle, a transcendental anthropologist would be advised to attend to sciencing as an accomplishment within the world. This is the most radical expression of the Mentor's perspective. The Student discerns the thrust of his Mentor's admonitions and in a clumsy fashion extends and pursues their implications. The Student suggests that even were he to make sciencing a phenomenon and examine, say, how 'science' manages to produce descriptions of reality which are deemed 'superior' to those produced by lay persons, he would nevertheless still participate in an idiom or discourse which maintained certain assumptions suspiciously like those employed by individuals in the world. To wit: his studies would entail the assumption that 'sciencing', whatever *it* might be found to consist of, has an objective structure and that the behaviors, practices and presuppositions comprising 'sciencing' can be explicated to varying degrees of adequacy. The Student wonders whether in accepting such an assumption would he not thereby reiterate an in-the-world feature which is perhaps as profound and subtle an aspect of worldly reason and practice as any noted by the Mentor. Would he not thereby formulate his relation to 'reality' as do worldly reasoners and thereby be usurped by worldly reason in a most subtle fashion?

The Student also raised a related methodological question. If mundane reason is to be the phenomenon, how does one study mundane reason without 'naively' participating within mundane reason? Even if we set about to study 'studies which suppose definite structure' are we not thereby once again back into the very discursive space which is the focus of inquiry? In terms of a familiar ethnomethodological distinction, is it possible to turn to mundaneity as a topic without naively (at some level) participating within mundane reason or using it as a resource? 'Where does one stand?' asks the Student. How does one attain a transcendental position, a position which is somehow unfettered by divisions, categories, suppositions and practices of the very order one wishes to address? Indeed, is there such a position or is it itself a dream from within mundane reason?

McHoul (1982) has argued that not only is the quest for a neutral presuppositionless method of describing reality, one free from the use of commonsense categories, fruitless but it is fundamentally misguided. Ethnomethodology, he argues, can never completely purge itself of members' knowledge but must necessarily rely upon members' knowledge as a constituent feature of being able to locate and explicate its subject matter. Moreover, the very attempt to eliminate commonsense knowledge as a resource partakes of a classical but now defunct notion of the sciences. The work of Kuhn (1970) especially demonstrates that 'natural scientific forms of life assume an overwhelmingly practical, socially managed and negotiated character in contradiction to the ideal scientific enterprises pursued by logical positivism' (McHoul 1982: 85) and, indeed, by certain forms of ethnomethodology insofar as they seem to strive for objective description. Ethnomethodology is unavoidably situated within commonsense knowledge. This fate, however, is only a problem insofar as one invokes a classical rather than a sociological model of science. Thus 'while ethnomethodology is firmly located in the practices it describes' it is not thereby undermined for it could not be otherwise and the demand to be otherwise is a worry constituted by a dated version of scientific practice.

McHoul proposes that ethnomethodology ought to have a dual vision. As a condition of being able to do its work ethnomethodology must assume the objective existence of the structures and practices it sets out to study, although those structures and practices are those through which reality itself is understood to be constructed.

In doing actual investigations, ethnomethodology might usefully rely upon the research heuristic ('myth') that the phenomena it treats comprise a real order of events, that they are objects in an independently existing world . . . However, in *addressing itself as such a phenomenon*, ethnomethodology can, by contrast, hold that these very objects and practices (which it takes as 'topic') in fact emerge as products of the concerted, reflexive work of the ethnomethodological tradition and discourse (p. 101).

Inquiry is constituted as a possibility within mundane discourse, that is, within a discourse which allows for the separation of 'knower', 'analyst' or 'inquirer' on the one hand and 'object' or 'world' on the other. The possibility of inquiry is constituted within that space as indeed are the derivative possibilities of truth, error, bias, subjectivity, and perception. Thus, for sociology or its boundary hunter, ethnomethodology, to somehow abandon mundane discourse as a resource is to ultimately undo the discipline and its topic. The price of relinquishing mundane reason may be very great. The discourse by which it might be replaced though intimated (Reiss 1982) is not known. And those (e.g. McHugh *et al.* 1974) who have been bold enough to experiment with another idiom in which aspects of mundane reason are suspended have begun to produce a discourse virtually unrecognizable as or to sociology. Thus, I would suggest, following McHoul (1982), that mundane reason is essentially and unavoidably part of the investigative attitude of ethnomethodology. Ethnomethodology necessarily takes up a position in an ontological space in which there is an 'analyst' on the one hand and 'practices' or 'structure' on the other. It is thereby graced with the possibility of truth and shadowed by the prospect of error. In some respects the ethnomethodologist is like the mundane actor within labelling theory: though they construct, they mask their own work and provide an autobiographical version of themselves as 'subject' over and against 'reality'. Ethnomethodology thus partakes of the retrospective illusion, remedial self-concern and the privileged self-exemption inevitably, unavoidably and as a constituent feature of being what it is.

To the Student, the Mentor might respond that the Student is confronted with a choice. On the one hand, if investigation of any sort is to occur, the Student must at some level naively participate within the mundane idiom and the mundane space of 'real structure', 'truth' and 'analyst'. Insofar as the Student is to continue his investigations, he has no recourse but to be a mundane inquirer. He thereby forfeits to an unknown extent the primordial non-objectified and non-objectifiable features of mundaneity, but he retains the possibility of a topic, i.e. worldly reason and worldly practice. Alternatively, he may pursue mundaneity radically. Every indication regarding radical inquiry suggests, however, while one may gain a deep insight into mundaneity, the price is mundanely intelligible description.[7]

While ethnomethodology is condemned to mundane 'structure' and 'practice' as a condition of its intelligibility, its understanding of the nature of those structures and practices must be informed by rigorous and daring efforts to move to the 'limits' of the mundane idiom. Although ethnomethodology cannot exempt itself from mundane discourse at the investigative level (which means that it *will* give itself a privileged exemption from the structures it uncovers and treat them as 'real') and is inevitably situated within commonsense resources, the nature of mundane reason and commonsense resources generally is visible only as a consequence of efforts to deconstruct to transcend them. They are constituted as objects of ethnomethodological investigation only and precisely to the extent that they are observable and formulable as that which could be actually or imaginably otherwise. Given that the mundane processes we have considered are operative at a profound level in society, discourse and consciousness, dereification requires ever renewed and ever deepening efforts toward radical reflection.

Notes

Preface

1 Heritage (1985) provides a lucid, insightful and sophisticated overview of the aims, achievements and prospects of ethnomethodology.

2 Several of the most important insights and incentives for taking this turn came from Harold Garfinkel's seminars. Two of Garfinkel's lectures were especially significant. In one, he discussed the 'essential properties' of practical action: these are features irremediably and necessarily implicated in practical action and yet curiously are glossed, disattended or treated as 'cause for complaint' by practical actors. In another, Garfinkel discussed the ways in which inquiry into practical action might necessitate criteria of proof and demonstration different from those invoked in inquiries which consisted of practical actions: he referred to these alternative criteria and concern as 'methodological insteads'. The 'essential properties' implanted an appreciation of the depth, subtlety and 'no time out' character, as Garfinkel put it, of everyday practices. The 'methodological insteads' cultivated the prospect that inquiry into essential properties might entail a transformation of the parameters of sociological discourse and demonstration.

3 Some of the analyses presented in this study were first developed in Pollner (1970; 1974a; 1974b; 1975; 1978).

4 In the following pages mundane reason is referred to as though it were an autonomous force or actor. The reification of mundane reason has two sources. First, it is a stylistic convenience. A statement such as 'Mundane reason assumes an objective reality' is a shorthand way of indicating that individuals insofar as they are guided by the mundane idiom assume a world independent of discourse and experience. Second, however, the reification of mundane reason signals the claim that the notion of 'person', 'ego' or 'subject' is constituted from within mundane reason. Accordingly, 'individuals' do not engage in mundane reason; it is by virtue of mundane reason that 'persons' or 'individuals' are constituted. One implication of this position is that ethnomethodology is not reductionist insofar as reduction is understood as explaining social phenomena by reference to the actions of individuals. For ethnomethodology, the 'individual' is a mundane construction.

1 The problem of mundaneity

1 Heidegger (1961) provides a useful discussion of radical or 'out of order' questions.

2 For an intuitive appreciation of the paradoxical problems, consider the consequences of critiquing, say, Bingo by using Monopoly as the model of what a game ought to be like. One might find Bingo to be inadequate because it does not employ dice, uses a peculiar sort of board and so on. Carried to its limits, such a critique leads to faulting Bingo for being precisely what it is.

3 Mannheim's (1955) discussion of the extra-rational structure of total ideological conflict complements Kuhn's (1970) discussion of the extra-rational structure of paradigm conflict.

4 Harvey Sacks also sought to make the practice of sociology strange and the current work partakes deeply of the ideas and attitude expressed in one of his early (1963) papers. Whereas Sacks sought to make the work of 'doing describing' problematic, the current effort is intended to make problematic the suppositional 'space' within which 'description' or any activity oriented to an objective reality is an intelligible possibility.

5 The mentor's responses are informed by my reading of Garfinkel's (1967) study 'policies' most especially his insistence that 'All "logical" and "methodological" properties of action, every feature of an activity's sense, facticity, objectivity, accountability, communality is to be treated as a contingent accomplishment of socially organized common practices' (p. 33). The Mentor and Student might be heard as pursuing the implications of 'all' and 'every' in the preceding statement.

6 The term 'near-radical' applies to the Mentor's recommendations until the very last exchange. Until this point, the recommendations are informed by mundane notions of analysis and knowledge. The last exchange represents a marked departure from the preceding character of the conversation in that it implies the possibility of an abandonment of these notions and the recognition of a more primordial, albeit yet-to-be-specified, phenomenon.

7 In actual practice it is not necessarily the case that the descriptions offered by elders, informants and so forth have the status of 'merely' another activity in the tribe. Informants, for example, are often given privileged positions in that their descriptions are permitted to stand as anthropological descriptions. The informant is conceived of as a research assistant who has lived out his life in the tribe in lieu of the anthropologist. In fact, the practice of raising the informant to the level of colleague or research assistant is not limited to anthropology. In survey research, for example, the respondent is often treated, albeit implicitly, as a social scientist *vis-à-vis* his or her own life. For a general consideration of these and related issues see Cicourel (1964), Zimmerman and Pollner (1970) and Sacks (1963).

8 It may be useful to distinguish between formal and substantive radicalism. Substantive radicalism consists of questioning or making problematic the suppositions and practices of a particular form of discourse or inquiry. Thus, the sociology of knowledge and the sociology of science are substantively radical as are most meta-sociologies. Formal radicalism consists of making

problematic the nature of discourse and inquiry as such. Thus, meta-inquiries may be substantively radical though formally conservative in that they naively participate in and reproduce mundane ontological space

9 Analysis of the nature or 'limits' of analysis often realizes the paradoxical nature of its project and asks or hopes for something other than a literal reading. Thus, for example, Wittgenstein (1961) wrote: 'My propositions serve as elucidations in the following way: anyone who understands me eventually recognizes them as nonsensical, when he has used them – as steps – to climb up beyond them. (He must, so to speak, throw away the ladder after he has climbed up it.)

He must transcend these propositions, and then he will see the world aright'. (p. 161).

10 For a discussion of the distinction between 'practical' and 'scientific' attitudes, see Alfred Schutz (1967: Ch. VIII); Husserl (1965: 149–78); Gurwitsch (1966: 397–412).

11 The 'underlaborer' conception of the task and role of philosophy to the sciences was formulated by Locke who, in considering himself in relation to Newton, found himself to be but 'an under-laborer, employed in clearing the ground and removing some of the rubbish that lies in the way to knowledge' (Winch 1965). Such a conception of philosophy denies it any positive or autonomous domain of its own such as envisioned by Husserl. The 'underlaborer' conception relegates philosophy to have its issues formulated for it by reference to the sciences. At its most adventurous level, 'house philosophy' criticizes the sciences, and in this way receives its issues by virtue of what it is against. For a further discussion of the underlaborer conception of philosophy, see Winch (1965: especially pp. 3–10).

12 Alternatively, the inadequacies of particular sciences *qua* science are displayed by revealing the affinities between the science in question and commonsense reasoning. See for example, John Passmore (1965) and Allan Mazur (1968).

13 In *Ideas: General Introduction to Pure Phenomenology*, Husserl (1962) refers to the relation of the world and the sciences in a fashion which we shall provisionally adopt as our own: 'Natural knowledge begins with experience (*Erfahrung*) and remains within experience. Thus in that theoretical position which we call the "natural" standpoint, the total field of possible research is indicated by *a* single word: that is, the World. The sciences proper to this original standpoint are accordingly in their collective unity sciences of the World, and so long as this standpoint is the only dominant one, the concepts "true Being", "real (*wirkliches*) Being", i.e. real empirical (*reales*) Being, and – since all that is real comes to self concentration in the form of a cosmic unity – "Being in the world" are meanings that coincide ... The World is the totality of objects that can be known through experience (*Erfahrung*), known in terms of orderly theoretical thought on the basis of direct present (*aktueller*) experience'(pp. 45–6; some italics deleted).

14 Merleau-Ponty (1968: 105) calls questions of this sort – that is, questions which manifest an implicit faith in the essential objectivity of the world which is thus interrogated – 'natural questions'. Even the apparently radical questions of conventional philosophy, 'Does the world exist?' are possessed of faith:

'There is something, and the only question is if it is really this space, this time, this movement, this world that we think we see or feel.' (p. 105).

15 At a later point we shall see the redundancy of this entire formulation of mundane inquiry. The term 'mundane' looks as though it discriminates one mode of inquiry from another. In fact, it does not.

16 As we shall see, the idea that the objectivity of the world may be formulated as a thesis, belief, faith and so on is inadequate. Minimally, it is a belief which, precisely insofar as it becomes available as a 'mere' belief, radically alters the status of that which is believed. The effects of the alteration are possibly like those encountered in moving from the academic speculation that man is essentially evil to a state of paranoia.

17 See Hubert Dreyfus' introduction to Maurice Merleau-Ponty (1964a: xiii). The idea of prejudice is also to be found in Husserl's writings. See, for example, Husserl (1962: 74–5).

18 In this way the *préjugé du monde* is differentiated from what Mannheim (1952: 185) called a 'World postulate', which is essentially the primordial premise of an ideology or *weltanschauung*. The 'prejudice' by contrast is a world postulate which postulates the world and is thus antecedent to any substantive categorizations.

19 To be sure, within the province of mundane inquiry the advent of the sciences heralded an unparalleled radicalism. With the institution of the ideals of scientific method as a means of expurgating the idols and biases of practical investigation, science set itself the infinite and hence ideal task of a determination of nature as it really is in and of itself for all times and for all men (Gurwitsch 1966: 406–12). Also see Husserl's (1962: 74) remarks on the 'intellectually practical radicalism' of the sciences. The relative radicalism of the sciences *vis-à-vis* practical inquiry is dramatically manifest when the ideals governing scientific inquiry are invoked in practical activities. See Garfinkel (1967: 262–83); Schutz (1964: 64–90).

20 We may note here the beginning of the paradoxes which will continually be imposed upon us by virtue of having to talk. Mundaneity is not an object; and yet, precisely insofar as we wish to explicate it, we must objectivate it. Use of the natural language does not permit mundaneity to be approached in any other way. Notice that even in this footnote we have had to objectivate mundaneity if only to say that *it* is not an *it*.

21 There are an immense number of aphorisms which suggest the elusiveness of mundaneity. A particularly poignant one is found in R. D. Laing's *The Politics of Experience* (1967: 90): 'The truth I am trying to grasp is the grasp that is trying to grasp it'. This is certainly the character of mundaneity. The Buddhists know such structures well, and we shall have occasion to turn to them later, particularly in Chapter 7.

There are a variety of synonyms for the ways in which mundaneity hides itself. Naivete, forgetfulness, illusion (Macomber 1967) are but a few of the terms, each of which emphasizes a different aspect or image of the ways mundaneity suppresses or disattends its constitutive work. Each of these terms is the product of the irony which comes from having obtained a fore-grasp of mundaneity while attempting to articulate mundaneity within the idiom which mundaneity supports.

22 If mundane concern with a world *per se* is the first-order state in which mundane inquiry finds itself, and if mundane concern with mundane-concern-with-a-world-per se is a second-order or reflective state, then the objects encountered in each order are substantively distinct. A first-order world may be the physical world *per se* which is composed of vectoral forces, particles and so forth. A first-order world may be the social world *per se* consisting of roles, norms, etc. A second-order world of physics is the world-*per-se*-as-considered-by-physicists. It is a meta-physical world which is now the object of concern. Similarly, a first-order social world *per se* may consist of Durkheimian social facts. The second-order world is the social-facts-as considered-by-the-sociologist; this is more or less the world of the sociologist of knowledge. And these second-order worlds may themselves be made the object of mundane concern, and so on *ad infinitum*. With each reflexive turnabout, however, the substance of the intended world retains its character as a world *per se*. This is to say that it presents itself as an essentially pre-constituted field of objects and relations which awaits explication. It presents itself in this fashion precisely to the extent that it presents itself as a world. As with all worlds (in the very way that they offer themselves as worlds) mundane inquiry becomes oblivious to the constituting work in favor of – indeed, in order to consider – the world *per se*, which is available only by virtue of that obliviousness.

23 The naivete of which we speak has an ambiguous status. Insofar as it is considered as part of a critique of the foundations of sociology, then it has definite pejorative implications. Husserl berated the sciences for their naivete with respect to their own primordial foundations, namely, the assumption of a pre-given world. When, however, one attempts to describe the foundations of sociology and mundane inquiry in general, the naivete proves to be an irremediable feature of all concern with a world precisely insofar as it is a concern with a world.

24 For an exegesis of Weber's suppositions from the standpoint of phenomenology, see Schutz (1967).

25 With respect to the presupposed availability of mundane structures, Durkheim and Weber are in agreement. Indeed, with appropriate terminological alteration – specifically the substitution of 'social meanings' for 'social facts' – Weber would not be uncomfortable with Durkheim's (1938) maxim 'Consider social facts as things' and its corollary, 'All preconceptions must be eradicated.'.

26 Heisenberg (1966) is always a particularly critical figure insofar as he represents 'second-order' mundane inquiry – that is, inquiry into a domain in which the observer is included as a constituent feature of the investigated domain. But the tradition which he represents is, in principle, no different from the tradition which he seemingly upsets. It is no different in that the new domain which includes observer *and* observed is treated as a preconstituted objectivity awaiting explication. The relative is absolutized.

27 Hubert Dreyfus' description of Merleau-Ponty's vision of the task of phenom-

enology is deeply resonant with the project of the current study. 'The object, we assume, is completely determinate and independent of our investigation of it. This is an inevitable prejudice, according to Merleau-Ponty. The basic task of phenomenology is to overcome this *'préjugé du monde'* by describing the way experience develops, uncovering the steps by which perception hides its activity of organization and thus leads us to see the object as an independent entity. Phenomenology, then is not simply the study of how objects appear to commonsense but is a description of the way objects *arise*. This shakes our perceptual faith in the independent solidity of objects – or rather, it calls our attention to the fact that it is indeed a *faith*. A study of the genealogy of objects reveals the fact that perceptual meanings can become stabilized but are never absolutely secure. It makes us aware that our experience is always meaningful yet always menaced by disorder and non-sense.' (Merleau-Ponty 1962a: xiii) One distinguishing feature of the current study, however, is that it is not a phenomenological explication of experience but a sociological analysis of the practices through which a community maintains the faith in an objective world.

28 This is not to say that the 'truth' or determining 'what really happened' is the only or even the primary concern of the judge or the defendant. Defendants, for example, are not necessarily concerned with 'truth' for its own sake but as a way of establishing the unfairness of the charge or unjustness of the fine. Nevertheless, to the extent and in the ways that their practical concerns require making claims about 'what really happened' they enter into mundane reason.

29 An arraignment is the legal occasion for informing the defendant of the charges and the entering of a plea. In practice, however, it is often the case that defendants are allowed to 'explain' the extenuating circumstances of their cases. Indeed, in the largest of the observed courts, a defendant could enter a plea of 'no contest' and the judge would adjudicate the matter on the basis of the defendant's account and the officer's comments on the face of the citation. Thus, though trials would presumably be the definitive source of illustrative materials, arraignments proved to be an equally rich and much more accessible vein.

30 For analyses of the interactional organization of court transactions see Atkinson and Drew (1979); Carlen (1976); Pollner (1979).

2 Mundane hermeneutics

1 The problem of the truth is generated from within mundane reason. In differentiating 'subject' from 'object' mundane reason establishes the problem as well the prospect of the subject 'knowing' the object. Thus, the formulation of mundane inquiry's plight is not an analytic characterization of the difficulties of producing a correct or objective account of reality but mundane inquiry's formulation of its plight. Put another way, my remarks are not intended as philosophy or epistemology but as ethnography.

2 While 'assertive languages' may stipulate against self-contradictory utterances, as Earle suggests, speakers nevertheless frequently make ostensibly

contradictory claims about reality. Whether the utterances are found to be in violation of norms of logical discourse or perfectly intelligible speech acts, turns in part on the interpretive reception of those utterances. Hearers may modulate the kinds of background knowledge they deploy as the context of another's utterances, with the result that the seemingly illogical and contradictory is heard as, say, metaphorical. Coulter (1979: 101–4) refers to the variation in the deployment of background knowledge as 'strategic contextualization'. A suggestive example of how background knowledge may be deployed is provided by Molotch and Boden (1985).

3 In Chapter III, we shall treat the relation between the idealization of the object and inter-subjectivity in far greater detail. For the moment, suffice it to say that the anticipated continuity and coherence of experiences within and among observers is predicated on the anticipated continuity and coherence of the object.

4 One specie of transcendental stranger, the young child, fully conforms to this expectation. For them (Piaget 1928) contradictions are not a source of puzzlement.

5 It should be noted that contrary to the implicit tenor of our discussion, mundane reason does not merely arise on the occasion of a particular problematic as when, say, accounts which purportedly describe the self-same scene are in open conflict. It is not a specific 'instrument' invoked to obtain closure on the 'in-itself' or 'the real'. Rather, the presupposition of the real, mundane reason, and the very problematic which mundane reason seemingly resolves, are vitally integrated features of mundane inquiry. Consider, for example, the fact that the problematic which contradictory accounts poses for mundane reason is a problematic which is formulatable as such only under the auspices of mundane reason. It is a reflection of mundane reason's anticipation regarding the relations which should obtain among accounts which describe the self-same event. In this sense, mundane reason furnishes in its own terms the problematics it is prepared to resolve.

6 The adumbrated presentation of the object is a phenomenological notion which we are using in a somewhat modified sense. We are concerned with the object as it manifests itself through language as opposed to the typical phenomenological concern with the object as it is given to consciousness. For a discussion of the concept of adumbration see Gurwitsch (1964: 202–27).

7 It is of interest to note the ways in which the aspects are treated as indications or expressions of typical possibilities which in turn are used to build up the scene as a possible mundane occurrence. Year of birth yields to 'oldster', 'no business address' to 'retired person', time and place to 'murderous traffic'. As isolated aspects, the time or place of the offense provide for innumerable developmental possibilities by virtue of their relative vagueness. Treated as indicative of the traffic conditions which obtained at the time of the offense, these particulars act as constraints upon subsequent determinations of motive. In this case, the attribution of motivation to the driver seems to be contingent on such a transformation. For example, the transformation of time and place to 'murderous traffic' provides for the possibility that the driver was simply confused as opposed to intentionally violating the law. In its initial

'raw' form, the aspects of locale signify 'merely another' time and place among times and places. As such, the motivational possibilities are relatively diffuse and large in number. As symptomatic of 'murderous traffic', however, time and place provide for a motivational attribution of a rather specific sort, one which is consonant with the fact that one who proceeded against such traffic would do so while undergoing possible risk, e.g. injury. Whereas the unmodified aspects yield to an almost endless number of motivational possibilities, the transformed particulars, in the very ways in which they constrain, also suggest and invite comparatively specific motivations.

8 The nature of mundane hermeneutics is probably far more complex than these elementary examples suggest. Consider, for example, that any aspect is not merely a detail of the described scene (though to be sure it is that as well): it is also contributory to the constitution of the possible scene of which it is a detail. The judge does not have any *a priori* report on the events analyzed by the accounts. Thus, the analyses of the defendant and the officer do not merely explicate a scene, but they simultaneously present the scene of which they are explications. The scene upon which they report is available only in the reportage. Thus, the ensemble of aspects leads a dual life. They are *contingent details* in the sense that they are features which may be altered without materially altering the intended scene. It may make no difference that the scene took place on Highway Y as opposed to Highway X. Yet the ensemble of aspects taken together realize the scene of which they are 'about'. In this sense, the aspects are *constitutive details*. To alter each presented aspect is tantamount to changing the scene of which the aspects were hitherto seen as merely contingent or incidental particulars. The particulars are at once documentary representations of the scene they intend and the vehicle through which the scene of which they are documentary instances is brought to light in the first place. The particulars are at once particulars 'about' or 'of' the scene and revelatory of the scene of which they are 'about' or 'of'. The citation simultaneously explicates a scene and reveals the scene of which it is an explication.

An appreciation of the 'dual life' of particulars or aspects permits a correspondingly deeper appreciation of the ways in which the accounts mutually explicate one another. Since aspects lead the dual life, 'what really happened on the highway' is made available through aspects which realize the scene of which they are also mere details. The citation intends a scene through pre-formatted and *ad hoc* specifications which subsequently become contingent particulars. A charge of speeding is at once that which allegedly 'happened' and 'about' that which happened. The specification 'speeding' may, for example, turn out to be 'wrong', and yet the scene may be envisioned in which speeding-did-not-take-place. Because the judge has no way of knowing what the scene to be considered consists of (apart from its consideration in the accounts of the officer and the defendant), these accounts provide the relational context in which the other accounts feature as talking-about-the-same-scene and as realizing a possibly existent state of affairs are constituted. Since the scene is available only in accounts, the accounts organize and elaborate their intended referent and, simultaneously, reveal their adequacy to realize their referent as an existential possibility (cf. Hilbert 1977).

9 See Gurwitsch's (1964: 287–92) illuminating discussion of the necessary and sufficient conditions of the perceptual process.

10 Upon subsequent examination of the citation, I found that the section of the vehicle code was not that having to do with speeding, but instead with 'unsafe entry onto a highway'. If the officer's comments are now attended to as an explication of the scene initially aspectuated by the 'unsafe entry' code instead of speeding, then the scene which the aspects collectively realize is a possible scene in the sense that the contradictions have been removed. An unsafe entrance onto the highway does not necessarily require that the defendant exceed the speed limit. But, more significantly, the alteration of a particular aspect has consequences for the sense of the ensemble of aspects in which it is embedded. It is not merely that the introduction of the correct section of the vehicle code removes the contradiction from an otherwise internally inconsistent ensemble, but rather with the correct section the sense of the now coherent ensemble is modified. The noted 'loss of traction' and the 'squealing tires', for example, no longer stand as further corroboration of the vehicle's excess speed, but rather they are rendered aspects which further develop and corroborate the lack of reasonable safety in entering the flow of traffic. Similarly, the sense of the officer's comment 'med. traffic' is also altered. It stands as the description of the flow of traffic into which the defendant entered and possibly disrupted as opposed to the flow within which the defendant's vehicle was speeding. Finally, the comment 'excessive speed' is rendered a relative assessment as opposed to the absolute character it possessed under the original interpretation.

11 There is an 'asymmetry' to the relation between the defendant's account and that of the officer. The citation, more particularly the charge, has a primacy *vis-à-vis* the defendant's account. The charge is the organizational reason for the defendant's presence. It specifies the matter to which he may speak if he is to speak relevantly. This is in contrast to, say, confessionals wherein it is the confessant who formulates the 'charges'. The citation's primacy resides in its announcement of the 'this is what really happened'. It specifies the matter which may or may not have taken place, the aspects which may or may not be in correspondence to their referent. It formulates the matter-to-be disputed. The accusation in its organizational context stands as the matter with which the defendant will have to come to terms if he is to relevantly come to terms with anything.

12 The contradictory aspectuation of a scene in this illustration is direct and unequivocal. The citation asserted that the defendant had aided and abetted drag racing: the defendant asserted that no drag racing took place. Contradictions between accounts are not necessarily as explicit. The discovery and formulation of a conflict may itself involve an explication of an accounted scene's tacit implications. Further, the relevantly notable horizon of further possible determinations is not given in advance of the juxtaposition of accounts. That is, what the explicable horizon of an

accounted object relevantly consists of awaits the juxtaposition of the other accounts.

As noted earlier, because of the horizon of potential determinations, the accounted objects are endowed with an openness. Their promise of more-could-be-said-with respect to inner or outer determinations may be pursued indefinitely. An accounted object, as the beginning of an indefinitely extendable chain of aspects, is capable of consuming the order of mundane existence, in which it is to take its place. It is by virtue of this open horizon of potential determinations that accounts – when considered under one another's auspices – reciprocally explicate and, in a sense, constitute one another's character as 'constraints'. Because the accounted scene is informed by aspects which are unspecified though implied, and because accounts in order to realize their objects must exhibit a congruence and conformity with one another in terms of both explicit and implied aspects, the accounts elaborate one another for their potentially congruent or incongruent character. That is to say, from the point of view of the judge, the accounts are the initial links of as yet undeveloped aspectual chains which must ultimately and throughout be joined. What the citation relevantly comes to, as an incipient aspectual chain, awaits the defendant's account. It is the first link of an infinite number of chains, the relevant chain being actualized by the one initiated in the defendant's account – which, of course, assumes its relevance by virtue of the citation.

13 Husserl (1960: 62) writes, 'an actual Object belonging to a world or all the more so, a world itself, is an infinite idea, related to infinities of Harmoniously combinable experiences – an idea that is the correlate of the idea of a perfect experiential evidence, a complete synthesis of possible experiences' (Italics deleted).

14 Sacks (1972a, 1972b) describes a host of ancillary features of categorization devices, such as their 'inferential richness' (which refers to that which may be warrantably asserted about a person by virtue of his membership in a particular class) and 'category bound activities' (which refer to those actions warrantably anticipated from person by virtue of category membership, e.g. 'babies cry').

The defendant stands as a further possible aspectuation of his own citation. In effect, he is a further potential determination which is implied by the explicitly noted particulars of the citation. The fact that the categorization 'student' is suggested is tied to the fact that the event happened on 'campus'. It is as if the scene realized in the ticket organizes the relevant categories under which the defendant might be subsumed. In turn, the categorization under which the defendant is subsumed modifies the sense of the realized scene. The defendant's relevant categorical identity awaits the grasping of the aspectuated scene, just as the sense of the scene awaits a grasp of the defendant's categorical identity (cf. Wieder 1974).

15 Similarly, the judge has knowledge of particular and general 'world circumstances'. As with the use of the categorization device as a means of establishing what an incumbent of a particular category might warrantably be expected to know or do, knowledge of worldly circumstances is employed as a

device to exhibit the incongruous and hence potentially 'impossible' character of the accounted scene. The judge may specify the typical and regular features of the environment in such a manner so as to display by juxtaposition the atypical, irregular, unlikely character of the accounted scene and its essential incompatibility with the natural facts of life.

3 The self-preservation of mundane reason

1 Bittner (1973) provides a penetrating analysis of the difference in regard for social reality by those who live it and those who would describe what it is like to live it. Insofar as the researcher views a group's reality as a construction, he is less likely to 'perceive those traits of depth, stability, and necessity that people recognize as actually inherent in the circumstances of their existence' (p. 123).

4 Mundane puzzles and the politics of experience

1 Perhaps the deepest expression of the ironic origins of subjectivity is to be found in the relation between modern physics and psychology. For a discussion of the ways in which psychology's understanding of what is to count as 'subjective' emerges from the mathematical specification of 'objective' reality furnished by physics see Aron Gurwitsch's (1966) 'The Place of Psychology in the System of Sciences' and 'The Last Work of Edmund Husserl'.

2 A related matter of more than passing interest is the way in which persons formulate themselves as insane. A major component of such work would seem to involve assumptions regarding 'normal me' and 'normal world', it is by reference to characterizations of what-I-am-like and what-the-world-is-like that inexplicable and unaccountable departures are made possible. For example, our versions of what we can expect from our bodies provides the possibility of being deeply surprised by our experiences of what we find them to be doing. Under certain circumstances the violation of body assumptions may be treated as an indication that one is 'out of her mind'. A report by Robert Kistler in the *Los Angeles Times*, 15 April, 1971, furnishes an illustration: 'A Hollywood woman and her son were hospitalized with hallucinations after eating a restaurant spaghetti dinner liberally dosed with LSD, police disclosed Wednesday.

The victims, who were treated at Kaiser Foundation Hospital for "drug intoxication", told police they had sprinkled their plates of spaghetti with grated Parmesan cheese from a container on the table in an Italian restaurant.

. . . Mrs. Jones, a waitress at a downtown hotel cafe, told officers she and her son had eaten out Sunday night then returned home when the pains began. "I had pains in my chest and I thought I was having a heart attack," the woman said. "After a while, I felt like there were strange animals of different colors coming from my skin and body" . . . Her son became hysterical because he thought his mother was dying, she added.

"He was acting funny, too, although I don't think he was as much out of his mind as I was."' Interesting hypotheses regarding self-labeling may be derived from Becker (1967).

3 Note that this case is recounted from the point of view of an already made 'choice'. The patient's problem is narrated in light of its solution. The problem of whether the patient was merely fabricating confessions to his wife or had in fact participated in the reported escapades has been decided in favour of the former possibility. Thus, for example, the patient is described as having 'felt that confession would be a way of satisfying her demands and of allowing her to reconcile with him, and he increased the fabrication of false confessions' . . . Presumedly, the patient in the midst of his problem did not have such a definitive formulation of himself for if he did he would not have a problem, i.e. if he knew he was 'fabricating', then he would know that the confessions were false.

4 The term 'cosmic reality' suggests that Leon may be proposing something other than Rokeach's inability to see what any competent person ought to be able to see. He may be introducing the possibility that the table is rising in some extraordinary sense in an extraordinary realm to which Rokeach, like most others, does not have perceptual access. If this is the thrust of Leon's proposal then while the disjuncture is thereby extended on one level, it is minimized on another. That is, while Leon is proposing the existence of an extraordinary realm to which Rokeach does not have access, he is also recognizing that the table in the mundane realm is on the ground. An interesting historical overview of the status accorded access to extraordinary realities is provided in Sarbin and Juhasz (1967).

5 Similar formulations apparently occur in the aftermath of paradigm revolutions when persons attempt to describe what they saw under the auspices of the discredited paradigm. According to Kuhn (1970) 'Looking at the moon, the convert to Copernicanism does not say, "I used to see a planet, but now I see a satellite." That locution would imply a sense in which the Ptolemaic system had once been correct. Instead, a convert to the new astronomy says, "I once took the moon to be (or saw the moon as) a planet, but I was mistaken."' (p. 114).

6 The controversy surrounding Castaneda's writings produced a multifaceted disjuncture. Some persons (e.g., DeMille 1980; Duerr 1985; Needham 1985) doubt that don Juan exists.

7 Analyses of the resolution of reality disjunctures in legal, scientific and everyday settings are found in Coulter (1975); Darrough (1978); Eglin (1979); Hilbert (1977); Gilbert and Mulkay (1984); Mehan (1983).

5 Mundane autobiography

1 It is important to distinguish between the collapse of particular systems of mundane reason and the collapse of mundane reason *per se*. In the former, one substantive version of the subject/object duality is replaced by another – as when for example Ptolemaic is replaced by Copernican paradigm or when a theological cosmology is superseded by a secular version of a reality. In such sequences, there may be a massive transformation of content and even of form

but the distinction of a subject, corporate or individual, confronting a determinate or objective order of some kind is retained. The collapse of mundane reason *per se* occurs when the very distinction between subject and object and the idiomatic possibilities and concerns which it founds are not reiterated. On the individual level the experience of such collapse may resemble either 'transcendental' or 'mystical' states on the one hand or psychotic states on the other. The radical dissolution of mundaneity often involves profound difficulties in describing the nature of the change as well it might given that what has dissolved are the very conditions for 'doing description'. Insofar as the subject-object duality cannot be reiteratively reconstructed, there is no subject to 'describe' and no object to be described. It is also of interest to note the low premium placed on introspection or describing by the various disciplines which seek to cultivate transcendence. The effort to describe, discuss, or even to desire non-dualistic states of consciousness are discouraged because such activities presuppose, invoke and reaffirm the very dualistic structures mundane practitioners intend to overcome. Thus, aspirants to alternative modes of being which completely dissolve subject/object space may be confronted with seemingly paradoxical demands to do something without doing it (cf. Herrigel 1964a, 1964b).

2 I shall be considering the ways in which Becker's formulation of labeling theory becomes conflated with the mundane autobiography of the deviance processing enterprise. While a modification of Becker's formulation affords an outside or constitutive vantage point and allows it to escape the snare of mundane autobiography on one level, the liberated version becomes 'ensnared' at another level. I shall consider the nature of the higher order mundaneity in a subsequent chapter.

3 In *The Trial* (1964) Kafka's K has an outside ontological view: K sees that actions which seem to be concerned with and directed to responding to infractions of the law simultaneously constitute the law, the infractions and the infractor. K is nevertheless enmeshed within the system while retaining his outside ontology.

4 For the most forceful treatment of the problems arising from a failure to distinguish clearly between commonsense or members' models and those employed by the sociologist, see Cicourel (1964).

For a seminal and illuminating discussion of mundane and constitutive positions as they apply to the relation of a psychiatric clinic to the 'real demand' for its services and the relation of the police to the 'real amount of crime', see the footnote in Garfinkel (1967: 215–16). Garfinkel notes that whereas for the police 'real crime' means that it occurs independently of the measures used to detect, describe, report, and suppress it, for the sociologist the 'real amount of crime . . . *consists only and entirely of the likelihood that socially organized measures for the detection and control of deviance can be enforced*' (emphasis in original).

5 Merleau-Ponty (1962), makes the following observation regarding the use of the concept of 'attention' in psychological theorizing: 'The object, psychologists would assert, is never ambiguous but becomes so only through our inattention. The bounds of the visual field are not themselves variable, and

there is a moment when the approaching object begins absolutely to be seen, but we do not 'notice' it. But the notion of attention ... is no more than auxillary hypothesis, evolved to save the prejudice in favour of an objective world' (p. 6).

6 This anomaly has been considered by others. See, for example, Gibbs (1966).

7 Wasserstrom (1961) has constructed a dialogue in a hypothetical system in which justice is achieved through judges' 'intuition' of the just and need not be justified in any other terms. The dialogue is suggestive of what a transformation (or disintegration) of mundane legal discourse might be like. The dialogue begins:

Q: 'On what grounds do you justify your decision in this case?'
J: 'The justification for this decision rests upon the fact that I have intuited this result to be the best possible one for this case.'
Q: 'Oh, you mean that there is some general moral principle which requires that a case involving this kind of fact situation be decided in this way?'
J: 'No, I mean simply that this decision is just because I have intuited to be just for this case' (p. 93).

8 The analysis in this chapter has its own 'inside' and 'outside'. From within, the chapter is predicated on the ontological validity of constructionism. From the outside, of course, the reality of constructionist work may itself be viewed as a construction. What kind of work is involved in the construction of constructionism? In part, the construction of constructionism requires a specific form of interpretation of the materials advanced as evidence of the relative character of deviance. The mere observation that different groups treat different acts as deviant, for example, does not necessarily lead to the conclusion of relativity. The same observation may be interpreted as evidence of the others' barbarism, incompetence or pathology. In actual practice in everyday life such attributions do indeed occur. To establish 'constructionism' as a 'real' feature of what members are doing, then, involves a choice between alternative interpretations (either of which may subsequently lay claim to merely reflecting or mirroring the obvious). The relativism which undergirds the constructive view is itself a construction.

9 Any conception which mundane inquiry entertains of itself cannot fully comprehend mundane inquiry. In whatever way mundane inquiry conceives of itself, it is always more than that conception, if only because mundane inquiry is also that activity which espouses that particular conception of itself. In this way, mundane inquiry is always more than it can say about itself in so many words – if only because it is the sayer of the words. As Karl Jaspers (1955) writes, 'I am not authentically myself if I am merely what I know myself to be ... Whenever I objectify myself, I am myself more than this object, namely, I am that being which can thus objectify itself' (p. 73).

10 Garfinkel (1967) has suggested that social scientific portrayals of social actors make them out to be cultural and psychological 'dopes' by ignoring the rich and complex nature of their practical decision making. I am suggesting that there is a sense in which mundane reasoners are ontological dopes in the ways they disattend or are oblivious to the organization of the mundane world.

Ontological dopiness, however, may be a necessary feature of the organization of that world.

6 Mundane reflection

1 Notice the affinity between Laing's characterization of psychotic experience and the following characterization by Merleau-Ponty (1968: 26) of the consequences of suspending a variant of the mundane model, i.e. the constancy hypothesis, as it applies to physiological research. 'As soon as we cease thinking of perception as the action of the pure physical object on the human body, and the perceived as the "interior" result of this action, it seems that every distinction between the true and the false, between methodic knowledge and phantasms, between the science and imagination, is ruined.'

2 For a dramatic illustration of a social object's constitution by the 'response' directed toward it, see Garfinkel's (1967; also McHugh 1968) experimental procedures for disclosing the properties of the 'documentary method of interpretation'.

3 This structure is foreshadowed by Garfinkel's (1967) discussion of the '"uninteresting" essential reflexivity of accounts' as a constituent feature of practical actions. Garfinkel notes that for a wide range of practical actions, one matter is specifically excluded from examination as a phenomenon in its own right – practical action. 'In no case,' Garfinkel observes, 'is the investigation of practical actions undertaken in order that personnel might be able to recognize and describe what they are doing in the first place' (p. 7).

4 Jaspers' (1955) notes that 'absurd stupidities have the same logical form for the understanding as a deep contact with the limits' (p. 116).

5 In this respect, these structures conform to the essential properties of speaking practices formulated by Garfinkel and Sacks (1970).

7 Social construction of mundane reason

1 Mackie's (1985) recent book includes a superb martialing and explication of resources for the 'reversal of the containment that comprises everyday consciousness' (p. 1). The second half of the book is a fascinating attempt to actually use the resources to experientially deconstruct 'the everyday' and secure a more inclusive mode of consciousness. My focus by contrast is upon the institutional, interactional and experiential organization of the 'containment'.

2 Coulter (1979) has distilled the implications of both Ryle's (1949) and Wittgenstein's critique of mentalism for sociology. Instead of naively making attributions of inner or mentalistic states, Coulter argues, sociology ought to 'take stock of the fact that members of a culture mundanely traffic in cognitive categories and predicates amongst each other, and have practical ways of making subjectivity-determinations' (p. 51). These determinations, the orderly ways in which members presuppose, use and attribute mental qualities, comprise the significant phenomena for sociology. Sociology is not to become a participant in the language game of mentalism by itself inferring

or attributing inner states: rather its task is to describe the grammar which provides for intelligible inferences about and attributions of inner states as they are formulated by and to members of the society.

3 Reiss' (1982) methodological remarks are of considerable interest. In developing his general definition of 'discourse' Reiss refuses to commit himself to the notion of a speaking subject. Rather, discourse is defined as 'a coherent set of linguistic facts organized by some enunciating entity' (p. 27). Reiss writes that he does not 'dare' write 'enunciating subject' (instead of 'entity') because it would imply a particular class of discourse 'based on the assumption of the identity of an I' and it is precisely the universality of this assumption which Reiss disputes (p. 28). What it is that speaks, 'the speaking entity', is a meaning which produces but is also produced by the discourse.

4 As mundane reason becomes more pervasive, subtle and differentiated, various 'pathologies' are made possible which do not necessarily involve the collapse of the entire idiom so much as intensification, permutations or elaborations of elements within the idiom. In constructing themselves as 'subjects' confronting an 'objective reality', mundane reasoners are thereby provided with the resources and opportunities for distinctive 'symptomatic' experiences. An especially interesting hypothesis in this regard is H. B. M. Murphy's (1978) conjecture regarding the shift in symptomology of depression, which seems to have occurred in Europe in the middle of the seventeenth century and very recently in Ashanti society (and not at all in many Asian and African societies).

5 For analyses of the 'individual' as a construct see Broughton (1980); Gergen (1984); Harding and Hintikka (1983); Heelas and Lock (1981); Henriques *et al.* (1984); Jaynes (1977); and Mackie (1985).

6 Needless to say, all of the resources which I have indicated suggest yet other resources, issues and possibilities. For example, the developmental rise of the subject-object dichotomy could be profitably augmented and deepened through G. H. Mead's (1938) analysis of the rise of the self and Piagetian analysis of the development of logical-analytic thinking. Yet these analyses might be tempered by an appreciation of the historical contingency of mundane reason. Insofar as mundane reason is an historically contingent idiom, Meadian and Piagetian accounts may not describe invariant stages in the development of a universal mind and self but aspects of the process through which individuals in specific historical configurations, which emphasize the mundane distinctions, are socialized. The actor implicitly celebrated in Meadian and Piagetian models is the autonomous, deliberating, self-contained actor. The description of the Canaques and speculation regarding the ancient Greeks suggest, however, that this model of the actor is not universally regarded as the epitome of development. Indeed, there are some indications that the 'individual' and the 'self' are not universally formulable categories. Commentaries on Piaget (1928) by Seltman and Seltman (1985), and Gilligan (1982) suggest that the Piagetian model of intellectual and moral development may derive from and hence be applicable only to males in Western, industrialized societies.

7 Merleau-Ponty (1962) writes that the lesson of phenomenology is that a

presuppositionless philosophy is impossible. In part, it is impossible because the presuppositionless philosophy would be virtually unformulable or unrecognizable as philosophy to those constituted within the tradition. In his review of the experience of 'mystical' states of consciousness, James (1958) noted that any number of eminent individuals felt they had been delivered of a profound knowledge yet were unable to convey to others the nature of their insight.

References cited

Atkinson, J. Maxwell. 1978. *Discovering Suicide: Studies in the Social Organization of Sudden Death*. London: Macmillan.

Atkinson, J. Maxwell and Drew, Paul. 1979. *Order in Court: The Organization of Verbal Interaction in Judicial Settings*. London: Macmillan.

Bachelard, Suzanne. 1968. *A Study of Husserl's Formal and Transcendental Logical*. Translated by Lester E. Embree. Evanston, Illinois: Northwestern University Press.

Barfield, Owen. 1965. *Saving the Appearances: A Study in Idolatry*. New York: Harcourt, Brace & World.

Becker, Howard. 1963. *Outsiders*. New York: The Free Press of Glencoe.

Becker, Howard. 1967. History, culture and subjective experience: an exploration of the social bases of drug-induced experiences. *Journal of Health and Social Behaviour*. 8: 163–76.

Berger, Peter and Luckman, Thomas L. 1966. *The Social Construction of Reality*. Garden City, New York: Doubleday.

Bernstein, Richard, J. 1978. *The Restructuring of Social and Political Theory*. Philadelphia: University of Pennsylvania Press.

Binswanger, Ludwig. 1968. *Being-in-the-World*. Translated by Jacob Neddleman. New York: Harper & Row.

Bittner, Egon. 1973. Objectivity and realism in sociology. In George Psathas (editor). *Phenomenological Sociology*. New York: Wiley.

Bleuler, Eugen. 1950. *Dementia Praecox or the Group of Schizophrenias*. Translated by Joseph Zinkin. New York: Interactional Universities Press.

Broughton, John M. 1980. Genetic metaphysics: the developmental psychology of mind-body concepts. In R. W. Rieber (editor) *Body and Mind: Past, Present, and Future*. New York: Academic Press, 177–222.

Caputo, John D. 1978. *The Mystical Element in Heidegger's Thought*. Athens: Ohio University Press.

Carlen, Pat. 1976. *Magistrates Justice*. London: Martin Robertson.

Carr, David. 1974. *Phenomenology and the Problem of History*. Evanston, Illinois: Northwestern University Press.

Castaneda, Carlos. 1968. *The Teachings of Don Juan: A Yaqui Way of Knowledge*. Berkeley: University of California Press.

Castenada, Carlos. 1971. *A Separate Reality*. New York: Simon and Schuster.

Cicourel, Aaron V. 1964. *Method and Measurement in Sociology*. New York: The Free Press of Glencoe.

Cicourel, Aaron V. 1968. *The Social Organization of Juvenile Justice*. New York: Wiley.

Coulter, Jeff. 1975. Perceptual accounts and interpretive asymetries. *Sociology*. 9: 385–96.

Coulter, Jeff. 1979. *The Social Construction of Mind*. Totowa, New Jersey: Rowman & Littlefield.

Darrough, William D. 1978. When versions collide: police and the dialectics of accountability. *Urban Life*. 7: 379–403.

DeMille, R. (editor). 1980. *The Don Juan Papers*. Santa Barbara: Ross-Erikson.

Dewald, Paul A. 1970. Folie à deux and the function of reality testing. *Psychiatry*. 33: 390–5.

Dodds, E. R. 1951. *The Greeks and the Irrational*. Berkeley: University of California Press.

Duerr, Hans Peter. 1985. *Dreamtime: Concerning the Boundary Between Wilderness and Civilization*. Translated by Felicitas Goodman. Oxford: Basil Blackwell.

Durkheim, Emile. 1938. *The Rules of Sociological Method*. Translated by Sarah A. Solovay and John H. Mueller. Glencoe, Illinois: The Free Press.

Durkheim, Emile. 1951. *Suicide*. Translated by John A. Spaulding and George Simpson. Glencoe, Illinois: The Free Press.

Earle, William. 1968. *Objectivity: An Essay in Phenomenological Ontology*. Chicago: Quadrangle Books.

Eglin, Peter. 1979. Resolving reality disjunctures on telegraph avenue: a study of practical reasoning. *Canadian Journal of Sociology*. 4: 359–77.

Elias, Norbert. 1978. *The Civilizing Process: The History of Manners*. Translated by Edmund Jephcott. New York: Urizen Books.

Elias, Norbert. 1982. *Power and Civility*. Translated by Edmund Jephcott. New York: Pantheon Books.

English, Spurgeon O., Warren W. Hampe, Catherine L. Bacon, and Calvin F. Settlage. 1961. *Direct Analysis and Schizophrenia: Clinical Observations and Evaluations*. New York: Grune and Stratton.

Escher, Maurits C. 1967. *The Graphic Work of M. C. Escher*. New York: Meredith Press.

Evans-Pritchard, E. E. 1937. *Witchcraft, Oracles and Magic Among the Azande*. Oxford: Oxford University Press.

Foucault, Michel. 1973. *The Order of Things: An Archaeology of the Human Sciences*. New York: Vintage Books.

Garfinkel, Harold. 1967. *Studies in Ethnomethodology*. Englewood Cliffs, New Jersey: Prentice-Hall.

Garfinkel, Harold, Michael Lynch, and Eric Livingston. 1981. The work of a discovering science construed with materials from the optically discovered pulsar. *Philosophy of the Social Sciences*. 11: 131–58.

Garfinkel, Harold and Sacks, Harvey. 1970. On formal structures and practical actions. In *Theoretical Sociology: Perspectives and Development*. Edited by John C. McKinney and Edward Tiryakian. New York: Appleton-Century-Crofts, 338–66.

Gasking, Douglas. 1965. Mathematics and the World. In Anthony Flew (editor), *Logic and Language*. Garden City, New York: Doubleday, 427–45.

Gergen, Kenneth J. 1984. Theory of the self: impasse and evolution. In Leonard Berkowitz (editor). *Advances in Experimental Social Psychology*. New York: Academic Press, 49–115.

Gibbs, J. P. 1966. Conceptions of Deviant Behavior: The Old and the New. *Pacific Sociological Review*. 9: 9–14.

Gilbert, G. Nigel and Mulkay, Michael J. 1984. *Opening Pandora's Box: An Analysis of Scientists' Discourse*. Cambridge, England: Cambridge University Press.

Gilligan, Carol. 1982. *In a Different Voice*. Cambridge, Massachusetts: Harvard University Press.

Grunwald, Ernst. 1970. The Sociology of Knowledge and Epistemology. In James E. Curtis and John W. Petras (editors), *The Sociology of Knowledge*. New York: Praeger, 237–43.

Guignon, Charles B. 1983. *Heidegger and the Problem of Knowledge*. Indianapolis: Hackett Publishing Co.

Gurwitsch, Aron. 1964. *The Field of Consciousness*. Pittsburgh: Duquesne University Press.

Gurwitsch, Aron. 1965. The phenomenology of perception: perceptual implications. In James M. Edie (editor). *An Invitation to Phenomenology*. Chicago: Quadrangle Books, 17–30.

Gurwitsch, Aron. 1966. *Studies in Phenomenology and Psychology*. Evanston, Illinois: Northwestern University Press.

Habermas, Jurgen. 1984. *The Theory of Communicative Action, Vol. I: Reason and the Rationalization of Society*. Boston: Beacon Press.

Hallpike, Christopher R. 1979. *The Foundations of Primitive Thought*. Oxford: Clarendon Press.

Harding, Sandra and Hintikka, Merrill B. (editors). 1983. *Discovering Reality: Feminist Perspectives on Epistemology, Metaphysics, Methodology and Philosophy of Science*. Dordrecht: D. Reidel.

Havelock, Eric A. 1967. *Preface to Plato*. New York: Grosset & Dunlap.

Heelas, Paul and Lock, Andrew (editors). 1981. *Indigenous Psychologies*. New York: Academic Press.

Heidegger, Martin. 1961. *An Introduction to Metaphysics*. Translated by Ralph Mannheim. Garden City, New York: Doubleday Anchor.

Heidegger, Martin. 1962. *Being and Time*. Translated by John Macquerrie and Edward Robinson. New York: Harper and Row.

Heisenberg, Werner. 1966. *Philosophic Problems of Nuclear Science*. New York: Fawcett World Library.

Helmer, Olaf and Rescher, Nicholas. 1959. On the epistemology of the inexact sciences. *Management Science*.

Henriques, Julian, Wendy Hollway, Cathy Urwin, Couze Venn, and Valerie Walkerdine. 1984. *Changing the Subject*. London: Methuen.

Heritage, John. 1985. *Garfinkel and Ethnomethodology*. Cambridge, England: Polity Press.

Herrigel, Eugen. 1964a. Zen in the art of archery. In E. Herrigel, *Zen*. Translated by R. F. C. Hull. New York: McGraw-Hill, 17–109.

Herrigel, Eugen. 1964b. The method of Zen. In E. Herrigel, *Zen*. Translated by R. F. C. Hull. New York: McGraw-Hill, 7–125.

Hilbert, Richard A. 1977. Approaching reason's edge: 'nonsense' as the final solution to the problem of meaning. *Sociological Inquiry*. 47: 25–31.

Homans, George C. 1958. Social behavior as exchange. *American Journal of Sociology*. 62: 597–606.

Homans, George C. 1961. *Social Behavior: Its Elementary Forms*. New York: Harcourt, Brace and World.

Hund, John. 1985. Insiders and outsiders models of deviance and jurisprudence. *Philosophy of the Social Sciences*. 15: 35–44.

Husserl, Edmund. 1960. *Cartesian Meditations*. Translated by Dorion Cairns. The Hague: Martinus Nijhoff.

Husserl, Edmund. 1962. *Ideas: General Introduction to Pure Phenomenology*. Translated by W. R. Boyce Gibson. New York: Collier Books.

Husserl, Edmund. 1965. *Phenomenology and the Crisis of Philosophy*. Translated by Quentin Lauer. New York: Harper Torchbooks.

Husserl, Edmund. 1970. *Logical Investigations*. Translated by J. N. Findlay. New York: Humanities Press.

James, William. 1950. *Principles of Psychology* (Vol. 2). New York: Dover.

James, William. 1958. *The Varieties of Religious Experience*. New York: New American Library.

Jaspers, Karl. 1955. *Reason and Existence*. New York: Noonday Press.

Jaynes, Julian. 1977. *The Origin of Consciousness in the Breakdown of the Bicameral Mind*. Boston: Houghton Mifflin.

Kafka, Franz. 1964. *The Trial*. New York: Random House.

Kerckhoff, Allan C. and Back, Kurt W. 1968. *The June Bug: A Study of Hysterical Contagion*. New York: Appleton-Century-Crofts.

Kuhn, Thomas. 1970. *The Structure of Scientific Revolutions*. Second Edition. Chicago: University of Chicago Press.

Laing, Ronald D. 1965. *The Divided Self: An Existential Study in Sanity and Madness*. Baltimore: Penguin Books.

Laing, Ronald D. 1967. *The Politics of Experience*. New York: Ballantine Books.

Langan, Thomas. 1966. *Merleau-Ponty's Critique of Reason*. New Haven: Yale University Press.

Leenhardt, Maurice. 1979. *Do Kamo*. Translated by Basia Miller Gulati. Chicago: University of Chicago Press.

Leesser, Issac. 1913. *Twenty Four Books of the Holy Scriptures*. New York: Jewish Press Publishing.

Lienhardt, Godfrey. 1961. *Divinity and Experience*. Oxford: Clarendon Press.

Lofland, John. 1966. *Doomsday Cult*. Englewood Cliffs, New Jersey: Prentice-Hall.

Mackie, Fiona. 1985. *The Status of Everyday Life*. London: Routledge & Kegan Paul.

Macomber, W. B. 1967. *The Anatomy of Disillusion: Martin Heidegger's Notion of Truth*. Evanston, Illinois: Northwestern University Press.

Mannheim, Karl. 1952. *Essays on the Sociology of Knowledge*. Edited by Paul Kecskemeti. London: Routledge & Kegan Paul.

Mannheim, Karl. 1955. *Ideology and Utopia*. New York: Harcourt, Brace and Company.

Mazur, Allan. 1968. The littlest science. *American Sociologist*. 3: 195–9.

McHoul, A. W. 1982. *Telling How Texts Talk: Essays on Reading and Ethnomethodology*. London: Routledge & Kegan Paul.

McHugh, Peter. 1968. *Defining the Situation: The Organization of Meaning in Social Interaction*. Indianapolis and New York: Bobbs-Merrill.

McHugh, Peter, Stanley Raffel, Daniel C. Foss, and Alan F. Blum. 1974. *On the Beginning of Social Inquiry*. London: Routledge & Kegan Paul.

Mead, George Herbert. 1938. *Mind, Self and Society*. Chicago: University of Chicago Press.

Mehan, Hugh. 1983. The role of language and the language of role in institutional decision making. *Language and Society*. 12: 187–211.

Mehan, Hugh and Wood, Houston. 1975. *The Reality of Ethnomethodology*. New York: Wiley.

Merleau-Ponty, Maurice. 1962. *Phenomenology of Perception*. Translated by Colin Smith. London: Routledge & Kegan Paul.

Merleau-Ponty, Maurice. 1963. *The Structure of Behavior*. Translated by Alden L. Fisher. Boston: Beacon Press.

Merleau-Ponty, Maurice. 1964a. *Sense and Non-Sense*. Translated by Hubert L. Dreyfus and Patricia Allen Dreyfus. Evanston, Illinois: Northwestern University Press.

Merleau-Ponty, Maurice. 1964b. *Signs*. Translated by Richard C. McCleary. Evanston, Illinois: Northwestern University Press.

Merleau-Ponty, Maurice. 1968. *The Visible and the Invisible*. Translated by Claude Lefort. Evanston, Illinois: Northwestern University Press.

Molotch, Harvey L. and Boden, Dierdre. 1985. Talking social structure: discourse, domination and the Watergate hearings. *American Sociological Review*. 50: 273–88.

Murphy, H. B. M. 1978. The advent of guilt feelings as a common depressive symptom: an historical comparison on two continents. *Psychiatry*. 41: 229–42.

Nagel, Ernest. 1961. *The Structure of Science*. New York: Harcourt, Brace & World.

Needham, Rodney. 1981. Inner states as universals: skeptical reflections on human nature. In Heelas, Paul and Lock, Andrew (editors). *Indigenous Psychologies*. New York: Academic Press, 65–78.

Needham, Rodney. 1985. *Exemplars*. Berkeley: University of California Press.

Norris, Christopher. 1985. *Contest of Faculties: Philosophy and Theory After Deconstruction*. London: Metheun.

O'Flaherty, Wendy D. 1984. *Dreams, Illusions and Other Realities*. Chicago: University of Chicago Press.

Onians, Richard B. 1954. *The Origins of European Thought About the Body, the Mind, the Soul, the World, Time, and Fate*. Cambridge, England: Cambridge University Press.

Ornstein, Robert E. 1975. *The Psychology of Consciousness*. Harmondsworth, England. Penguin.

Palmer, Richard E. 1969. *Hermeneutics*. Evanston, Illinois: Northwestern University Press.

Passmore, John. 1965. Explanation in everyday life in science and in history. In George H. Nadel (editor), *Studies in the Philosophy of History*. New York: Harper Torchbooks, 16–34.

Piaget, Jean. 1928. *Judgment and Reasoning in the Child*. Translated by Marjorie Warden. New York: Harcourt, Brace and Company.

Pirandello, Luigi. 1952. *Naked Masks*. Edited by Eric Bentley. New York: E. P. Dutton.

Polanyi, Michael. 1964. *Personal Knowledge: Towards a Post-Critical Philosophy*. New York: Harper Torchbooks.

Pollner, Melvin. 1970. On the foundations of mundane reasoning. Unpublished doctoral dissertation. Santa Barbara: University of California.

Pollner, Melvin. 1974a. Mundane reasoning. *Philosophy of the Social Sciences*. 5: 35–54.

Pollner, Melvin. 1974b. Sociological and common sense models of the labeling process. In Roy Turner (editor). *Ethnomethodology*. Middlesex, England: Penguin, 27–40.

Pollner, Melvin. 1975. 'The very coinage of your brain': the anatomy of reality disjunctures. *Philosophy of the Social Sciences*. 5: 411–30.

Pollner, Melvin. 1978. Constitutive and mundane versions of labeling theory. *Human Sciences*. 31: 285–304.

Pollner, Melvin. 1979. Self-explicating settings: making and managing meaning in traffic court. In George Psathas (editor), *Everyday Language: Studies in Ethnomethodology*. New York: Irvington Press, 227–55.

Pomerantz, Anita. 1981. Speakers' claims as a feature of describing: a study of 'presenting the evidence for'. Paper presented to the 76th Annual Meeting of the American Sociological Association, Toronto, Canada, August.

Pomerantz, Anita. 1984. Giving a source or basis: The practice in conversation of telling 'how I know.' *Journal of Pragmatics*. 8: 607–25.

Reiss, Timothy J. 1982. *The Discourse of Modernism*. Ithaca, New York: Cornell University Press.

Rockwell, Don A. 1971. Some observations on 'living in.' *Psychiatry*. 34: 214–23.

Rokeach, Milton. 1964. *The Three Christs of Ypsilanti*. New York: Random House.

Rorty, Richard. 1979. *Philosophy and the Mirror of Nature*. Princeton, New Jersey: Princeton University Press.

Rosenthal, Robert. 1966. *Experimenter Effects in Behavior Research*. New York: Appleton-Century-Crofts.

Ryle, Gilbert. 1949. *The Concept of Mind*. New York: Barnes & Noble.

Sacks, Harvey. 1963. Sociological description. *Berkeley Journal of Sociology*. 8: 1–17.

Sacks, Harvey. 1972a. An initial investigation of the usability of conversational data for doing sociology. In David Sudnow (editor), *Studies in Social Interaction*. New York: The Free Press, 31–74.

Sacks, Harvey. 1972b. On the analyzability of stories by children. In J. J. Gumperz and D. Hymes (editors), *Directions in Sociolinguistics*. New York: Holt, Rinehart and Winston, 325–45.

Sacks, Harvey. 1972c. Notes on police assessment of moral character. In David Sudnow (editor), *Studies in Social Interaction*. New York: The Free Press, 280–93, 444–6.

Sarbin, Theodore R. and Juhasz, Joseph B. 1967. The historical background of the concept of hallucination. *Journal of the History of Behavioral Sciences*. 3: 339–58.

Sartre, Jean-Paul. 1966. *Being and Nothingness*. Translated by Hazel E. Barnes. New York: Washington Square Press.

Scheffler, Israel. 1967. *Science and Subjectivity*. Indianapolis: Bobbs-Merrill.

Schegloff, Emanual A., Gail Jefferson, and Harvey Sacks. 1977. The preference for self-correction in the organization of repair in conversation. *Language*. 53: 361–82.

Schilder, Paul. 1935. *The Image and Appearance of the Human Body*. London: Kegan Paul, Trench, Trubner.

Schrag, Calvin O. 1980. *Radical Reflection and the Origin of the Human Sciences*. West Lafayette, Indiana: Purdue University Press.

Schutz, Alfred. 1962. *Collected Papers I: The Problem of Social Reality*. Edited by Maurice Natanson. The Hague: Martinus Nijhoff.

Schutz, Alfred, 1964. *Collected Papers II: Studies in Social Theory*. Edited by Arvid Brodersen. The Hague: Martinus Nijhoff.

Schutz, Alfred. 1967. *The Phenomenology of the Social World*. Translated by George Walsh and Frederick Lehnert. Evanston, Illinois: Northwestern University Press.

Seltman, Muriel and Seltman, Peter. 1985. *Piaget's Logic*. London: George Allen & Unwin.

Shapere, Dudley. 1964. The structure of scientific revolutions. *Philosophical Review*. 73: 383–94.

Simmons, J. L. 1964. On maintaining deviant belief systems. *Social Problems*. 11: 250–6.

Snell, Bruno. 1960. *The Discovery of the Mind*. Translated by T. C. Rosenmeyer. New York: Harper Torchbooks.

Sorokin, Pitirim A. 1964. *Sociocultural Causality, Space, Time*. New York: Russell and Russell.

Spencer, Martin E. 1982. The ontologies of social science. *Philosophy of the Social Sciences*. 12: 121–41.

Stolzenberg, Gabriel. 1984. Can an inquiry into the foundations of mathematics tell us anything interesting about mind? In Paul Watzlawick (editor), *The Invented Reality*. New York: Norton, 257–308.

Sudnow, David. 1965. Normal crimes. *Social Problems*. 12: 255–76.

Tulku, Tarthang. 1977. *Time, Space, and Knowledge*. Emeryville, California: Dharma Publishing Co.

Wasserstrom, Richard A. 1961. *The Judicial Decision*. Stanford: Stanford University Press.

Watts, Alan W. 1957. *The Way of Zen*. New York: Vintage Books.

Weber, Max. 1964. *The Theory of Social and Economic Organization*. Translated by Talcott Parsons. New York: The Free Press.

Wieder, D. Lawrence. 1974. *Language and Social Reality*. The Hague: Mouton.

Winch, Peter. 1965. *The Idea of a Social Science*. London: Routledge & Kegan Paul.

Wittgenstein, Ludwig. 1951. *Philosophical Investigations*. Translated by G. E. M. Anscombe. New York: Macmillan.

Wittgenstein, Ludwig. 1961. *Tractatus Logico-Philosophicus*. Translated by D. F. Pears and B. F. McGuinness. London: Routledge & Kegan Paul.

Wittgenstein, Ludwig. 1969. *On Certainty*. Translated by Denis Paul and G. E. M. Anscombe. Edited by G. E. M. Anscombe and G. H. van Wright. New York: Harper & Row.

Zimmerman, Don H. 1969. Record-keeping and the intake process in a public welfare agency. In Stanton Wheeler (editor), *On Record: Files and Dossiers in American Life*. New York: Russell Sage, 319–54.

Zimmerman, Don H. and Pollner, Melvin. 1970. The everyday world as a phenomenon. In Jack Douglas (editor), *Understanding Everyday Life*. Chicago: Aldine, 80–103.

Index